P9-DFV-901

Achieving Excellence Through Customer Service

John Tschohl
with
Steve Franzmeier

PRENTICE HALL
Englewood Cliffs, New Jersey 07632

Prentice-Hall International (UK) Limited, *London*
Prentice-Hall of Australia Pty. Limited, *Sydney*
Prentice-Hall Canada, Inc., *Toronto*
Prentice-Hall Hispanoamericana, S.A., *Mexico*
Prentice-Hall of India Private Limited, *New Delhi*
Prentice-Hall of Japan, Inc., *Tokyo*
Simon & Schuster Asia Pte. Ltd., *Singapore*
Editora Prentice-Hall do Brasil, Ltda., *Rio de Janeiro*

10 9 8 7 6 5 4

Library of Congress Cataloging-in-Publication Data

Tschohl, John.
Achieving excellence through customer service / by John Tschohl with Steve Franzmeier.
p. cm.
Includes index.
ISBN 0-13-005125-X
1. Customer service. I. Franzmeier, Steve. II. Title.
HF5415.5.T83 1991
658.8'12—dc20 90-22449
CIP

ISBN 0-13-005125-X

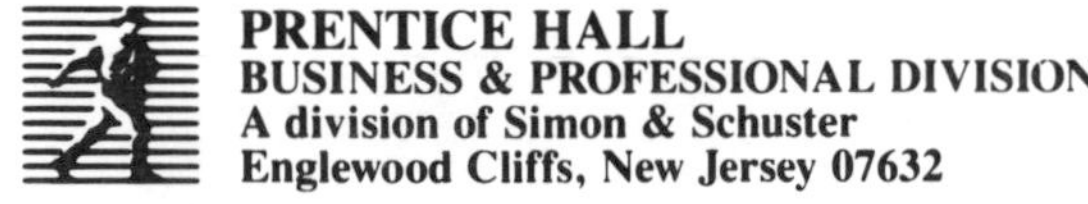
PRENTICE HALL
BUSINESS & PROFESSIONAL DIVISION
A division of Simon & Schuster
Englewood Cliffs, New Jersey 07632

Printed in the United States of America

Introduction

WHAT THIS BOOK WILL DO FOR YOU

If you've heard and read all you want to know about how bad service is in America and how important service is to customers and to your bottom line, you may be ready for a little *action*. This book is for you.

After many recent articles and books dealing with the need for quality service, few business managers remain unconvinced. Many, however, remain *unequipped* to express their commitment in action. The mission of this book—is to *equip* the already convinced to implement the already proved: service is a strategy as powerful as marketing and as potent as quality product itself in the ongoing effort to realize the full profit potential of a company.

This book gives you detailed, step-by-step knowledge that you can use in establishing profitable customer service strategies.

The profit-producing capability of an organization derives from impressions made by *all* employees upon the organization's customers. The means of creating these impressions are the quality and efficacy of the product or service that the employees sell: the quality, accuracy, dependability, and speed of their service—and the warmth of their human relationships with customers. All employees, from CEOs to minimum-wage hourly workers (some more than others) influence a company's reputation and form the attitudes of customers and other "influentials." Therefore, these employees—especially front-line service employees—must be trained to deliver service. The service mentality and the desire to provide service are not native traits. Once trained, employees' motivation (commitment) must be renewed.

In 1979, long before customer service came into vogue, I designed a customer service training program that organizations could use to change the attitudes and the behavior of employees.

I saw organizations spend millions on advertising, trying to attract customers. But, then, they used baseball bats (figuratively) to drive them away. This was bizarre behavior, I felt. If these organizations would just provide good service, making their customers feel special, wanted, and appreciated, they would keep the customers their advertising attracts.

The learning system developed in 1979 has been used by millions of people throughout the world. It is cost effective and user friendly, and is written to be understood by the employee participants, not just management and trainers.

This book is written for managers—for senior and middle managers who influence the service quality of a company by deciding what employees who deal directly with customers will do, how they will do it, and, initially, *whether they* will do it at all. They tell employees what is expected of them in terms of customer service; and they evaluate and report to them their service performance.

But, to imply from the significance of management in the service scheme that only management needs training would constitute a significantly counter-productive oversight, no matter how elegant the rationalization supporting it. The reason is that an estimated 95 percent of the factors that determine reputation of a company among customers and prospects are in the hands of front-line service employees. Even though a manager may harbor low esteem for the personal qualities of front-line workers, a grossly uninformed and unfair view, the fact remains that they still are *primarily responsible for delivering* service. They *create* impressions that form an organization's reputation. They *especially* must be trained. And money must be spent training them.

But, today, many organizations don't train front-line employees in service at all. Instead, they advertise that they have good service. Apparently they hope that employees will read the ads and feel constrained to live up to the promise. Training and motivation for the people who actually deliver service, and how-to-do-it implementation instructions are the twin I-beams supporting the substance of this book. They are:

- The reason the book was written.
- The features that distinguish the book from other books on service.

Among key benefits to readers of this book are:

- Hands-on ideas, skills, and techniques that can be used *immediately*.
- Knowledge about shaping employee attitudes, a powerful competitive force moving a firm toward greater market share, customer loyalty, and profitability.

HOW THIS BOOK IS ORGANIZED

The book presents information in building-block fashion. Each chapter helps you to understand and to use information that follows properly.

The first chapter presents facts and statistics and logical narrative to use in persuasive internal reports and memos on service. Chief among benefits of quality service itemized in Chapter 1 is the positive impact of service upon the bottom line. Customer service is *not* an expense. It is a high-yield investment.

Chapters 2 and 3 deal with getting started—Chapter 2 with planning and Chapter 3 with organizing.

Chapter 4 presents essentials of a basic subject, knowing what your customers want—in other words, knowing what you have to do to win their satisfaction and their continued patronage. This step is essential to the development of any company's service strategy. Know your customers. Factoring results of national surveys of consumer needs and wants into your plan simply isn't good enough.

A quality service program stalls quickly without employees to implement it aggressively. That's why a chapter (Chapter 5) on finding service-minded employees is included. The message of Chapter 5 is that trainable employees with native service ability generally are born, not made (with exceptions).

But, even high-potential employees need to be remotivated. So, we present Chapter 6, dealing with the function of employee motivation in a service strategy.

The following three chapters (7, 8, 9) are the meat and potatoes of the book. Herein lies information that a reader would need months or years to assemble from diverse sources. These chapters are brightened by ideas in action—case histories from all over the country and the world.

Chapter 7 primes the reader's imagination with treatment of essential loyalty-building service programs. Chapter 8 contains more "basics of quality service" from which readers can select practices most appropriate for their organizations. Chapter 9 covers projects with the most tangible, profit-making results—results that even the most hard-nosed manager would admire. From this chapter should come the heavy-caliber ammunition for use in winning support for a service program of hesitant VIPs in the organization.

Once a program is underway, the next concern should be with maintaining momentum and with practicing "preventive maintenance." According to Chapter 10, you must give a new service program a boost to get it up to speed, measure service performance, stay alert to customer dissatisfactions and eliminate them, and identify and perpetuate reasons for *satisfaction*.

Chapter 11 deals with soliciting and encouraging complaints, with preventing them when you can, and with converting and retaining as customers as many dissatisfied customers as possible.

The final chapter gives you the tools to design your own in-house training system. Chapter 12 presents the most up-to-date information on training dealing with technology, packaging, persuasive communication, and group dynamics.

In this book you will find a blueprint for a quality service program that increases profit by developing customer satisfaction and loyalty. Satisfied customers buy more, and they buy more often. They don't switch to competitors. The larger base of loyal customers that is the yield of a quality service program reduces the need for advertising and marketing. Why? Because fewer customers abandon a company for its competitors, leaving behind a need to replace them with new customers attracted by advertising and marketing.

Contents

1

Exceptional Service—The Secret Weapon

MAKING MONEY WITH CUSTOMER SERVICE

> The battle for repeat business is critical to long-term success in today's intensely competitive marketplace. Customer service is not just a competitive edge. In many industries it is *the* competitive edge. Service is the new standard by which customers judge an organization's performance.
>
> —*William Band, partner with the Strategic Management Practice, Coopers & Lybrand Consulting Group, Toronto*

"Most businesses don't understand that customer service is really selling," says N. Powell Taylor, manager of consumer communications and telephone operations for the GE (General Electric) Answer Center in Louisville, Kentucky. Service is "selling" because it inspires customers to return more often, and to buy more. Business done by loyal customers who return to buy again and again because they are satisfied with service yields 65 percent of a typical organization's volume, according to a study by the American Management Association.

One of the biggest problems in customer service is the reluctance of managers to look on customer service as a marketing strategy. Too many see it as an after-sale service, something relating back to the previous sale rather than ahead to the next one.

Studies prove that service actually is *more* effective in many companies at enhancing volume and profit than is marketing, promotion, or advertising. We suspect that in companies with comprehensive, highly professional service strategies, service adds more to bottom-line results than research and development, product innovation, capital improvements, broad selection, credit services, or any other strategy.

As noted in *Electrical Contractor* magazine, "In our service-oriented society, quality of service has become more significant to company success than quality of product. And, those companies that lead the way in service excellence will have a powerful competitive advantage over those who lag behind."

To make this true for your company, meet these conditions:

1. Management Commitment. This is the most vital prerequisite to the success of a quality service program. There should be no advertisements flaunting "We Love You" service unless top management believes in personal, helpful service as strongly as it believes in family values, patriotism, and profit.
   Management words and deeds must continuously communicate management commitment to employees. Unfortunately, in my years of customer service experience, I have been consistently surprised by management commitment . . . to lip service.
2. Adequate Funding. The organization enthusiastically spends all the money needed to develop and to maintain a professional service program.
3. Conspicuous Improvement in Service. Service improves so much that customers notice and, as a result, feel as if product (tangible or intangible) quality has improved. The organization's service must be noticeably better than service provided by competitors.
4. Training. Employees are thoroughly trained to implement a service strategy keyed to special needs of an organization's customers or clients. Since 1980 I have been encouraging businesses and organizations to train all their employees. Unfortunately, businesses usually ignore service training though it is likely to have greater impact upon earnings than anything else a company can do.
5. Internal Service. In a retail store the display department and the merchandising department must help each other present merchandise and service in ways that win the satisfaction and loyalty of customers.
   In a manufacturing company, maintenance and production departments must interact amicably and helpfully to deliver to customers products that maintain their loyalty. Departments must help each other instead of sniping at each other.
6. Involvement of All Employees. All employees should feel that their work affects customer perception of service quality and even product quality, no matter how far they are removed from the "front line" and from direct communication with customers.

Remember: No matter how much a company spends to enhance service, the expenditure will pay off *only* if customers and prospects are *aware* of service quality. Quality must be noticeable. It must benefit many customers or clients continuously, not occasionally. And customers must be told that the company provides service and they must be regularly reminded to use it.

Awareness of quality service by customers and prospects is a great advantage to salespeople who are far more likely to make a sale when they can say, knowing that it's true: "If you buy from me, I will never let you down. Servicing your company will be my top priority."

Jan Carlzon, president of Scandinavian Airlines (SAS), wrote in his book, *Moments of Truth* (Ballinger, 1987): "Last year, each of our 10 million customers came in contact with approximately five SAS employees. Each contact lasted an average of 15 seconds. Thus, SAS is 'created' in the minds of our customers 50 million times per year, 15 seconds at a time."

These 50 million "moments of truth," when customers are made aware of the quality of SAS service, are the moments that ultimately determine whether SAS will succeed or fail as a company.

Any manager can apply the same analysis to his or her company.

COMPETITIVE EDGE

Because quality service is an effective "selling" tool, it is also a long-term competitive advantage. In fact, often it is the only competitive advantage available to an organization in a service economy in which many organizations provide essentially the same service.

"Virtually all customers make buying decisions based on the service they get from a company," says Terrell J. Harris, managing partner, Chicago Consulting. "When service slips, sales fall. It's that simple. Conversely, even small improvements in service can result in increased profits for a company."

Put yourself in the shoes of a housewife standing at the end of a long row of white refrigerators. They look alike. They do the same thing. But chances are that the housewife will walk over to one refrigerator first—the one bearing the brand name that warms her heart with memories of friendly, helpful, knowledgeable salespeople or with visions of a company's considerate responses to her inquiries. True?

Yes, we do live in an era when the only difference between many products and services discernible to customers often is no more than a distinct difference in service quality. That difference—that margin—is manifested in a friendly, low-key feeling of approval for an organization or for its product or service.

This is the competitive edge.

The Feeling of Approval

When customers are presented with a choice between companies, the "low-key feeling of approval" becomes as effective in persuading them to buy from one company and not from another as the advice of a close friend.

The effect of this feeling of approval for a company is "powerful," says Jan Carlzon. "It is the power of consistent profit."

Jan Gates, service manager of Chef Francisco, a frozen-food manufacturer in Eugene, Oregon, knows about the competitive edge of customer service. "In our field, as in others," she says, "the market is maturing. My company always has sold quality. But now there are other companies out there with quality products, and pricing is about equal.

"So, we have to sell service," she says.

Banks, too, know that they must sell service more than ever because prices for banking services usually are similar. They know that larger corporations do business with 20 to 30 banks around the world. And they know that service is the key to business retention, and to differentiation.

Bank management traditionally has considered its industry to be very good at service. But consumers usually rate banks very low in customer service, often at the same level as car dealers.

MARKET DOMINANCE

When a company makes the momentous discovery that customers are really "people," and when they give customer service at least as much power and influence over decisions as they give financial and statistical considerations, then they are well on the road to achieving a competitive advantage and even market dominance. That's means money.

But many companies are ruled by "number crunchers" unfamiliar with the value of loyal customers who buy for years and years and tell their friends how much they enjoy doing business with an organization. Even as renowned an authority as W. Edwards Deming, famed management consultant who taught quality to the Japanese and whose reputation was built on statistical control, said in a lecture that if you run a company on figures alone "you will go under . . . because the most important figures aren't there."

Deming asked: "What about the multiplying effects of happy customers in either manufacturing or in service? What about the effect of an *un*happy customer?" The fact that a majority of companies are ruled by financial or by sales departments is precisely why service is so noticeable, appreciated so highly by customers, and so effective in boosting volume and profit.

In my years in the customer service field I have consistently found that manufacturing firms often are more committed to service than are so- called service firms. If a manufacturing firm accepted the failure rate in its service that a service company does, it would be out of business in a short time.

The reason that manufacturing firms are more committed to service, I think, is that they have a limited number of customers. Service firms, on the other hand, wrongly believe that their customers are unlimited. Lose one and you can always get another!

I have trouble understanding why service firms whose future is totally dependent upon service quality blithely go about their business ignoring service quality.

Service Is Salvation

There's knockout value in service even for companies with reputations for indolence, insolence, ignorance, insincerity, indifference, and aloofness . . . or for hollow promises . . . or for vanishing whenever a customer has a complaint.

Good service and customer education programs, you see, restore brand loyalty, confidence, and repurchase intention of customers who experience service problems with a company. This finding was the result of research by the Technical Assistance Research Corporation (TARP) of Washington, D.C. Results were reported in a paper entitled "The Bottom Line Implications of Unmet Customer Expectations." TARP is the leading research organization in the service field.

In the intensely competitive atmosphere of the twentieth century's closing years, companies must train service-delivery employees to look for the service element in everything they do.

The question that anyone employed by any organization with customers must continually ask is: "How can I do this work to further the interests of the customer?"

Service is the energy and the strength needed by an organization struggling just to stand still instead of falling behind. With service, the company can begin running downhill toward greater profit, gaining momentum as it goes.

PREDICTABLE PROFIT INCREASE

So real is the feeling of approval—the competitive edge—that increases in customer satisfaction can be measured in terms of added increments of profit. Bell System companies, among my first clients, were measuring customer satisfaction with the Telsan Survey before the AT&T breakup and long before anyone else thought of customer service surveys. Fortunately I can say that the surveys consistently revealed improved customer satisfaction after customer service training.

One of TARP's claims to fame is a pioneering study of complaint handling for the Coca-Cola Corporation in 1981. That study found that people are at least twice as likely to complain about negative experiences as they are to discuss positive experiences.

In another study, TARP determined that average return from service activity for makers of consumer durables such as washing machines and refrigerators is 100 percent. In other words, if a company spends $1 million on a service program, the company receives $2 million in bottom-line benefits.

For banks, return on service is as high as 170 percent.

Payoff can be even higher—as high as 200 percent—in the extremely competitive retailing field. Here, high-quality personal service is the star of the team, and customer loyalty is the first-round draft choice. A change in gears is called for at this point because it occurs to me that I have not defined the primary term, "customer service." I've been using the term as if all readers define service as I do. In an attempt to situate readers and writer on the same dimension, I present my definition of customer service. Some of you will agree with it. Some of you will want to expand upon it. And some will define service differently.

WHAT IS QUALITY CUSTOMER SERVICE?

Note these differing customer service concepts:

- To some, service is product repair and a middle-aged lady in a wash-and-wear dress delivering oh-so-glib responses to questions and complaints from a centrally-located "customer service booth."
- Some managers feel that they have service when employees dutifully declare "Have a nice day" as if their mouths were wired to tape recorders.
- A liberal return policy is enough for other managers to brag about their "customer service." Dayton Hudson Corporation, a large nationwide retailer, wrapped its customer service in a tidy no-questions-asked return policy. Consequently, the company lost touch with many other facets of service. Now, however, Dayton Hudson has begun to offer the full gamut of customer services.

No matter what form it takes, some managers view service as a bonus—a "feel-good" extra that a company adds on to a purchase out of generosity.

The newsletter *Quality Assurance Report* states that only when a company knows exactly what kind of service its customers expect, delivers on those expectations 100 percent of the time, at a price that customers are willing to pay, while still getting an acceptable return, can the company claim to excel in customer service.

So it seems that the bottom-line definition of service is "whatever your customers think it is." This is the definition that we favor.

At Lands' End, even our guarantee comes as close to a simple Wisconsin handshake as it can in two no-nonsense words:

GUARANTEED. PERIOD.®

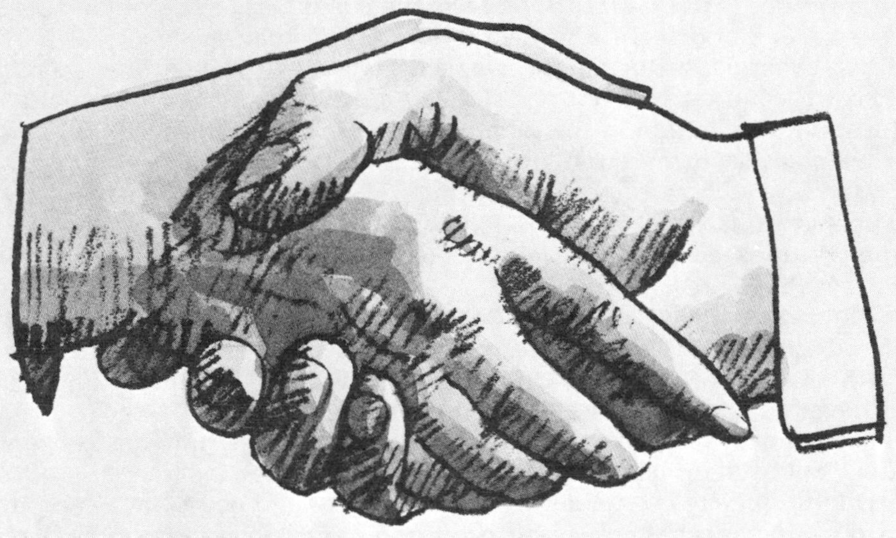

The world is full of guarantees, no two alike. As a rule, the more words they contain, the more their protection is limited. The Lands' End guarantee has always been an unconditional one.

It reads: "If you are not completely satisfied with any item you buy from us, at any time during your use of it, return it and we will refund your full purchase price."

We mean every word of it. Whatever. Whenever. Always. But to make sure this is perfectly clear, we simplify it even further, in the two words above.

Binding as a handshake.

Please send free catalog.
Lands' End Dept. HV-35
Dodgeville, WI 53595

Name __________

Address __________

City __________

State _____ Zip _____

☐ Please send information about your new international service.

Write or call toll-free:

1-800-356-4444

THIS ADVERTISEMENT
PREPARED EXCLUSIVELY FOR
LANDS' END
by THE PEER GROUP CHICAGO, ILLINOIS
AD NO. LE 35 HANDSHAKE
REVISED 5/3/90

Lands' End, the mail order clothing company, knows that a few people take advantage of their unconditional guarantee. But that doesn't stop them from offering it to you. The benefits of a no-hassle return policy, Lands' End realizes, far outweigh the consequences of a small proportion of dishonest returns. (Reprinted courtesy of Lands' End.)

Whatever Customers Want

Many insurance companies have invested heavily to improve service levels. Yet, sometimes, these investments have provided little or no return, since superior service provides competitive advantage only when the improved service is in an area that affects the customer's decision and when the customer can discern a measurable improvement.

For example, reducing the elapsed time to issue a group accident and health contract will not affect a buying decision nearly as much as will a similar reduction in the time spent issuing a claim check. Reducing price calculation turnaround from overnight to four hours won't be appreciated as much as providing on-line services that can be sensed by a prospect during a sales call. It follows that you must know what your customers think customer service is. For guidance in learning what your customers think, see Chapter 2.

This much is certain: What the consumer defines as service has changed radically. Today's definition includes convenient location, breadth of selection, category dominance, and speed of transaction. It can even mean competitive prices.

Still, much about service remains unchanged—employee courtesy, product knowledge, helpfulness, and enthusiasm, for instance.

Quality service is orientation of *all* resources and people in a company toward customer satisfaction—*all* people—not just those who deal face to face with customers or who communicate with them by phone, by fax, by letter, or in other ways.

Service is selling, warehousing, delivery, inventory, order selection, labor power, employee relations, adjustments, correspondence, billing, credit, finance and accounting, advertising and public relations, and data processing. There is a service element in any activity pursued by any employee because ultimately it all impacts the real or perceived quality of the product purchased by the customer.

Service involves maintaining old customers, attracting new customers, and leaving all of them with an impression of the company that induces them to do business with the company again.

The general purpose of quality service is

- Customer maintenance
- Customer retention
- New customer development

Expressed in terms of attitude, service is

- Thoughtfulness
- Courtesy
- Integrity
- Reliability
- Helpfulness
- Efficiency

THE GRAEBEL COMPANIES

CUSTOMER SERVICE GUIDELINES

- ★ We will meet the needs of our customers.
- ★ We will meet every commitment we make.
- ★ We will communicate well.
- ★ We will do it right the first time - every time.
- ★ We will treat every customer with courtesy and respect.
- ★ We will treat every article as if it belonged to our mother.
- ★ Our services will be on-time, efficient, effective, and dependable.
- ★ Our customer's needs vary; we will adapt our services to meet them.
- ★ We will follow up, measure our efforts, and encourage feedback.
- ★ Policies and procedures will guide us and not rule us.
- ★ Slogans, buzz words, and a list of guidelines do not make superior customer service happen -- our professionalism, dedication, and commitment do!

To Graebel Van Lines, quality customer service means "being responsive to (customer) needs." (Reprinted courtesy of Graebel Van Lines.)

- Availability
- Friendliness
- Knowledge
- Professionalism

All this having been said, most complaints are caused by the shabby, impersonal, even insulting way that customers are treated. Being treated in a way that makes them enjoy their shopping experience is even more important to customers than is reliability or value of product, merchandise, or service. Yet we allow ourselves to go on believing that employees were born with the skills needed to provide quality service.

Is Service Mere Benevolence?

It's a source of wonder that many companies actually see no connection between customer purchases and service. They believe that a company has fulfilled its unspoken contract when the customer gets the goods. Service is seen as an unearned and mostly unnecessary bonus.

Zenger-Miller, Cupertino, California, developer of training systems, found that many businesspeople view service in the same way that car dealerships do. Service means repair. Employees service (repair) a product (the car) at the customer's request.

For these organizations, service improvement consists of making better repairs more efficiently. Whether or not the customer is satisfied is something that's dealt with later, in questionnaires and How'd-we-do? phone calls.

These observations were based on a study of service programs in financial services, health care, retail, and manufacturing industries and in public sector organizations by Zenger-Miller.

The teachings of Deming, Philip Crosby, and Genichi Taguchi about the importance of product quality in customer service are fine, as far as they go. A company should make certain, however, that its product quality effort is not the sum total of the customer service program. Product and service quality are interdependent. That is, a wonderfully manufactured product with poor sales and service support still will exasperate customers.

Many companies are concerned only with tangible factors such as repairs. They overlook the most important factor, as far as customers are concerned—reliable and responsive service. This is also the conclusion of a study by The Forum Corporation, a large international consulting firm that has worked with more than 700 companies in the areas of management consultation, training, and research. The Forum study determined that companies that change only tangible elements in their operations—elements that are "visible and easiest to change" such as formal complaint systems—are unsuccessful in achieving lasting, significant benefit from quality service.

The Intangible Difference

Intangible elements are vital to successful customer service. Chief among these intangibles are reliability, responsiveness, and empathy.

Reliability implies that employees have the ability to establish goals for themselves that, when attained, meet or exceed customer expectations.

Service means different things to different people, as we've observed. At the lowest level, service is something a customer is not entitled to, but you may give it to him or her as a gift. At a somewhat higher level, service means focusing on customer transactions but only fixing something if it is broken.

At the highest level, The aim of service *is* to deliver more than the customer expects, which probably is what he or she needs.

Many companies assign customer service a selling role, viewing it as a function that allows salespeople more time to sell. That's the way it's practiced at Ore Ida Foods in Boise, Idaho, says Dick Johnson, general manager of customer service. This is the prevailing function of service in many companies. Certainly, seeing service as selling is appropriate. It's just not a complete view of service.

In a sales-oriented service environment, everyone works to make the sales rep's time more productive. Someone else answers questions that salespeople would have to take time to answer otherwise. Someone else schedules deliveries.

To do their jobs in a company where sales support is a service function, employees learn to ask themselves questions such as

- "How can I process the order sooner?"
- "How can I deliver the quickest?"
- "How can I improve my performance to support the customer?"
- "How can I enhance product quality with service?"

Supervisors and managers should continually retrain employees to monitor themselves by asking themselves questions such as these. The day that pressure to maintain quality is released is the same day that quality in customer service will disappear.

Quality service often is seen as a function that makes it easy for people to buy. Ordering and stocking are responsibilities for service. Many organizations have formal definitions of service standards, either as a mission statement or as an operational rule.

Global Imperatives

Generally, these definitions take the form of global imperatives. "The customer is always right," and "Excellence in creating customer satisfaction" are typical. However, stockholders are the only people who see these statements, sometimes. They are printed in the annual report. Or, if we share our expectations with employees, we review these "standards" with them once and assume that this will be enough to change their lives and the way they do their jobs.

In service companies the narrowest definition of service quality is "accuracy and efficiency in completing a transaction." An order-entry clerk gets the order right and does it quickly and efficiently. Or a retail clerk makes many sales transactions with few returns or complaints. At the other end of the spectrum are definitions of service that focus on the customer, the product or the transaction. Service practices are expressed in terms of imperatives such as: "Meet the customer's expectations" and: "The only difference between stores is how they treat customers."

The latter "global imperative" reflects the belief that service is a competitive edge when competing companies offer similar products and services to the same consumers.

More advanced, sophisticated customer service thinking can be illustrated with the IBM philosophy stated by F. G. (Buck) Rodgers, retired IBM vice president, marketing: "No magic formula or guarded secret keeps customers 'married' to IBM long after their equipment is installed and their check deposited. IBM simply approaches the customer, after the sale, with the same interest and attention as when he was the prospect being courted."

Still, some competitors can't seem to figure out why IBM is a consistently high performer, even though the company freely attributes much of its success to customer service.

After all these definitions and interpretations of quality service, we still adhere to the belief that service is whatever one's customers think it is. Service employees *deliver* the services that *create* the impression that *build* the reputation—that *pays off* in repeat sales, in more sales, and in customer satisfaction and referrals.

IS IT CUSTOMER SERVICE OR CUSTOMER RELATIONS?

In practice, customer service deals with policy and with operations, whereas customer relations is day-to-day customer contact.

Customer service establishes a level of service that customers receive. Then, customer relations delivers it.

At food processing companies such as Del Monte, it is "customer relations" people who answer the phone, take orders, and ship car loads and train loads of fruit salad to Kroger's, Safeway, and A&P. A food processor's customers who have complaints also call customer relations.

Ethel Peterson, who was President Carter's director of consumer affairs, also was director of consumer affairs at Giant Foods before her stint with the government and again after it. Her job was a customer relations position, mainly involving response to complaint letters, keeping Giant out of trouble with the law and with government agencies, and providing services to customers such as mailing recipes.

Pat McDonough, director of customer service at the Reader's Digest Association, technically is in customer service because she establishes policies. The 500 or so employees who report to her handle people who call in about subscriptions, contests, adjustments, and so on.

HIGH TECH, HIGH TOUCH

Quality service, by whatever name, is *more* essential now, at a time when hands-off technology is so popular, than it ever was.

The more we are faced with "high tech," the more we want "high touch," says consultant John Naisbitt. "High touch" is translatable for our purposes as "personal service."

What Naisbitt says is that the fewer contacts we have with the people in an organization, the more important the quality of each contact becomes. Also, the more often we are forced to interact with a machine, the greater our yearning for human contact becomes.

So, machines that do not offer the immediate option of recourse to a warm, breathing, intelligent employee just won't do—if a company is determined to win the satisfaction and loyalty of its customers.

Automatic teller machines (82,000 of them by 1989), electronic transfer of funds by banks, and airline ticketing machines are likely to prove counter-productive in terms of customer disloyalty (readiness to switch to competition), insensitivity, and even alienation.

The same is true of computer-generated car rental agreements, closed-circuit TV hotel bill review, automatic credit card bill payment, and phone systems that require callers to wait until a recorded voice reads a list of options before connecting to the extension desired.

Voice Mail Equals Nonservice

A comment about these so-called "voice mail" systems. They are a perfect example of nonservice. There's no service in them for many customers, just for the sponsoring company. The telephone company benefits, too, because callers often end up making more than one phone call after reaching a dead end and a disconnect, according to a study of these systems. The manufacturer of this kind of equipment benefits, of course. The manager in charge of systems at the user company benefits also because he or she becomes a hero by saving so much money in the elimination of human operators. But elimination of human operators is precisely the reason that the systems manager should be reprimanded, from a customer service point of view.

Finally, the personnel department benefits because payroll amount declines.

The only loser is the customer who is put to a lot of trouble trying to complete a call. One waits 30 seconds for a recorded message and then another 30 seconds for another message before giving up.

People contacts usually are the most memorable of our buying experiences, not our contacts with optical readers or electronic robots. However, *all* contacts with an organization contribute to our perceptions and judgments about that organization.

Tom Peters agreed, in *Thriving on Chaos* (Alfred A. Knopf, 1987), that people contact in a high-tech society is more important now than it was before we became a service/information economy. Remember this: People will continue to appreciate and to reward warm, helpful service by other living, breathing human beings, no matter how computerized the society becomes. They will smile when you address them by name or when you give them information or help that they didn't expect. They will tell their friends about fast service by friendly, helpful employees who knew what they were doing and enjoyed doing it.

The competitive edge will continue to go to companies with personal, personable service.

The Little Things

But too many organizations in service industries will continue to overlook basic, human technique such as calling regular customers by name—the "little things."

Roger Longtin, Chicago personal injury lawyer who travels nine months a year, says: "I find it incredible that you can go to a city and stay at the same hotel 30 or more nights out of a year and each time you show up they don't know who you are. There's no system for keeping track of frequent customers."

I have gone to the same convenience store twice a week for more than four years to buy gas. I always present my name to the clerk: It's on the credit card that I submit. But not once have I ever been called by name. Not once has anyone in that store seemed to recognize me.

Most other convenience stores are the same. As a result, I do what I suspect many other people do—I select my gas pumps on the basis of convenience and price because service is unattainable. I've lost my loyalty.

Another reason that personal service by a live human is superior to any technological marvel is that flawless, zero defects, perpetual motion machines that never break down or misbehave haven't yet been discovered. If they have, they probably serve only small numbers of people.

The shift from smokestack economy to service/information economy requires transformation in the way organizations are managed to help prevent sacrifice of personal service upon the altar of economy by technology. Management and organizational change needed to achieve professional, company-wide transformation into a service-oriented company is described in Chapters 2 and 3.

HOW TO BENEFIT FROM SERVICE ENHANCEMENT

Customer service, to use the term as a general description of the quality service field, exerts a multiplier effect: it multiplies results achieved by advertising, marketing, and sales.

The basis for this "multiplier effect" is a positive feeling about a company that quality personal service places in the minds of customers and, thereby, in the minds of people motivated by personal service to recommend the company.

When a company advertises against a backdrop of consumer goodwill for the organization and its products, the company's cash registers ring a merry tune after advertising.

On the other hand, if a company's employees routinely sentence customers to long waits, and then behave as if they were doing customers a favor by helping them complete their purchases, a week's worth of the prime time commercials on network TV would have little effect on sales.

Even in the absence of advertising and other marketing, when a business successfully adopts a professional service strategy, then sales, profit, and return on investment usually improve geometrically—not just proportionately. Customer satisfaction and loyalty increase dramatically, too. And customer complaint numbers drop.

Customer service, you see, is the first-string quarterback. With customer service playing, the rest of the team performs better and the team wins most of the time.

If a company treats its customers right, makes customers feel at home, and gives them the distinct impression that the company values their patronage, then profit is the quite certain result. But, if the company treats service as "nice to do if you have the time," then the company will find that other strategies, such as advertising, achieve only anemic results and fall short of expectations or potential. No matter how new a store or how creative its displays or how professional its advertising, the store's sales-per-square-foot goals will not be achieved.

Because of the "enhancement effect" of service, some companies begin major expansions of marketing programs just as new quality service programs begin to take effect. It's a smart move: service augments normally anticipated results of marketing.

BENEFITS OF SERVICE

To clarify the value of quality service, we can say that service retains the customers you already have, attracts more customers, and develops reputation that induces customers and prospects alike to do business with you in the future.

This objective is achieved by satisfying customers who then recommend your company to friends, relatives, and acquaintances and who, by their comments, develop and then augment your positive reputation in the marketplace.

John E. Kelly, vice president of Kelly Electrical Construction, Inc., of Upper Marlboro, Maryland, knows about the enhancement effect of quality service. He says: "About 20 percent of our business is referral."

Many businesses derive virtually all of their business from referrals—and then from repeat business.

"Studies show that satisfied customers can give you two or three referrals to other jobs," says Lew Tagliaferre, director of marketing services, National Electrical Contractors Association. (NECA)

Word-of-Mouth Recommendations

So, cultivate positive word-of-mouth comment on service if you want to achieve a very profitable reputation for good service. Word-of-mouth recommendation often is more effective than product advertising in influencing purchase decisions.

The Technical Assistance Research Program (TARP) found in a study that customers who have a good experience with a company on a small-ticket item tell an average of 5 other people. But customers tell an average of *9 or 10* other people about *bad* service experience. Here's a good argument for a customer satisfaction effort if there ever was one.

Break out from TARP research the customer reaction to bad service involving big-ticket items only and you find that 8 additional people hear about a good experience by a customer, but a whopping 16 people hear about unresolved problems.

Conclusion: Word-of-mouth communication about bad service is more likely to suppress sales results than good service talk is likely to enhance them.

Increased Employee Productivity

A major benefit of service is increased employee productivity. (See Chapter 6 for guidance on increasing productivity.)

Example: After Bio-Lab Inc., of Decatur, Georgia, installed a customer service system, productivity climbed steadily. Says Anne Pinkerton, director of customer service, "We processed $5 million more in orders in (one year) than in (the previous year) with the same number of employees."

Customer Complaints

Another benefit of a quality service system can be more customer complaints. Customer service encourages complaints, and that's good. Complaints are opportunities. They are opportunities to correct problems that a company might never hear about unless its customer service program encouraged them.

But employees avoid complaints because they've never been educated in handling them. Indeed, 80 percent of the complaint letters that I write go unanswered—like one I wrote to the president of Marriott Courtyard hotels. During the first (and last) time I stayed at a Courtyard hotel, my father-in-law had a heart attack. The hotel didn't deliver an emergency message left for me. What's more, they didn't make the wake-up call that I left the night before.

Indeed, a service system that simplifies and encourages complaints tends to increase profit. Why? Because customers who can complain to the company are less likely to spread their complaints throughout the community, thereby turning away a certain amount of business.

Richard Gamgort, customer service representative at Armstrong World Industries, says: "We have brought on some very loyal customers whose original contacts with our company originated with a complaint."

So, it's a wise move, indeed, to make it very easy for customers to express their opinions. (See Chapter 11 on complaint systems.)

Don't deny, out of misplaced pride, that you receive complaints. *Admit* that the complaints that you know about probably are just the tip of an iceberg of complaints. It's almost always true.

Don't, figuratively, execute the messenger when the messenger (employee) brings you news of customer complaints.

Summary of Benefits

Benefits of quality service, all of which will be discussed later in the book, can be condensed into this list:

1. Customer loyalty and increase in market share and return on sales.
2. Increased sales and profit.
3. More frequent sales. Repeat business. Larger sales. Order upgrading. Reordering.
4. Higher customer count and more new customers.
5. Savings in marketing, advertising, and promotion budgets.

6. Fewer complaints in an environment receptive to complaints. More complaints resolved. Customers stay.
7. Positive company reputation.
8. Differentiation.
9. Improved employee morale and productivity because customers respond positively to them.
10. Improved employee relationships: people talk to each other because they are in better moods, doing work they more often enjoy.
11. Fewer employee grievances, absenteeism, and tardiness.
12. Less turnover.

CUSTOMER LOYALTY

One of the greatest benefits of customer service is customer loyalty. This is true because most business is repeat business. Loyalty is a hedge against competition's erosion of your customer base.

"What is more important than customer service?" asked Bruce Bolger, editor of *Incentive* magazine. "Few companies can depend upon a continuing flow of new customers. Sooner or later most must build a loyal base. The better the service, the bigger that base." Loyal customers who continue to buy are the foundation for long-term success.

"It's well known," says Marva McArthur, customer service executive for Waddell and Reed Services of Kansas City, "that it is a financial benefit to a company to get repeat business from the same customers instead of having to go out into the market and find new customers."

Indeed, it's a lot smarter—and cheaper—to emphasize customer service, thereby keeping many of the customers a company already has, than it is to spend a large part of the budget to attract new customers.

Francis Tritt of Kansas City, Missouri, who conducts seminars on customer service, says that businesses that used to throw all their energies into creating new products and luring new customers are beginning to realize that they ought to be doing more to keep the customers they already have.

It's instructive to note that the business philosophy of L. L. Bean, Inc., purveyor of outdoor clothing and supplies, includes this phrase: "treat your customers like human beings and they'll always come back for more."

Eastman Kodak Corporation views its customer service program as a key to customer retention. Retaining customers is vital in staying ahead of the competition and in remaining profitable, the company believes.

Jan Carlzon wrote in *Moments of Truth*: "We have oriented ourselves to become a customer-driven company that recognizes that its only true assets are satisfied customers, all of whom expect to be treated as individuals and who won't select us as their airline unless we do just that."

There's no better illustration of the value of customer loyalty than the consequences of disloyalty and loss of customers. Take a 100-store supermarket chain as an example. If each of those stores alienated only one customer per day, how much money do you think the 100-store chain would lose annually?

For one such chain the loss estimate was $94.4 million.

Cost of Lost Customers

"Studies have shown that hotels may be losing as much as 12 percent of their annual revenues when dissatisfied customers switch to other hotels," says William Sheehan, president and CEO of Omni Hotels.

I can testify to the validity of that statement. I stayed at a Miami Doubletree Hotel. These hotels have been promoting their responsiveness to service, but I left a completed Doubletree Response Card and I still haven't received acknowledgment.

Look upon every customer as a potential lifelong patron—as equity in your marketing investment. Satisfied customers generate word-of-mouth referrals; so every time you lose a customer, you weaken your sales base. But the longer you *keep* a customer, the greater is the equity in your marketing investment.

Attend especially to intangible traits of a product or service. Over the long haul, relationships, based upon perceptions formed over time, are more important than are so-called tangible traits.

But service certainly is more than smiles. At the very best it is attitude and all the supporting systems.

Loyalty, however, is fleeting. Customers always ask, subconsciously: "What have you done for me *lately*?"

"Three key facts about customer loyalty are that it is circumstantial, it is fragile, and it is fleeting," write Karl Albrecht and Ron Zemke in *Service America!* (Dow Jones-Irwin, 1985).

The transitory nature of customer loyalty is the best reason to make service an established corporate strategy constantly reinforced by follow-up training and supported by highly visible management commitment that is communicated.

The American Management Association found that successful companies spend about 20 percent more money on personnel, including personnel training, than unsuccessful companies do. The finding held true for companies of all sizes in every industry.

Customer loyalty is very effective in muffling the Lorelei call of new competitive products and services. It takes a lot more effort by competitors to lure away a loyal customer than it does to attract one who is loyal no more as a result of the unreliability of a company and the hostility of its employees.

Peggy F. Haney, vice president of consumer affairs for American Express: "As a result of our customer service program, both satisfied customers and those who have problems that we can work out quickly are much more loyal."

Substantiating Haney's view is Roger Nunley, director of industry and consumer affairs for Coca-Cola USA. He says: "In terms of brand loyalty it is in the company's best interests to influence not only the half [of customers] who intend to change brands but all of those who wouldn't normally contact us."

Service Can Restore Loyalty

Service not only maintains loyalty. It restores loyalty. A TARP report cites documented evidence that good service and customer education programs can restore brand loyalty, confidence, and repurchase intention of customers who experience problems.

A group of Michigan hospitals discovered the truth in the assertion that service can restore loyalty. The hospitals experienced a serious problem with malpractice suits. So, a hot line was established to answer calls from people who planned to file suits.

The hot-line staff discovered that the former patients now intending to become litigants were motivated to file by bad employee attitudes and personal behavior, not by low quality of medical care. After the staff began dealing with the real causes of the malpractice threats—the way the staff treated patients—many of the planned suits were dropped.

Bottom-Line Value of Service

Is customer loyalty important to the bottom line? Your local supermarket expects at least $4,400 to $22,000 from each consumer during the five years that market research shows that the consumer lives in the same neighborhood. Appliance manufacturers figure brand loyalty is worth more than $2,000 in profit over 20 years. In banking, the average customer represents $80 a year or more in profit. All these figures rise with inflation.

Auto industry studies have found that a brand-loyal new car dealer's customer represents average revenue of at least $140,000 over the customer's lifetime. You can see that it's ludicrous for a service department manager to stand toe to toe with a customer and argue about who should pay for a $40 part. It's ludicrous because the car dealership stands to lose much more in the future than the profit on a $40 part.

HOW SERVICE INCREASES CUSTOMER LOYALTY

Service enhances perceived value of a tangible or intangible product. When consumers perceive that the value of a product has increased without a corresponding increase in price, loyalty, purchase amount, purchase frequency and amount usually increase also. This is a truism in business.

So, often it is unnecessary to court customer satisfaction by reducing prices. Just improve service.

Service that's responsive to customer needs is *value added* to a product, at a bargain rate. Prompt service and delivery, helping a customer find solutions to problems, treating each customer as an individual—these practices are just reorientation of effort that would be expended anyway. So they are practically free.

The GE Answer Center

The General Electric Answer Center is a sophisticated customer service marketing tool that contributes heavily to the bottom line. Answer Center reps answer up to 15,000 calls per day from information in a computer data base containing a lode of information on 120 product lines with 85,000 models and 1,100 operating and repair procedures. The result is that the Answer Center enhances unit volume and also customers' perceived product value.

"Perceived value" is the operative term in this context. Real value does not increase, of course. Service, you see, creates impressions articulated in comments such as these:

- "This company delivers what it promises."
- "I always feel welcome."
- "If I have a problem and I don't know what to do to solve it, my account manager at The Timberwolf Corporation always seems to have time to help me out."

N. Powell Taylor, manager of the GE Answer Center, says: "We are trying to build a bond with the customer, not just to answer a question—a bond that'll last many years and give us a real competitive advantage. Every opportunity offered by a customer contact gives us a chance to enhance brand loyalty."

So, with service, one achieves a *perceived* addition to product quality without spending money to add real quality. Payoff: Long-term increases in market share that lead to economies of scale that, in turn, reduce cost.

A penny saved is a penny earned.

The Zenger-Miller study mentioned earlier found that a combination of service and price determine the value that a customer perceives in a product. Credible evidence even indicates that improved service quality actually reduces total cost of running a business.

Improved service, then, "drives" price and customer perception of price.

BAD SERVICE NULLIFIES ADVERTISING

Richard Israel, retailing consultant, found that much of a huge advertising investment by a major furniture chain evaporated at the moment a customer entered a store and walked smack into a "nonsupportive psychological environment." (Translation: Salespeople initially ignored customers and failed to respond to questions and requests.)

All your company's promotion, advertising, marketing, and good will can be ruined by one rude or indifferent employee. Money spent on advertising is largely wasted when customers show up in response to it and are turned away by indolence, insolence, ignorance, insincerity, indifference, and aloofness.

"The whole purpose of advertising," says Israel, "is to get the customer to come in the front door. After that, advertising can't do anything more for you. *It's up to the people in the store to take over during the last four feet.*"

But we tend to assume that employees know from birth what to do for customers during these last four feet. If they do know, they aren't applying their knowledge. No, employees do not arrive on the job with a full-blown set of service skills.

I believe that advertisers should allot a portion of their ad budgets to development of learning programs for employees in order to reinforce media programs with customer service knowledge and skill.

Advertising brings customers in the door, all right, but bad customer service sends them right back out the door again.

One of the nation's largest manufacturers, looking for a way to cut down on erosion of market share without spending much money, "found that its advertising sold only 17 percent of its products," says Richard Seltzer, a leading customer service consultant. "The other 83 percent was sold by the company's reputation—past consumer experience, word of mouth, magazine stories about the company, and so on.

"In other words, when (the manufacturer) looked at all the money that had been sunk into advertising, it wasn't selling as many products as it thought," said Seltzer. "As a result, they expanded into a complaint handling program."

It's tough, today, for many manufacturing companies to understand that they are in service, too. It is difficult for managers of these companies to realize that service has a powerful impact on the bottom line.

These companies must make the transition to a service orientation, or they'll be left behind by competitors who do—competitors who realize that service adds product value and customer loyalty.

CUSTOMER SERVICE: A PROFIT CENTER

Item: When nothing was changed but service level, Woolworth's of England saw an 18 percent increase in sales at four stores.

Item: Computer terminals lit up at Zellers, Inc., third largest retailer in Canada, with a system-wide $20 million sales increase when the only change was a new customer service system led by a training program for employees featuring reinforcement and review. This 12.5 percent increase in sales at Zellers stores continued for months. Increased volume occurred despite declining sales and customer traffic throughout the retailing industry at the time.

Item: Warren Blanding, customer service pioneer, describes how he knows that service produces profit. "In my business (Marketing Publications, Inc.), publishing, we know that it costs 'X' dollars to obtain a customer. We know, too, what it costs to service a customer. So, we project revenue for 10 years, based on subscription renewal rate.

"One of our publication's renewal rate is 70 percent. So, for every thousand dollars we take in we know that 10 years from now we will have made a profit of about $4,000 with almost no selling expense other than a few letters requesting renewals.

"If we jump renewal rate to 80 percent by providing a higher level of service, that $4,000 becomes $6,500—more than a 50 percent increase in total revenue with only a 10 percent increase in service level."

Item: The GE Answer Center produces at least twice the return that GE forecast in planning for the Center. Until recently, the company spent only $2.50 to $4.50 on a typical call. (Only 15 percent of calls are complaints, by the way.)

Facts like these verify the marketing impact of service and whet the appetite of business for customer service programs.

So it seems to be true that an increase in customer satisfaction yields a measurable increase in profit.

Profit Contribution of Service

Indeed, profit contributions of customer service show up at many points. Order upgrading is one way.

Let's say that a customer calls in an order for 3,000 pounds of material and the employee taking the call says: "If you buy 5,000 pounds you get a 10 percent discount, you know."

Says the customer: "I'll take it."

That's order upgrading. That's volume and, presumably, profit contributed by customer service.

Does profit vary in direct proportion to degree of customer satisfaction? Wc think that it does.

It is true that when you do something for a customer, even when it's as simple as a refund or deduction, you're rewarded with far more than the cost of providing the service in future business attributable to the good will that your gesture engendered.

Cost of Service

It costs money to start a customer service program. Unfortunately, some companies can't see beyond initial expense to long-term results; so they put off new service programs.

But spending money on something that pays off in profit should not be a sticking point for a business. Most executives in most kinds of business enterprises don't reject good ideas because they're expensive. Price shouldn't be the crucial consideration when it comes to developing or to maintaining a positive business relationship with a customer.

"The best kept secret in the global economy today is that if your service is awesome you get so stinking rich you have to keep buying new bags to take all the money home," wrote Tom Peters in *Thriving on Chaos*.

Some—just a few—well-known companies with "awesome" service are Disney, Domino's Pizza, Federal Express, Wal-Mart, First Chicago National Bank, The Coleman Company, and Honda. In one recent fiscal year, British Airways posted one of the largest net incomes of all international airlines ($189 million) on revenues of $7 billion. But six years earlier it had been one of the biggest money losers in the skies.

What happened? Customer service happened. During the same time that the company was getting so profitable, it ranked at the top in customer satisfaction.

Profitable carriers satisfy unhappy customers by "giving a full explanation if they can't comply with a request," says Dan Smith, director of consumer and industry affairs at the International Airline Passengers Association in Dallas.

Growing evidence that customer happiness shows up on the bottom line is one reason that companies such as GE, Whirlpool, Coca-Cola, and British Airways spend millions to improve complaint handling.

Maryanne Rasmussen, vice president of worldwide quality at American Express, says: "The formula I use is: Better complaint handling equals higher customer satisfaction equals higher brand loyalty equals higher profitability."

CUSTOMER SERVICE SAVES MONEY

Not only does customer-satisfying service *make* money. It also *saves* money. Keeping customers, you see, reduces marketing expense. Money unexpended on marketing equals profit retained.

A professional customer service program enables a company to reduce marketing expenditures because fewer customers are lost. Fewer former customers need to be replaced.

Club Industry magazine, edited for management of membership businesses such as health clubs, notes that with a 2,000-member cap and a 40 percent attrition rate a club must pick up 800 new members a year to stay afloat. The cost of recruiting 800 new members can put a big dent in a budget, the magazine continues.

"Good service may cost money, but not as much as a major annual recruiting drive," the magazine observes. "If that same club can cut its attrition rate in half through better service, it would need to attract only 400 new members per year."

The Multiple of Five

So there's yet another relevant equation here: Money spent on customer service equals customers retained. Keeping customers is very important to business success because customers are five times more likely to switch vendors because of perceived service problems than for price concerns or for product quality issues. This was one finding of research by The Forum Corporation. The study involved 2,374 interviews of customers and employees from many different companies.

It's interesting that this multiple of five also shows up as the rate at which dissatisfied customers switch their business to competitors.

The 5-to-1 ratio shows up once again when we compare cost of obtaining a new customer with cost of keeping a customer you already have. This has been a rule of thumb in customer service for years. The difference in cost between "getting" and "keeping" a customer becomes clear when you measure cost of customer acquisition through marketing (advertising, direct mailings, field sales calls, and so on) against the cost of maintaining an account in house.

Field sales calls alone (part of "customer acquisition" expenses) cost $64.80 each, according to information released in late 1989 by The Dartnell Corporation. Cost of maintaining an account in-house varies widely by company, but it is a very safe guess that the cost would be far less per contact than $64.80.

Service Yields Savings

Savings are achieved with good service this way: Employees improve service performance and thereby *prevent* dissatisfaction and complaints. This reduces or eliminates cost of correcting problems such as payroll for a larger customer relations staff. Furthermore, service saves marketing costs because it's easier and cheaper to sell to present, satisfied customers than it is to sell to mere prospects.

Many business managers are unaware of the fact that service saves marketing costs. What's more, quality *work* (doing things right the first time) that is part of quality service saves other costs such as the cost of doing a job over again, cost of repairs and replacement, and the simple administrative costs of complaints that would not be made if an organization practiced quality service delivery.

Of course, good customer service drastically reduces the number of lost customers to be replaced. Poor service is responsible for 40 percent of customer defections, according to study results announced in 1990 by Booz, Allen & Hamilton Inc., management consulting firm.

Some managers even believe that quality service is expensive, notes Ronald L. Vaughn, Max Hollingsworth Professor of American Enterprise at the University of Tampa and president of Atlanta-based Strategic Testing and Research Co.

But courtesy, friendliness, and positive interchanges with internal and external customers, those quality service hallmarks, are free!

Service Doesn't Cost, It Pays

Another way of looking at the initial cost of a service program is that the cost of a dissatisfied customer is much greater than the cost of providing service, says Kenneth L. Pia, Vaughn's colleague at Strategic Testing. So customer service doesn't cost, it pays.

Here's one way it pays: Lorna Opatow, president of Opatow, Inc., New York marketing research company specializing in consumer affairs and public relations, finds that if you keep your customers happy, you have an "easier sell"— thereby saving marketing expenses.

Selection of a brand or a product, or choosing a company to do business with, says Opatow, isn't so much a conscious choice, in many cases, as it is a knee-jerk choice. The knee jerks in the direction of the good-service company, when a consumer has a good "feeling" about a company that derives from the company's quality service, she says.

Any businessperson should recognize the wisdom of giving customer service status at least as high as marketing, and certainly as high as any other business program, once a customer base has been established.

We predict that service of the future will be known as a facet of marketing, not as a frill or a customer bonus as it often is known today.

IT'S FIRST CLASS TO BE SECOND

Despite all the benefits of quality service, experienced managers often shrink from starting a formal quality service program when a competitor rolls out a program before they do. Most reasons for this inaction can be grouped under a single word: *pride.*

Now, pride is a valuable ingredient of any company's culture. But occasionally pride is a handicap, as it is when it justifies turning thumbs down and noses up on service because a competing company was first with a service program. In these situations managers are disabled by the "Not Invented Here" syndrome. (If it's somebody else's idea, the reasoning goes, it can't be very good.) Executives may say: "We aren't interested in being followers."

Middle managers think that they'll look bad in the eyes of senior managers—and competitors—if they seem to copy a competitor's strategy.

A department may have been developing a customer service program for months. Management shies away from instructing the department to implement a competitor's wildly successful plan because they want to avoid demoralizing employees.

These emotional reactions are the reasons that most of the time a company that installs a customer service program will not be challenged in the customer service area for at least two years by its competitors. Other companies don't want to embarrass employees who were bested by the innovative firm. Companies in the airline and automobile industries nurture no such reservations. Within one or two days of a special price promotion, all the companies in an industry will have copied the strategy.

Stanley Marcus, retired chairman of The Neiman Marcus Company, says that the only thing that forces a company to become service driven is a competitor. A *competitive service* program stands a 50 percent chance of failing because commitment will be weak or nonexistent. But service is so important that ego should not be allowed to interfere with speedy use of a customer service program.

This same kind of intellectual and emotional baggage interferes in other ways with implementation of quality service practices.

1. A manager accustomed to applying sophisticated management and financial tools sometimes is incapable of understanding that something as simple as customer service can actually increase profit.
2. Management wants to avoid offending those who were responsible for service by suggesting that they develop a new service system similar to a competitor's.
3. Company management in an industry dominated by a single competitive corporation widely admired for service often can't believe that something as inexpensive and fundamental as customer ser-

vice could be the reason for dominance such as return on investment as high as 20 percent.

4. Service that develops long-term customer satisfaction and loyalty is hard work—too much work for some companies. This may be the major reason most firms do not focus on service.
5. Service is a "soft issue"—intangible and abstract. It's hard for some managers to believe that a customer service program is worth their time. Service doesn't require tangibles such as million-dollar computers, a fleet of trucks, industrial robots, numerical control machines, or new buildings, so it's difficult for managers to imagine it. Therefore, customer service couldn't be very important.

But the benefits of a quality service program—once they have been achieved—simply "blow away" all empty rationalizations.

It's a fact of life that many companies leave customer service leaders unchallenged in their industries. Years and even decades pass before they take up the gauntlet in the coliseum of customer service.

Among beneficiaries of this unintended accommodation have been companies with stellar customer service reputations such as Trammel Crow, Neiman-Marcus, National Steel, Sheraton Hotels, Dow Chemical Co., Miles Laboratories, Eastman Kodak, Polaroid, Woolworth's of England, Byerly's, Federal Express, Disney, McDonald's, and others.

Companies with good customer service steamroll the competition, continuing for years to confound competitors with poor customer service by out-performing them no matter what they do.

You'd think competitors would catch on.

CALCULATING RETURN ON SERVICE

TARP, the Washington, D.C., service consultants and researchers, developed economic models that predict return on dollars invested in handling complaints and inquiries. The models apply to buying patterns, profit margins, and dozens of other factors.

Another TARP service model provides a way to document value of an existing service system—and also to determine how to improve service in cost-effective ways.

The Market Impact of Service Model determines the effect of reaching dissatisfied customers and concluding contacts satisfactorily. It provides executives with the actual dollar impact of existing service and service improvements, it quantifies economic impact of service levels, and it indicates which service should be changed to achieve greatest bottom line impact.

This service model also enables executives to determine the amount that profit and return on investment would increase for each increment of decrease in "unarticulated dissatisfaction"—complaints unexpressed.

It also determines impact on profit and return on investment of reduction in cost per customer contact and of an increase in percentage of customers satisfied by the service system.

This model is the salvation of company service departments and service systems because it gives them the figures to document their roles as corporate profit centers generating sales.

The Service Model assumes the following returns on service costs:

1. Increased sales and return on investment from better service. Service gets better as a result of improvements made to prevent customer dissatisfaction.
2. Reduction in service cost. The result of *preventing* dissatisfaction.
3. Positive market impact, the result of satisfaction that good service causes among a larger proportion of customers. Using the model, TARP comes up with specific information for a company such as incremental cost versus incremental benefit.

Increments are expressed in terms of employees and equipment added in one location to achieve, for example, a 3 percent increase in customer loyalty. Bottom-line value of a 3 percent increase in loyalty would be calculated.

To estimate increased sales and return on investment resulting from service, the model combines company-provided data and data obtained from surveys of a sample of all customers. The result is calculations such as

Net purchases by customers whose complaints were satisfied.
New purchases resulting from positive word of mouth.
Profit on sales from complaint handling and resultant word of mouth recommendation of the company.
Return on investment from money invested in service.

In real life, the service model produces figures such as those contained in "Close to the Customer," an American Management Association Research Report on Consumer Affairs:

1. " . . . a small firm that sells software to *Fortune* 500 companies spent $110,000 on mail/phone questionnaires, $100,000 on consumer education materials, and $300,000 to educate its own employees in customer relations—and grew by 30 percent . . . (in one year).
2. "A mid-sized chemical processor spent $350,000 to leap over its retailers and put its salespeople directly in touch with their consumers. The company increased sales by 20 percent!
3. "A billion-dollar chain of convenience stores—a business that does all its selling over the local counter and that takes no phone

> orders at national headquarters —nevertheless spent $200,000 on an 800 line to field customer queries and complaints. Sales revenues increased by 19 percent in one year."

The TARP model can predict benefits such as those experienced by Procter & Gamble, the nation's largest producer of consumer products (Ivory soap, Folger's coffee, Crest toothpaste, Pamper's disposable diapers, Tide detergent, and many more). P&G answers more than 750,000 telephone calls and letters from customers each year. A third of these replies are complaints about products, ads, and even about the plots of soap operas that the company sponsors.

If only half of those complaints, according to TARP's model, relate to products with 30 cent margins, and if only 85 percent are handled to the customer's satisfaction, the benefit to the company in one year would exceed half a million dollars. Such a sum would have represented a return on customer service investment of almost 20 percent in a recent year.

MAINTAINING QUALITY SERVICE LEVELS

Once you've hired people with good service tendencies, and once they've learned to apply your service system, then your concern becomes maintaining a high level of service.

Pride is your best tool for maintaining service level.

Employees are proud to work for a company with a president and other senior managers who support the need for good service often and then prove their support with their actions. They are proud of a company that maintains in training and in every other relevant contact with employees that it is committed to service excellence and then proves it by providing financial support for service.

Bad Service Causes Employee Turnover

A study by The Forum Corporation found employee turnover to be inversely proportional to employee perceptions of the quality of service provided by their employer. That is, turnover drops when employees feel that the company is providing high-quality service. On the other hand, when a company's service is perceived as bad, not only do consumers not like to patronize the firm, but also employees don't like to *work* for it.

A report on the Forum study states: "The highest turnover rates are associated with companies possessing the lowest employee ratings of service quality. . . . Factors such as length of service with the company, job function, and frequency of contact with customers demonstrate little influence (upon turnover rate)."

The results of the Forum study add relevance to the lack of pride in work that is rampant today. This is an issue that must be dealt with by companies determined to maintain a quality service reputation.

Says Thomas Kelly, an assistant professor at Cornell University's School of Hotel Administration: "In our culture, these [service] jobs are not considered a worthwhile occupation. When workers view giving service as beneath them [revealing lack of pride], it shows." Pride in job and in employer is promoted at The Coleman Company, Inc., of Wichita, Kansas. Coleman is the world's largest manufacturer of camping and outdoor recreation equipment. "Outstanding Employee" performance recognition programs and articles in the company newsletter report outstanding customer service performance.

The underlying message in this book is that customer service is something that you can achieve. Once an organization's chief executive officer is committed to a professional level of real (not claimed and nonexistent) service and once the CEO has communicated his or her commitment to the organization's managers, then it's time for commitment to be translated into action. That's what the rest of this book is about—action.

We will be suggesting action that you can take to achieve results obtained by some of the most successful companies in America from their service programs.

So, read on.

2

In the Beginning Was . . . the Plan

REMOVING THE BLINDFOLD

> The most effective business *strategies* developed today are those that take a service orientation. Customer service is a vital function of any well-run company's operation.
>
> —*Eric Jones, former president, Data Systems Group, Texas Instruments*

> The best way to sell is to make it convenient to buy.
>
> —*Anon.*

The pride that motivates professionals to demand excellence of themselves and of others is the same pride that often becomes a blinder concealing shortcomings such as poor service that are left to chip away at a company's reputation.

Pride is the reason that executives don't react to high marketing costs. (Those high costs are needed to attract new customers to replace those lost to poor service.)

Pride is the reason that a steady slide in sales is *not* attributed to unreliability, slow delivery, resistance to customer requests, or unresponsiveness to customer complaints.

Pride prevents perception of embarrassment and discomfort of employees who must deal continually with hostile customers fed up with bad service, and pride prevents the realization that this embarrassment is a primary cause of low employee morale and high turnover.

The pride that believes in either the infallibility or in the untouchability of management or that harbors fundamental faith in overall superiority of an organization vis-à-vis *all* competitors is a blindfold that must be removed from the eyes of an organization's managers before effective customer service planning can begin.

How? Determination to define needs and benefits sought—in unemotional, harshly objective terms—is effective.

Short-Term Profit: A Blindfold

Service often is not a priority for management. I place a substantial portion of the problem of underemphasis on service at the feet of corporate leaders.

A common feature of corporate service mentality, besides pride, that blindfolds managers developing a service strategy is short-term emphasis on profit at the expense of long-term service quality.

Part of the difficulty is their short-term orientation. If you are evaluated on quarterly or yearly profits, that's what you will pay attention to.

Pride, misplaced priorities, short-term orientation, and also failure to understand realities of the service economy all are reasons that service often is given short shrift.

After years during which our economy has been more service oriented than industrial, many managers still don't understand the significant difference between the old world of manufacturing and the new world of service, says Alden Clayton, head of Marketing Science Institute, Cambridge, Massachusetts, a nonprofit business think tank.

Only Lip Service

Granted that service is a veritable triumph for some leading organizations, still a large proportion of managers have made virtually no adjustment to the new service climate except to pay lip service to it with boring slogans:

"The Customer Is Always Right," "Satisfaction Guaranteed," and "The Customer Is King."

They may install a service program, give it a noisy send-off, then publish a quarterly motivational article in the company magazine, paper the walls with posters, and send an annual letter to employees extolling the importance of service.

They may launch a battle of platitudes with competitors. They boldly commit the company to a larger lobbying budget. They noisily herald a new, strongly worded corporate philosophy or mission statement that asserts unqualified commitment to service. Ad and promotion budgets are boosted for the purpose of creating a service *image*. (Managers expect that employees will read the ad and spontaneously deliver good service. They are dreamers!)

But that's not service. Service is service.

Stand guard against this self-deception. Learn to recognize it. And reject it in favor of pro-active development of a long-term service plan that becomes your professional guide to quality service performance.

Where the Plan Begins

Begin by completing a professional assessment of the company's service status and needs, evaluating customer views on service, developing service standards, objectives, and actions—and writing it all down in a Service Plan.

The consequence of an all-talk and no-effective-action approach to service is delay of serious effort to install a customer service program. Some people consider General Motors to be an example of this approach. Except in the case of Cadillac, General Motors long took a cosmetic approach to customer service. The company sent service managers through a training program in which they were taught how to refuse requests for service politely. It used "800" numbers to field complaints.

This approach backfired. Customers concluded that General Motors was "supercilious" and that "they were very courteous but didn't want to fix your car."

However, in 1987 Oldsmobile offered a customer satisfaction program that we customized for dealers. Those who adopted it realized a 4.8 percent average improvement in their customer satisfaction index (CSI). Training works. It's just hard to convince management that it works.

"Polite evasion" antagonizes people more than saying right out that you can't do what the customer asks. Tactically, nothing's wrong with "800" numbers, but it didn't lead to improvement in customer satisfaction because of GM's lack of service strategy.

SERVICE: VALUABLE BUSINESS STRATEGY

Service is valuable for companies hard pressed by competition. The most successful companies today push quality service, not price. After all, competitive pricing brings shoppers, but not necessarily customers. Anybody can lower price. But give a customer something worthwhile, like service that treats him or her in a personal, individual, sincerely concerned manner, and he or she will gladly pay the asking price and return to buy again and again.

Home appliance manufacturers increasingly depend upon service to distinguish them from competitors. Whirlpool's "Cool Line" information-complaint (800) number began in 1967. In 1985, General Electric began the same type of service, "The GE Answer Center." (800 numbers and similar information-complaint systems are discussed in Chapter 9.)

Marva McArthur, when she was a customer service representative at Waddell and Reed Services, Kansas City financial services company, said: "Our company recognizes that many companies offer basically the same kinds of mutual funds and options that we offer. So, to be more competitive, we try to be faster in servicing accounts, and we try to provide better quality."

We've found the experiences of one fitness club to be applicable to virtually all businesses interested in increasing profit: A formal survey by the Homewood/Flossmoor Racquet and Fitness Club near Chicago found that 72 percent of members considered "speed of service and atmosphere the staff creates" the most important aspects of the club. Value for the money was rated third, supporting the idea that club members, and by extension customers everywhere, want service *first* and are willing to pay for it.

Isn't the fact that customers think that service is important reason enough for any business to consider service to be worth significant investment in time and money?

"Service, service, and more service is what counts today," says Harold Saper, director of Corporate Service for Budget Rent-A-Car Corp.

THE BEGINNING

Some companies should begin planning for a service program by understanding what's important to their customers—and all companies should include this information in their plan. They need research. (See Chapter 4.)

Other organizations should begin by evaluating their own performance. They may discover glaring shortcomings in authentic, tangible efforts to fulfill customer expectations.

What Customers Want

Customer expectations: This is a significant concept. A common problem at the beginning of customer service planning is customers' "level of expectation." An organization must know its customers' level of expectations for these reasons: Do less than customers expect and service is bad. Do exactly what customers expect and service is good. But do more than customers anticipate, and service is perceived as superior.

I urge you to do more than your customers expect if you plan to retain them. Doing so sets the positive word-of-mouth process moving.

The realities of customer expectations are the primary determinants of expectation level. Few patrons of luxury hotels can be led to expect anything other than luxury service; so the hotel shouldn't waste its time and reputation trying to lower expectations.

Likewise, trying to set expectations that vary widely from the realities that customers perceive is futile. Martin Stein, auto industry analyst, observes: "General Motors' advertising campaign for Mr. Goodwrench, GM's mythical service expert, doesn't work. People doubt that the quality of service being advertised will be available. They may be looking for a Mr. Goodwrench, but they aren't finding him."

The job of bringing service strategy in line with customer expectations is basically the same as positioning a company or product in the marketplace. Service positioning starts with four givens:

- The segments targeted.
- Expectations of customers within those segments.
- Strategy for exceeding expectations.
- Expectations of service level that has already been created by *competitors* in the minds of your customers. (The goal is to exceed these expectations.)

Federal Express's strategy is to meet expectations for all the actions and reactions that customers *perceive* they have purchased, including not only pickup and delivery but also documentation and shipment information.

A winning service position meets two criteria: it distinguishes a company from its competition; and it leads customers to expect *slightly less* service than the company can deliver. Network Equipment Technology (NET) actually disciplines salespeople for "overpromising." NET realizes that keeping expectations at just the right level—slightly below perceived performance—is a constant challenge.

Years ago Avis positioned itself as the second-place car rental company that had to try harder. The company is doing the same thing today by portraying itself as the rent-a-car company that tries harder because the employees own the company.

Maytag positions its washing machines as being so reliable that the Maytag repairman is bored to death. The result is high expectation of service. It is to be hoped that customers receive at least as much as they expect.

Positioning Service

Communication tools used to position customer service are the same communication tools used by any marketer—advertising, promotion, public relations, and so on. Since service is intangible, communication must dramatize service in ways that make service benefits real and clear.

All forms of communication must tightly focus upon target markets because customer expectations are strongly influenced by any impression of the other kinds of customers they visualize in loosely focused advertising.

Reaching the wrong segments can be disastrous. A business traveler checking into a budget motel revises his or her expectations radically if a drunk is seen sleeping in the lobby.

Positioning customer service, in a service plan, differs from normal positioning because customers are hypersensitive to tangible service clues such as uniforms, repair trucks, brochures, and lobbies.

Often, customers are hard put to tell that a service has been performed without additional visual evidence such as the elaborate receipts that auto garages make out or the paper that hotels wrap around toilet seats to tell guests that the toilet has been cleaned. Customer expectations of service rise and fall precipitously in response to these seemingly minor clues.

There's a message in this that should be reflected in your service plan: make sure that it is easy for your customers to notice that they've received good service.

Foundation of the Service Plan: Service Strategy

When organizations know what's important to their customers and when they realize the shortcomings of their present service, then they are ready to write a Service Plan.

The foundation of a Service Plan must be a clear service strategy. You need, in the strategy, a strong vision of the values of service to your organization and also a well-planned, coherent, well-executed plan for achieving those values. All the pieces of the puzzle must be present.

A service strategy describes your customers, reports their evaluations of different aspects of service, estimates budget for achieving customer satisfaction, and projects profit increases. Without a strategy it is difficult to develop a concept of service that rallies employees or to arrest conflicts between corporate strategy and actual customer service or to come up with ways to measure service performance and perceived quality.

In short, without a strategy you can't get to first base. Developing a service strategy is an essential step toward choosing an optimal mix and level of service for different customer groups. Provide too little service or the wrong kind and customers will become more responsive to the blandishments of competitor sales messages. Provide too much service, even the right kind, and your company might price itself out of the market and struggle to balance the books at the end of the year.

Service: No Afterthought

A Service Plan is a proper part of every new marketing plan: a new product never should be introduced until service has been thought out and tested. Service is not an afterthought. It is an important original part of a marketing plan.

Every corporation that acquires another corporation ought to plan how it will achieve customer satisfaction and allot money for that purpose at the same time that it is preparing financial and operating plans. What often happens, however, is that millions are spent on brokers' fees and on new signs, new uniforms, and golden parachutes, but not one red cent is spent on the organization's implied service responsibility to the customers who will make or break the organization's financial plan.

Guidelines

Use these guidelines in making decisions about the features of your service plan:

1. Underpromise and overdeliver. Set customer expectations at the right level.
2. Research customer needs thoroughly. Only the customer knows what he or she wants.
3. Segment the market and design core products and core services to meet the needs of the customer base. Not all customers who buy the same service or product have the same service needs.

Follow these steps in developing a service plan:

Gather Information

Describe your customers in terms of their needs and wants. If you don't know who it is you're trying to satisfy and what their needs are, it will be difficult, indeed, to satisfy them. Gather information needed to set goals such as average revenue per customer and the market share you seek.

In planning sessions, ask and answer questions such as

- What do our customers want and need from us? (Answering this question is covered in detail in Chapter 4.)
- What services can we provide customers that the competition doesn't?
- How can we improve *existing* service?
- How can we improve customer *awareness* of good service? (Service loses impact when customers don't know about it or notice it.)

Set up a system for on-going information gathering from customers and for assigning ratings of service performance. Rate:

1. Time spent resolving typical problems.
2. Ease of access to the corporation and to its services.
3. Quality of employee performance.
4. Customer satisfaction with action taken.

5. Degree of difficulty experienced by customers in attracting attention of employees and obtaining responses.
6. Content of the company's response to the customer in terms of accuracy, completeness, and effectiveness.

In addition, each of the foregoing attributes of service must be broken down into component parts. The elements of "ease of access," for example, may be seen, from the customer's point of view, as:

Ability to get through with the first phone call
Being placed on hold
Time on hold
Awareness of the number to call to get the desired service
Availability of service when needed—including evenings and weekends
Being assisted by the first person reached versus being transferred one or more times

In the Service Plan specify action called for by each of the component parts in your attributes of service.

Evaluating present level of performance is a legitimate part of this information-gathering phase. So is establishing a means of keeping your finger on the pulse of your service program.

Observe and evaluate continuously by asking questions such as:

- Is the company really making and delivering the quality product or service it says it is?
- Do customers see it that way?
- How can we do it all better—answering customer needs in a way that expands the business?

One of the best ways to find out what customers want is to ask them. So do it. Then analyze their answers.

Details on methods of determining customer needs and wants and updating your knowledge are found in Chapter 4, but we will cover here some of the points that are most essential to preparation for drafting a Service Plan.

Service Audits

Make sure that surveys to learn customer wants and expectations—call them service audits—are thorough and objective assessments of interactions between the organization and the customer at all known points of contact. You want to know what customers think and you want to use that information to develop an effective service strategy.

It's important to update customer surveys, though, so you can update your strategy. If you don't update, you may end up on a customer service treadmill—running at sprinter speed but moving at a snail's pace.

Plan to conduct customer surveys incessantly. Don't worry that customers might tell you to get lost. Customers usually are quite willing to tell you what they want and to rate the service they've already received.

The trouble is that most companies conduct one-shot surveys and base decisions upon their results for years afterward. This practice belies customer expectation of service meeting *current* needs 365 days a year.

Mailed Questionnaires

Jack Shaw, director of Quality Assurance and Field Operations for Northern Telecom Co., telecommunications manufacturer headquartered in Nashville, did some research to find the most effective way to extract information from his company's customers. He found that they responded most willingly to periodic mailed questionnaires. Shaw also discovered a bonus from mailed questionnaires: they enhanced customer opinions of the company because they demonstrated that the company was interested in their ideas.

Another company has each manager call one customer per month to ask "How are we doing?"

Ask Employees What Customers Think

You can also obtain valuable information, believe it or not, by simply asking employees what customers think. Employees are very good at estimating overall service quality. However, employee information should not be considered a substitute for data collected directly from customers. It's helpful, though. After all, employees deal with customers directly, day after day.

Employees are consulted at Omni Hotels. Every month department managers select specific service problems from customer comment cards and ask every employee reporting to them how they would remedy the problem.

How Not to Use Surveys

The main problem with surveys is that many managers have cotton in their ears: they don't hear what customers say. They pay for surveys, then they "pooh pooh" the results when they don't fit their preconceived notions of what they will or ought to reveal.

Another problem with the way surveys are handled is that impersonal and incomplete toll-free phone lines and comment cards are used. Phoned-in or written information that is volunteered by customers is an anemic substitute for group focus interviews.

"The problem with such methods [comment cards and phoned-in comments] is that they measure only the extremes," says Christopher Hart, assistant professor at Harvard Business School, who studies service industries. "You hear from Mr. Grumpy and Ms. Smiley but not from Mr. or Ms. Average."

Nevertheless, determining your customers' needs and wants is an essential preview to a Service Plan.

After Surveys—Objectives

After you know what those needs and wants are, establish objectives and strategy to achieve them. Line up resources including employees that are needed to implement strategy to achieve objectives. This alignment is more important than any other organizational move. It is critical to customer focus—to establishment of an infrastructure, a corporate culture. In a customer-focused infrastructure, leadership, managers, and systems all are lined up to serve the interests of customers.

This may mean passing up perfectly good business ideas because they don't fit in with objectives. Accepting them would dissipate corporate resources, making it more difficult to maintain focus on service goals.

With a clear reading of customer opinion in hand, you are equipped to begin writing down plans for meeting customer expectations.

But first, let's discuss plan structure.

Model for the Service Plan

We suggest the "Market Impact of Service Model" developed by the Technical Assistance Research Program (TARP) as an additional guide in developing the structure for a Service Plan.

The model specifies action needed to achieve a selected objective such as ease of access to services. It places executives in position to determine the most effective means of increasing ease of access or of achieving other objectives.

When phone or fax services are being considered, access might be increased by adding lines, by adding staff to reduce the frequency if busy signals, and so on.

This "Market Impact of Service Model" can be used to identify improvements in service that are needed to increase market share or to boost revenue *by a predetermined amount.*

The model produces "weights" indicating effect of the component parts of service on the overall effectiveness of service.

These weights then are incorporated into simple formulas that can be used in planning.

Timothy W. Firnstahl, founder and CEO of Satisfaction Guaranteed Eateries, Inc., of Seattle, developed his own service plan and wrote about it in the *Harvard Business Review*. His strategy for ensuring customer satisfaction "has worked wonders in our business" (four restaurants in the Seattle area). The strategy can, he's convinced, work wonders in other businesses as well.

His three-step system is

1. A guarantee . . . that customers will be satisfied with everything about the company's products and services
2. A mechanism for giving employees complete responsibility and authority for making the guarantee stick
3. A process for identifying system failures—the problems in organization, training, and other internal programs that cause customer dissatisfaction

His "game plan," as he calls it, rejects "cryptic mission statements, unreviewed strategic plans, and the hidden dreams of management."

Here are Firnstahl's suggestions for formulating a "game plan":

1. Develop a simple, easy-to-understand service guarantee. In writing it, think about the company's primary customer benefit and how to achieve it.
   "In our case," says Firnstahl, "the principal benefit is enjoyment. For many it will be dependability. For others, it will be low cost or flexibility."
2. Make sure employees know how to use their authority to do anything needed to keep customers happy. Make sure they don't underuse their power. Advise them to take action *before* a guest must ask for a remedy.
3. Make progress visible. Make graphs instead of written progress reports, for instance.

Set Realistic Objectives

Consider applying management-by-objectives theory in a Service Plan. Employ MBO theory in writing the plan, or use a similar methodical planning mechanism based upon achievement of objectives (making them realistic), application of standards, enunciation of individual responsibilities, and evaluation of performance.

Among benefits of MBO are motivation, communication, and managerial control.

Authorities whose works will help you during this stage of Service Plan development are William G. Ouchi, John Naisbitt, and Tom Peters. Ouchi wrote *Theory Z: How American Business Can Meet the Japanese Challenge*. Naisbitt wrote *Reinventing the Corporation*. And Peters is author of *Thriving on Chaos*.

The Service Plan, in summary, should incorporate:

1. Aggressive efforts to determine customers' wants and needs
2. A staff trained and motivated to deliver those wants and needs
3. Active follow-up that includes efforts to obtain customers' appraisals of service quality—feedback

A Mission Statement

A mission statement is a motivational document, a fine way to focus a philosophy of service, but inadequate by itself.

The Customer Service Department of Bio-Lab has a mission statement that contains a list of business functions that have impacts upon customers that should be controlled by a customer service department. The statement reads:

> The mission of the customer service department is to retain and to encourage *increased business* from customers by efficiently and courteously satisfying their needs with respect to ordering, shipping, invoicing, handling claims and adjustments, and responding to inquiries, complaints, and related activities.

Continuing with objectives of customer service, the Bio-Lab mission statement reads: "As a principal point of contact between customer and the company, the customer service department is a vital element in assuring and maintaining profitability."

Bio-Lab's Anne Pinkerton, director of customer service, comments upon the statement: "We represent the company to the customer, so the way we handle a customer largely determines that customer's impression of us."

Refocus Existing Policies and Procedures

Top management must continually evaluate organizational environment and make improvements and adjustments in it to optimize the service performance of all employees.

A survey by The Forum Corporation of Boston revealed several important implications about long-term competitive advantages in continually adjusting company policies and procedures to make them more customer oriented. Forum is a leader in helping organizations create customer focus and has worked with more than 700 companies around the world.

Forum concluded, on the basis of survey results, that it is important to convey to employees the skills associated with reliability, responsiveness, self assurance, and empathy.

Reliability implies that employees have the ability to set accurate expectations so that actual delivery of service meets or exceeds the customers' expectations.

Armstrong World Industries, Inc.
Consumer Affairs Department

The mission of the Consumer Affairs Department embraces five general activities:

1. Understand Armstrong's Consumer.

2. Respond Effectively to Consumer Inquiries and Specific Concerns.

3. Improve Company Response to Consumer Claims.

4. Monitor Activities that Preserve Corporate Credibility and Standards.

5. Promote Armstrong's Consumer Interests Outside the Company.

Within the Consumer Affairs Department, the Customer Response Center has been established to respond to:

A. Requests for literature and information generated by corporate ads and publicity.

B. Complaints and concerns involving Armstrong products.

C. Routine care, maintenance and installation information prompted by 800 number positioning on floors, cartons, instruction sheets, and literature.

D. Requests for convenient retail locations that inventory our products and participate in our marketing promotions.

The Center's performance standards include:

A. Fulfill standard literature requests within 2-3 weeks.

B. Respond to consumer complaints within 24-48 hours.

C. Offer easy, free access to consumers in continental U.S. from 9:00 a.m. to 8:00 p.m., Eastern Time, Monday through Friday.

D. Provide up to three retail sources for our products.

All contacts are coded and reports are prepared monthly for the Consumer Affairs, Advertising and Marketing Departments. These reports help us determine how we can improve on our products and services.

Mission statement of the Consumer Affairs Department of Armstrong World Industries, Inc. (Reprinted courtesy of Armstrong World Industries, Inc.)

Kemper Group Consumer Credo

Recognizing that the consumer is the lifeline to our existence, the Kemper Group and its employees will be guided by an attitude of service. That attitude embodies every effort on the part of our employees to conduct business fairly, openly, courteously, efficiently and in a manner that is responsive to the needs of our consumers. Each manager and supervisor will be held accountable for achieving established objectives aimed at promoting and maintaining that attitude.

We will:

1
Conduct business in an ethical, lawful and responsible manner.

2
Provide insurance products and services which are responsive to the needs of present and prospective consumers while fulfilling our responsibilities to our owners.

3
Respond to consumer grievances fairly, promptly, informatively, courteously and as we would wish to be treated while retaining the right to maintain our position if we deem it correct.

4
Initiate corrective action in our operations where needed to provide better consumer services.

5
Maintain mutually productive relationships with consumers and consumer groups.

6
Develop, implement and encourage insurance education programs internally and externally to bring about greater awareness and understanding of insurance.

7
Strive to develop greater consumer responsiveness among our employees and within the insurance industry and business community.

8
Continually review and revise our consumer relations policies and practices and search for ways to become increasingly consumer-oriented.

The "Consumer Credo" of the Kemper Group of insurance companies states that employees "will be guided by an attitude of service." Eight consumer objectives are listed in the credo. (Reprinted courtesy of the Kemper Group.)

Tell Employees What You Expect

Companies must be accurate and specific about what employees do to improve service quality. If companies merely tell their employees to improve service quality, employees may choose strategies that are "suboptimal." For example, customers often place the highest value on reliability, but employees often choose to emphasize responsiveness.

When problems occur, solve them to the satisfaction of the customer not to the satisfaction of supervisors and managers. Companies must attend to *all* dimensions of service quality. Many companies try to improve customer focus by implementing programs that change only tangible elements, those that are most visible and easiest to change such as name badges that say, "Have a nice day." But these efforts are "suboptimal," since customers also want to be served reliably and with responsiveness and assurance. Truly, companies need to recognize the service element in everything they do during these intensely competitive closing years of the twentieth century. Anyone employed by any company must continually ask: "How can this job of mine be done to further the interests of the customer?" Anything done in the interests of the customer, of course, is beneficial to the organization.

A few companies that analyze activities and refocus them toward the goal of achieving total customer satisfaction are Allstate, PepsiCo, The Coleman Co., and McKerley Health Care Centers.

To refocus policies and procedures, create special relationships between company and customer by

- Connecting people and systems to customers.
- Focusing on reliability.
- Preventing complacency.
- Retaining existing relationships.
- Paying attention to service quality.

Manage managers so that they

1. Value employees, particularly front-line employees. (Employees should know that they are valued.)
2. Develop employees.
3. Listen to employees and solicit their comments.
4. Set customer-focused standards.

Lead and motivate all employees in the company so that

- Everyone helps create positive customer experience.
- Systems support features important to customers.
- Leadership "enables" employees to act for customers.

Incorporate into the Service Plan policies such as a no-fault approach to claims and credits below a certain dollar amount that yields overall savings in processing cost for minor claims and substantially improved customer goodwill. In most industries more than 90 percent of claims or requests for adjustments are justified so investigation wastes money. Dayton Hudson Corporation (DHC), fifth largest U.S. nonfood retailer headquartered in Minneapolis, long practiced a no-questions-asked return policy. Ken Macke, chairman and CEO, considers the return policy and the company's spectrum of enlightened consumer relations practices to be very helpful in achieving his company's volume and profitability records.

But—I'll say it again—there's much more to quality service than an enlightened return policy. Dayton Hudson tripped on its apparent ignorance of this fact.

On the other hand, the management of one DHC division, Target Stores Inc., reminded employees that it was a self-service organization and that they were not to take time to talk with customers or to help them. Target's management felt that service *costs* money. They limited service to a money-back guarantee.

Since 1988 Target has seen fit to change this philosophy dramatically and to focus on service. Impetus for the change was provided by competition. Still, Wal-mart leads discount and low-margin chains in service.

Symbolic Acts

If the job is to refocus policies in pursuit of quality service, then management commitment is especially important. Commitment is best demonstrated by "dramatic, symbolic acts."

An innovative technique for corporate executives and staff was the first national "Hyatt in Touch Day" in 1989 at Hyatt Hotels Corporation. Hyatt closed corporate headquarters for a day and company executives worked alongside line employees in 67 hotels. Four hundred corporate employees, from president to mail room clerk, carried bags, bused tables, and made beds. President Darryl Hartley-Leonard worked at Hyatt Regency Chicago as a doorman, front desk clerk, and bartender. Tom Pritzker, chairman of Hyatt Corporation, spent the day at Grand Hyatt Washington as a front desk clerk and bellman. Jeff Lang, corporate mail room clerk, was a valet parking attendant at Park Hyatt Chicago.

Any company that chooses to adopt Hyatt's tactic ought to tell the press about it, as Hyatt did. The result for Hyatt was spectacular nationwide positive publicity, which certainly doesn't hurt business.

Jerre Stead, president of the Square D Company, said that one of the objectives of his company's customer service program is to have each officer spend at least 20 percent of his or her time working with customers every year. "And that includes the HR director, the chief financial officer . . . everyone. I feel very strongly about that and we work at it very hard."

Stead says that the chief financial officer is one of the best salespeople: "He has contacts all over the world."

In another kind of dramatic act that symbolizes management commitment, the Tennant Company cut the number of rework mechanics, the firm's highest-paid assemblers, in half, from 20 to 10. The message in this carefully calculated move was this: Our goal is to eliminate rework. We intend to do our work correctly the first time. At last report Tennant had only two rework mechanics, and *their* jobs were in jeopardy.

Apply Basic Management Techniques

Zenger-Miller, the Cupertino, California training and consulting firm, has developed a list of basic elements of good management directly applicable to administration of a Service Plan. The consulting firm assumes existence of high-quality basic product or products ("product" is "service" too), and then goes on to define relevant "common elements of good management" as management leadership, training, employee participation, communication, measurement, and reward and recognition.

Zenger-Miller matched this list of good management methodology with methods and with authorities who wrote about the methods.

Methodology: Employee participation in quality teams and circles.
Methods: Idea generation and problem investigation. Graphing and data gathering.
Authority: Kaoru Ishikawa

Methodology: Cost of management leadership.
Methods: Quality audit. Teams discover and track cost of quality.
Authority: Philip Crosby

Methodology: Statistical quality (process) control.
Methods: Statistical process control. A 14-step plan is suggested as a prerequisite to implementing statistical process control.
Authority: W. Edwards Deming

Methodology: Quality assurance engineering.
Methods: Design of high-quality products that are manufacturable to consistently high standards. Emphasis is on engineering applications. Includes 10-step plan to identify and to catalog opportunities.
Authority: Joseph Juran

Methodology: Inventory and supplier management (just-in-time).
Methods: Shifting focus from supplier and management emphasis to a strong customer focus. Each workstation delivers perfect work to the next workstation, its "customer." The last station becomes the driver of the system. The system and the external customer becomes the driver of the last station.
Authority: None

Methodology: Total quality control.
Methods: Essential elements from all management approaches. Apply executive leadership and passion about quality issues.
Authority: Armand Feigenbaum

Clearly, a service plan should conceive of service as much more than a broad smile and competent reaction to customer requests.

Implementing the Service Plan

The Forum Corporation drew upon its own consulting experience, current research, and a comprehensive data base to identify action that is taken most often by successful companies to implement service plans. Forum concluded: Companies best at implementing, monitoring, and modifying a service plan understand

What customers expect and what they get.
What management says and what they do.
What employees need to do, and what they are doing.

At Zayre Corporation, a major retailer, part of the implementation of service programs involves each department's awareness of the service plan of each department just below it. The Consumer Affairs Department supervises dissemination of plans throughout the company.

Haney of Amex says: "It's our job to inform managers about consumer concerns. In this way, they can build consumer objectives into their individual business plans. We are part of decision making at all levels."

Perpetuating the Service Plan

Service, of course, requires ongoing effort. The hit-and-run approach to service management has no place here.

Ray Stone, who retired in 1989 as the Marriott Corporation director of consumer affairs, knew this. He said, while he was still at Marriott: "We do a lot with the statistics we receive. Every four weeks we circulate a report that goes to Bill Marriott, our board chairman and president, to our hotel general managers, and to everyone in between. We have a 'Guest Satisfaction Index' that's one factor in determining bonuses for top hotel management. Hourly employees—even the engineering staff—are hooked into this index. It's their score card every four weeks." So Marriott monitors its service activities. Improvements are rushed in whenever service lags.

At Zayre, no one is shielded from what customers think. The company keeps the service plan fresh by preparing service reports that go to senior management, including the CEO, as well as to front-line employees, merchandisers, department managers, and store managers who then review the reports with employees.

Job objectives of all Zayre executives and middle managers require a fixed number of visits with customers every year.

Developing Customer Service Infrastructure

Companies that manage to stay close to their customers streamline communications among departments, buy new technology or adapt what they have, and discuss the values they wish everyone in the organization to share. The result is a service infrastructure—a service *culture.* Where it exists, customer satisfaction is *everybody's* business.

The "culture" of an organization is best defined as a consensus favoring good service. It is understood and routinely accepted that customers will receive satisfaction and value for their money, that they will be treated like friends and not as antagonists, and that questions and complaints will be handled quickly. This kind of thinking pervades all decision-making considerations.

What companies with a service culture have in common is their "legacy," "tradition." Talk of service permeates every management meeting, every plan and report, every decision. Employees know that the CEO is big on customer service. Everybody knows that the company gives outstanding service. That's the company's reputation, its image.

Service, in a company with a service culture, can be visualized as a membrane that envelops the entire corporate structure.

This is an important point: a service culture won't develop without the commitment of senior management. Commitment must be genuine. It must be demonstrated by word and deed. It must be continuous. And it must influence every employee.

Unyielding, highly visible management commitment to quality service that creates a pervasive "service culture" in the organization yields organizational pride.

One food processing company executive says: "Enthusiasm about good service starts with management. It radiates from us to the people who work for us. They know that we're committed because we communicate our commitment by talking with them in person, not with memos."

Drive the Program

Management must drive a customer service program with continuous training for all employees (a revolutionary concept for most organizations), with reinforcement by means of rewards for high-performing service employees, and with management standards that are enforced and regularly reinforced. And top managements must demonstrate by their own actions that they believe in customer service.

At EDS Corp., the company's culture is characterized by a strict code of ethics and a well-established philosophy of customer service.

When management is committed to customer service by daily word and deed, the result is a well-established infrastructure that facilitates free communication interchange internally and that yields organizational "culture."

Ralph H. Kilman, Ph.D., professor of Business Administration at the Joseph M. Katz Graduate School of Business, University of Pittsburgh, observes that commitment promotes a service culture and that culture, in turn, promotes commitment. Management commitment and service culture reinforce each other.

Customer service must be seen virtually as a religion at the top, says William H. Davidow, general partner in Mohr, Davidow Ventures, a venture capital firm in Menlo Park, California. "But," he continues, "since customer service is hard emotional work, the front-line employees who do that work must be given a lot of credit."

He cites the Embassy Suites hotel chain where employees do count. Authority and responsibility are pushed as far down into the company's structure as possible. General managers support middle managers. A complaining customer is always right.

Conveying Dedication to Employees

How can your senior management influence employees with their dedication to service? Train and retrain employees. Publish stories in the company paper about customer service. Maintain poster and bulletin board displays and update them regularly. Make sure that supervisors mention customer service regularly in employee meetings.

At companies that pay mere lip service to quality service, splashy customer service campaigns run for 30 days or, at the most, 90 days. Everybody feels great! They've "got" customer service. However, service disappears from print and oral communication after the initial splash and effort to win customer satisfaction wanes.

When management is committed to *long-term* service, however, and when a Service Plan is followed and renewed continuously, procustomer behavior becomes traditional and largely (but never completely) self-perpetuating.

"The constancy of the message is what's important," says James D. Robinson III, chairman and CEO of American Express. "After years of being hammered in, it (customer service) becomes part of the company culture. Employees eventually realize that things are done for the customer and not just to make things easier or cheaper for the company. Consumers and the community realize it, too. The company has a 'good reputation.'"

One message that committed CEOs should convey to employees is that anything done in the interests of the customer is, by definition, beneficial to the company and to them. Employees should have no trouble motivating themselves to pursue the service element in their work if they really believe this. (Commitment is discussed later in this chapter.)

A company can promote a service culture with actions such as these, taken from "Close to the Customer," an American Management Association research report on consumer affairs.

Quarterly awards by marketing to production personnel who provide outstanding service to customers
Regular, reinforced communications to employees that describe customer service techniques
Management leadership by example
Realization that if you believe your service is merely acceptable, you're not improving as you should
Monthly posters emphasizing importance of the customer

LONG-TERM STRATEGY

Strategy must be developed and then implemented by hardheaded analysis, talented management of people, intense concentration and commitment—and serious spending.

Fortune magazine defines service strategy as "knowing exactly which customers (companies) you want to serve and figuring out what kind of service will loosen (customers') purse strings."

Analyze:

1. All policies and procedures. Review them. They must be customer oriented.
2. Sales costs, including shipping expenses. Decide how to provide service in the most cost-efficient way.
3. Work flow. Develop strategies to level work load in a warehouse, for instance, so customers won't be subjected to slow delivery periods.
4. The company's capability to react to unexpected events. Develop a "disaster" contingency plan that helps determine how to maintain service to customers when the computer blows up, or a tornado blows in.
5. Customer wants and needs. Make arrangements to have your customers' points of view represented in your meetings. You know your customers better than anyone.

The strategic program that guides my company's (BTMC) customer service consultants is based upon a top-down, whole organization approach that begins with consideration of the nature of the customer experience and creates strategies and tactics that maximize the quality of that experience.

I believe that the goal of a service strategy should be to "systematize" (to "institutionalize") a customer service program. Everyone needs a long-term program, well-established in the *culture* of the company.

Albrecht and Zemke say in *Service America!* that service strategy is "a unifying idea" and "a guiding concept." They say: "This guiding concept finds its way into all that people do. It becomes a rallying cry, a kind of gospel, and the nucleus of the message to be transmitted to the customer.

"Every executive in the company, and every employee who works for every executive, must follow the same road map toward the same objectives," say Albrecht and Zemke.

But benefits of customer service last only a short time after assertive application of the service strategy ends or, more likely, fades away. Customer service must not be viewed as a quick fix that will last forever. It's not a boulder on the mountain top that you give a push, confidently expecting that it will roll on and on.

Regard customer service as a long-term strategy on a par with other strategies and in line with the most advanced management thinking. It requires unremitting management commitment and employee enthusiasm to survive over a long period so it can continue to work its magic on customer loyalty.

Here are three important long-term customer service strategies. Call them "attitudes," if you wish.

1. *Service as the product.* Most buyers don't have the technical knowledge needed to make the best choice in products such as electronic equipment, motor vehicles, or office machines. They want reassurance that support and service will be available if problems arise.
   So maintenance and service, if you sell hard goods, are very important parts of a service strategy. It must be fast. And it must be good.
2. *The customer is the boss.* This slogan—The Customer Is the Boss—appears on signs in every office of Bio-Lab.
3. *Strive for reliability.* Reliability means *consistent* performance that meets the expectations of all your customers all the time. Admittedly, this is ideal. But a superior service program will come very close to achieving the ideal.

Consumers rank reliability as the key ingredient in good service, says Richard C. Whiteley, President of Forum Corp., the Boston consulting firm specializing in customer service. But he warns companies not to try too hard to be reliable and to end up over promising.

He even advises that if you can finish a job in three days, promise it in five days. If, then, you finish it in *three days* you are likely to achieve "customer delight," a goal also favored by Colby Chandler, chairman of

Eastman Kodak. (If speed is important to the customers, however, this might not be an advisable tactic.)

Likewise, if you must provide an estimated bill, don't do as most people do and keep it unrealistically low. Instead, err on the high side so that you can "delight" the customer when the bill is less than the estimate.

This tactic is somewhat "gimmicky"; so examine it through customers' eyes before implementing it.

Other Important Long-Term Strategies

1. React immediately to customer dissatisfactions. Reacting immediately to customer dissatisfactions is a short-run goal, however. It's a point acknowledged by Richard Gamgort, director of Quality Assurance and Customer Affairs for Armstrong World Industries. "The long-run goal," he says, "should be to get enough feedback from our customers to really get a feeling for how our product is meeting customer needs." "A customer service program is a tremendous opportunity to stay in touch with customers to clearly understand their needs," says Gamgort.
2. It is critically important to examine and to correct anything that gets in the way of superior employee performance such as difficult communication or poor logistics. Even in companies that aren't customer focused, most employees believe in the value of providing excellent service. So the company shouldn't get in the way with ironclad rules that employees are forbidden to deviate from, for instance.
3. Work hard to retain customers who report that they are satisfied, all right, but who still credit your company with only fair or poor service.

In one Forum Corporation study, "wishy-washy" customers amounted to 40 percent of all customers. Although these people report that they are basically satisfied, they are vulnerable to competitors that provide high-quality service.

"Long-term strategy" has lost out in many board rooms in recent years because of merger mania. Managements are intensely aware that corporate raiders might be lured to their companies by sagging earnings. So management focuses on short-term financial results and on savings (money not spent) that fatten the profit figure.

This Wall Street mentality means that management in general seems unable to sacrifice next quarter's earnings for long-term objectives, such as quality service, which can be achieved only through long-term commitment.

Armstrong

OPERATING PRINCIPLES

- To respect the dignity and inherent rights of the individual human being in all dealings with people.
- To maintain high moral and ethical standards and to reflect honesty, integrity, reliability and forthrightness in all relationships.
- To reflect the tenets of good taste and common courtesy in all attitudes, words and deeds.
- To serve fairly and in proper balance the interests of all groups associated with the business — customers, stockholders, employees, suppliers, community neighbors, government and the general public.

Armstrong

CORPORATE STRATEGY

1. To build on the existing strengths in our core businesses.
2. To continue searching for ways to expand into related businesses through technology that is either developed in-house or acquired.
3. To attempt to acquire companies in related businesses.
4. To look outward to our markets and customers using the Quality Management Process to continuously improve the value of our products and services.

Armstrong World Industries executives carry a card in their wallets that has operating principles printed on one side and corporate strategy printed on the other. Strategy 4 is: "To look outward to our markets and customers using the Quality Management Process continuously to improve the value of our products and services." (Reprinted coutesy of Armstrong World Industries.)

MANAGEMENT COMMITMENT

As essential as strategy, objectives, and support systems (infrastructure) are as foundation for a service program, the entire program probably would wilt like an unwatered lily without (1) a corporate culture to sustain it and (2) a chief executive who, every employee notices, is just as committed to customer satisfaction as he is to stockholder satisfaction.

A finely honed strategy will turn yellow inside its three-ring binder if management is not committed to service and if it doesn't demonstrate faith in the value of customer service by word and deed. Management must preach service and require service until it becomes the veins and arteries of the company.

The most important factor in outstanding customer service, then, sits in the corner office.

In their book, *Passion for Excellence* (Random House, 1985), Tom Peters and Nancy Austin, write: "we propose leader . . . as cheerleader, enthusiast, nurturer of champions, hero finder, wanderer, dramatist, coach, facilitator, builder." We couldn't say it better.

The president, chairman, and other top executives must frequently be heard and seen pushing the values of service *and taking their own advice.*

Visible management attention rather than occasional management speeches or articles gets things done. Action may start with words, but it has to be backed by symbolic behavior that gives life to words.

Persistence

Perseverance is a vital element in commitment, says James D. Robinson III, chairman of American Express. "Constancy of the message is what's important," he says.

Develop a mechanism for *maintaining* commitment, like regular executive conference sessions. Assign the job of *expressing* the customer point of view to one executive. All executives should know and react to customer interests, as a matter of course. The general purpose of conference sessions should be to inspire and to maintain commitment of managers to the customer service strategy—and to train them in techniques of implementing the strategy.

American Express has an executive group such as this. A Customer Service Task Force is made up of key people from each section's customer service division. The Task Force is a clearinghouse where individuals meet to discuss problems that come up in their departments. The relevance of these problems to the entire corporation is discussed, too.

IBM continuously drums into employees that their work must be done to satisfy customers. Even after the sale, employees approach customers with the same interest and attention as when the customer was the prospect being courted. Though IBM works hard to get a new customer, the company works even harder to hold on to the customers they have. That's management commitment in action.

We agree with what Michael Durik, executive vice president of personnel for The Limited Stores, Inc., says about perseverance in management commitment: "[Commitment] is a conscious effort that begins at the top and requires constant reinforcement and rewards to employees who excel."

Constant reinforcement usually involves changes in the Service Plan—improvements. Once you've tested a plan against day-to-day realities, changes are sure to be needed. Welcome them. They are your opportunity to maintain *quality* service.

Management Isolation

Isolation is the opposite of commitment. Unfortunately, isolation is more common than commitment, in customer service. Management often is out of touch with day-to-day activity that creates the company's reputation for good service or that creates a reputation for rotten service, instead.

Kenneth Bernhardt, business professor at Georgia State University, tells this management isolation story.

With his family he moved to Boston in 1983 to become a visiting professor at Harvard. After repeated attempts to resolve a problem with his moving company through established channels, Bernhardt called the president of this national moving firm. When he explained to the chief executive's secretary that he was a professor at Harvard, she asked if he was calling about business or a personal matter. When Bernhardt said that he was having trouble with the company's movers, the secretary said: "Oh, the president doesn't talk to customers."

Says Bernhardt about senior executives: "They don't shop. When they fly, they fly in corporate jets and ride in limos. Their hotel rooms are reserved for them by someone else, and another someone checks in for them. At the highest levels, their Christmas presents are bought for them by an assistant." They certainly don't wait at home for the cable TV man to show up.

"And most of them don't talk with customers."

Bernhardt says: "When top management is concerned with customers, you won't find clerks who won't help you."

Preventing Isolation

Some companies such as IBM and Digital Equipment Corporation require top management to spend at least 30 days per year with customers. When Robert Townsend was president of Avis, top executives spent one week per year in customer-contact positions. Competitor Hertz has a policy that requires managers to spend a month a year on the line. The idea is spreading in hospitality industry companies.

Commitment is magic. Rosemarie B. Greco, president of Fidelity Bank of Philadelphia, once placed a phone call to a retired customer who had serious problems with his IRA account statement: "He was beside himself with gratitude. That taught me an important lesson about letting customers know that management is personally involved with their problems."

Benefits of Commitment

When management's commitment by example achieves the expected result, companywide commitment, then every employee instinctively looks for the service element in everything they do. The question, "How can this job be done to further the interests of the customer?" guides their actions and decisions.

If management makes it very clear that fast, courteous, helpful service is expected and even demanded, it is a rare employee who will determinedly oppose management's standards. Outstanding service becomes routine.

This is what leads to awesome, bigger than life status for companies with service at the "heroic" level. Customers not only are satisfied. They are "delighted." So they tell their friends about the company's service, at every opportunity, recalling their own favorite stories.

A company with this kind of a service reputation gets by with mistakes. Customers forgive and overlook. What's more, such companies often receive credit for better service than they really have. But windfalls are earned.

No Lip Service Allowed

In group interviews some people speak with fervor about the importance of service quality. But the same people report in surveys that service ranks "moderate" to "low" in their action priorities.

Companies sometimes say they have service even when they have taken no action whatsoever to install a service program, like drafting a Service Plan. Maybe they've taken no action because high-quality service delivered consistently is a condition that is not easy to achieve, and because it costs real money up front.

Only a handful of organizations have achieved a level of consistently excellent service.

I've found that 70 percent of customer service initiatives are lip service. People basically want to improve service, but they don't want to invest in it.

Instead of investing in service, companies add veneer to existing programs to make them *appear* more responsive to consumers. So it is that an organization will smugly congratulate itself on its new service "program" achieved with the master stroke of merely renaming the "Complaint Department" the "Consumer Affairs Department" or "Office of Public Responsibility."

The prevalence of this "lip service" in the service field was confirmed in a study of the state of customer service in more than 200 corporations by Zenger-Miller, the Cupertino, California, management training company. Ronald Dumas, when he was at Zenger-Miller, reported that the study uncovered the fact that "this problem [poor service] draws much more talk than action."

Why? No company wants it to be known that it doesn't have customer service. So when they don't have it they say they do and expect customers and prospects to believe them.

But commitment must be real. It must be honest. It cannot resemble a false front on a store, a mirage, or sleight of hand. It cannot be a customer service veneer on existing programs.

Unfortunately, there is plenty of veneer being applied these days.

Surveys Are Not Service

Hotels, hospitals, airlines and other businesses flood customers with service quality surveys. But for too many firms, that's as far as the project goes.

Everywhere you look these days you see customer contact people wearing buttons in their lapels that say things like "We're No. 1 in Service" or "We Try Harder."

Some stores seem to specialize in lip service. They have a booth just inside the front door with a sign hanging over it. On the sign in large letters are the words "Customer Service." Ask the employee running the booth what she or he does and you'll get: "Give refunds, tell people where they can find merchandise, answer questions. . . ."

When I wanted to buy tires at a discount store one evening I couldn't find a salesperson. I asked Customer Service three times to call over the loudspeaker for a salesperson. I'd already rung the bell eight times. Finally, a salesperson emerged from the background to help me spend money.

Too often the message that management just wants to make a show of providing service comes through loud and clear. One executive of a large banking system proudly extolled the incentives his firm offered employees for both sales and service. High sales brought a cash bonus, but good service earned a lapel pin.

The message in the contrast in reward value tells employees a lot about management's values. The result, of course, is that employees don't take the occasional reminders to "treat customers as you would want to be treated" very seriously.

Slogans as Service

Slogans are very popular veneer. Delta Air Lines painted itself into a corner when it vowed: "Delta is ready when you are." So did Holiday Inn with its slogan: "No excuses. Guaranteed."

These companies were begging for grumblers, and they got them. Eventually the companies switched to less "omnipotent" slogans.

"The correlation between service and slogans is essentially nil," wrote Karl Albrecht and Ron Zemke in their book, *Service America*.

"It's quite common," they note, "to find a sharp disparity between slogans of advertising people and the realities of the customer-contact front line."

Slogans may lead an organization along a detour that bypasses real solutions. Slogans and advertising hype create customer expectations that go unmatched by service. One result is wasted advertising budgets. Shoppers become disillusioned and take their business elsewhere.

Companies, from multinationals to the corner photo studio, must realize that the quality of the company's relationship with its customers won't improve just because the CEO has made a speech or because three articles have appeared in the company newsletter—or because a sign behind the cash register says "Customers Count."

Proper procedure was followed by Bruno's, supermarket chain based in Birmingham, Alabama. Angelo Bruno, chairman of Bruno's, reports that the company has been one of the most consistently profitable supermarket chains in the United States.

Harry Bressler, executive vice president of Steiner/Bressler, the advertising agency that handles the Bruno account, proposed a major advertising campaign stressing service and friendly, knowledgeable employees. It was a smart move, considering the fact that Bruno's already dominated the market in low prices.

The smartest move of all, though, was to train all employees *before* the ad campaign began. Bruno's wanted to make sure that they would deliver that which they were about to promise so they called us in to train employees.

We demonstrated at Bruno's that it takes only 1 to 5 percent of an advertising budget to train all employees to deliver the customer service message. Companies that truly focus on service can "own" their markets.

None of Bruno's competitors caught on to the powerful impact of quality service promised *and* delivered for nearly two years. Only then did they begin to copy Bruno's strategy. Just saying that you have customer service and doing no more than distributing an annual customer service memo to employees exhorting them to practice good service is not enough to install customer service as a permanent part of a management system.

It is my observation that firms that advertise customer-friendly service most loudly are *least likely* to have it. Quality service is its own best publicity agent.

Put Your Money Where Your Mouth Is

Senior executives I have known nod vigorously in the affirmative when the need for service that attracts customer loyalty and increases sales and profit is mentioned. But in the quiet moments after the bustle of a business day, they often let slip their belief that customer service is nice but that it isn't really worth spending much money on. Retail companies, particularly, are loath to spend money training employees in service delivery.

Other companies have the foot-in-mouth disease, too. The president of one of the largest computer firms in the United States recently told the trade press about his commitment to focussing on customer service. So I mailed a letter to him asking for a meeting to discuss our service technology. His secretary told me by phone that he wasn't interested.

"Many companies spend huge sums to lure new customers but pay little more than lip service to taking care of the ones they have," wrote Bruce Bolger, editor of *Incentive* magazine.

"Most executives claim," wrote Bolger, "that their companies stress good service, but how much do they spend in dollars and top management time on customer service?"

They're all for service as long as it's free . . . or cheap.

Zenger-Miller reported: "We find that few people are trained or educated to do anything about service. The typical investment in creating quality service is about $2.58 per year, a token amount compared with the tens of thousands to millions of dollars spent on other issues."

Ask yourself: "Does our budget compare favorably with the advertising and capital investment budgets?" And "How involved do senior executives get in programs specifically designed to improve customer relations?" I've never heard of a senior vice president of Customer Service. Every large company has senior vice presidents for marketing, finance, legal affairs, operations, and other functions, however.

Lip Service: Counterproductive

Mere lip service to customer service not only is useless but also counterproductive. Why? Because customers notice insincerity and interpret it as a deliberate attempt to deceive. Frequently, they react by reducing the amount of business they do with a company or by straying to competitors.

Remember Abe Lincoln's adage: "You can fool some of the people all of the time and all of the people some of the time, but you can't fool all of the people all of the time."

As a result of the talkativeness of the people you can't fool, your reputation for bad service becomes common knowledge. Your competition prospers.

Planning, drafting, and implementing a Service Plan requires sincere management commitment, a long-term strategy, and continual effort to improve service. There's a lot of truth in the statement that when you are not actively trying to make service better it tends to get worse.

Also required: organization. It's the topic of the next chapter.

3

Let's Get Organized

HOW TO GET THERE FROM HERE

The purpose of a business is to create and keep a customer.

—Theodora Leavitt, Professor of Marketing, Harvard University, in The Marketing Imagination

Stew Leonard, Jr., proprietor of Stew Leonard's grocery store in Norwalk, Connecticut, comments: "Nobody walks in the door thinking 'What can I do for Stew Leonard today?' They walk in here thinking 'What can Stew Leonard do for me today? If he doesn't do it, I'm not going to come back.' And I don't blame them. Why should they?"

The point is, as they say, well taken.

The logical inference from the point is that every company had better organize its service delivery system to answer every customer's implied question: "What are you going to do for me today?"

Stew Leonard's grocery store, by the way, has gained nationwide notoriety because of the huge boulder located at the entrance with these words chiseled in it:

Rule No. 1:
The customer is always right.
Rule No. 2:
If the customer is wrong, see rule no. 1.

Let us establish at the outset that the purpose of an organizational plan for the customer service function is continuous, companywide service quality. *Conspicuous* commitment to exceptional service by senior management helps achieve this companywide quality. So does a service culture in a company.

Centralized Reporting

A harbinger of the future may well be the organization of the General Electric Motors Division that manufactures a wide range of electric motors. Here all aspects of production, distribution and after-sales support of the product line report directly to the manager of customer service operations. Only the sales department does not report to the customer service manager.

Terry Gautsch, customer service manager, spent most of his GE career in marketing and engineering. He says: "People needed to realize that customer service no longer meant only how fast you answer the phone. It meant quality of the product, on-time delivery, responsiveness to complaints, after-sale service, support—everything.

The funneling of previously disparate elements through a common manager, says Gautsch, "has made relationships tighter and more open between departments that never used to relate."

Gautsch continues: "There's an enormous gap between saying you work closely with traffic and actually having all of the company's logistical functions reporting to one boss."

In the new setup, says Gautsch, "Typical communication barriers have been erased."

A Service Plan, employee training, consistent reinforcement of training, employee motivation, and service-level monitoring followed by adjustments to elevate service level whenever it droops—all this contributes to maintenance of a consistently high level of exceptional service.

Needed: Consensus

But, in addition, as a result of organization, a certain "consensus" sustains good service in all parts of the company just as a consensus supports the idea of democracy in America. The consensus favors treatment of customers as friends and not as opponents. Consensus favors giving customers satisfaction for their money. This kind of thinking hovers above every decision whether it's made over the counter or over the board room table.

After a well-organized Service Plan has been in action for some years, service becomes a tradition, as it is in Dayton Hudson's department stores, and at IBM and American Express, and at Disney World and Marriott Corporation, and at Maytag and the Coleman Corporation.

Traditionally good service takes on a life of its own: it helped Dayton Hudson's department stores ward off a 1988 takeover attempt. And a reputation for good service was a major reason why the Minnesota state legislature passed an antitakeover bill, according to news reports and commentators.

When an organization promotes the service approach throughout the company, you augment the impact of service upon sales. The reason that leading companies emphasize service so strongly is that service strengthens sales.

SIX ORGANIZATIONAL COMPONENTS

Six organizational components enable a company to establish a strong customer service base. They are

- Strategy. A service plan.
- Executive leadership.
- Well-trained and motivated front-line personnel.
- Product and service design.
- Infrastructure.
- Techniques for measuring effectiveness.

SERVICE STRATEGY

Developing the service strategy/policy, a process described in Chapter 2, comes first. Policies segment the customer base into service expectations of customer groups. This equips a company to match the expectations of all consumers more effectively with the company's ability to deliver expected service.

In a Canadian hospital, for instance, it is policy for patients who are able to do so to walk to operating and recovery rooms instead of being required to sit in a wheelchair and to allow someone to push them around. Also, they take their meals in a common dining room instead of in hospital rooms. That's the way they like it.

Another service policy is the four-part quality strategy of First National Bank of Chicago. It includes performance measurement, employee involvement, decentralized customer service, and a variety of employee recognition programs. First National Bank won the 1988 Award of Excellence from the International Customer Service Association. It's the largest bank holding company in the Midwest.

Good service policies are predictable. Customers know what to expect. It goes without saying that they should not be disappointed. For instance, the service policy for The Paty Co., called "The Paty Promise," consists of easy refunds, professional advice, convenience, rain checks on service, speedy delivery, free estimates, low prices, and quality products. Customers have come to learn that they can count on receiving this kind of service. The Paty Co. is a seven-store retailer in eastern Tennessee and western North Carolina.

Write a policy and communicate it to your customers. Even before customers benefit from the policy, their loyalty toward you may move up a notch just because you have been considerate enough to write such a customer-oriented policy and to tell them about it. But you'd better follow through and really give customers what you promise, or the customer fallout will be a terrible thing to see.

EVERY BUSINESS MUST IDENTIFY ITS "MOMENTS OF REALITY"

Tom Winninger, who conducts seminars and delivers speeches throughout the country on customer service, says that all business executives who want a reputation for great service must identify the "moments of reality" (MORs) in their businesses. Then they must train employees to react during these MOR times in a way that will achieve customer satisfaction.

A MOR, says Winninger, is the point when the expectancy level of a good customer contacts the service delivery level of a business.

For instance, when a customer calls on the phone, an encounter occurs between expectancy level and service delivery level. If an employee picks up the phone by the fourth ring and says, in a caring tone, "How may we help you?" then the customer's expectations have been met or exceeded.

An answer by the fourth ring is an average customer's expectation in America. More than four rings and a business has disappointed a customer.

MORs vary by business, by type of customer, by product category, and even by time of year. Identifying the MORs in a business requires research through focus groups made up of customers. And it requires application of the sophisticated awareness of customer reaction that's characteristic of most businesspeople.

Make your service even better than your customers expect. That way they are sure to notice it, to commend it to friends and relatives, and to want more of it.

PREVENTING SERVICE

Ironically, a company may have a fine service policy, but certain business methods and development practically *prevent* good service. For instance, a business might find itself in a marketplace where competitors offer poor service because cost-reduction measures are given higher priority. As a result, there's little impetus actually to deliver on good service promises.

Or a company may find itself offering a product for which there is heavy demand but insufficient supply. Inability to deliver a product certainly is poor service.

When a company grows very fast, concern with expansion often overtakes commitment to service and, in effect, negates service policy. Or service policy can be suddenly deemphasized by new management or ownership that stresses other areas such as new products.

ERECTING THE CUSTOMER SERVICE STRUCTURE

After you've drafted a policy, convene an executive conference session to develop the organization's commitment to the policy. Top management should lead these sessions in which decisions are made about establishing service objectives and committing resources to them.

Objectives:

1. Make sure they're realistic—that you can achieve them.
2. Make them logical extensions of the Service Plan.

Manager Seminars

After the executive conference session, conduct seminars (typically a half-day long) that introduce all line supervisors and managers to the service program and that encourage them to lead by example and to provide a climate conducive to implementing the system.

Department Objectives

At Zayre's, a low-margin department store, each department, including "customer relations," identifies its annual objectives. Each plan gets passed up through the company and reviewed at each level until it reaches the top, where it becomes part of corporate objectives. In this way, customer service becomes an element of the management process at every level.

Bio-Lab Inc. of Decatur, Georgia, lists this general objective: "To retain business and to encourage increased business from customers by efficiently and courteously satisfying their needs with respect to ordering, shipping, invoicing, handling claims and adjustments, and responding to inquiries, complaints, and related activities."

Every organization should have specific objectives that deal with how the work is done at the front line. Objectives might be to answer the phone by the fourth ring, to mail orders on the day promised or before or to contact the customer with an explanation, to complete repair orders within two days or to provide free "loaners," or to achieve a zero defects condition in manufactured product within a given period.

Customer Service PERFORMANCE STANDARDS

Page 1

Performance Period:

30 days from ______to______
90 days from ______to______
6 months from ______to______
(New employees should be evaluated after 30 days; regular employees with frequent customer contact every 90 days; and those with less contact every 6 months.)

Employee:______________________________
Average hours per week: ______________________
Position/Job Title:______________________________
Date attended last program: ____________________
Evaluator's name:______________________________
Position: ______________________________
Today's Date: ______________________________

Instructions: In each category circle the number for the statement that best describes the behavior or attitude of this employee. Please make a rating for each item.

Attitude Toward Customers:

1 Inconsiderate/Indifferent
2 Polite but reserved
3 Warm, friendly, and outgoing

Comments: ______________________________
____

Says "Thank You" and Smiles:

1 Rarely
2 Occasionally
3 Always

Comments: ______________________________
____

Recognizing Customers:

1 Doesn't remember customers
2 Recognizes customers but doesn't verbally communicate those feelings to the customer
3 Very good at recognizing customers with good facial expressions and verbal feedback

Comments: ______________________________
____

Uses Customers' Names:

1 Doesn't know or call the customer by name
2 Uses customers' names but not often enough
3 Remembers customers' names and pronounces their names correctly

Comments: ______________________________
____

Customer Oriented:

1 Shy, uneasy with customers
2 Helpful, but does not seem completely comfortable
3 Outgoing, helpful, and extremely comfortable

Comments: ______________________________
____

Customer Oriented Pressure Situations:

1 Experiences frustration, usually makes no attempt at handling a situation
2 Attempts to handle situation then refers problem to manager
3 Attempts and usually succeeds in handling situation on his/her own

Comments: ______________________________
____

Treats Customers as being Real:

1 Shows boredom and coldness
2 Sometimes is tense, cold, and abrupt with customers
3 Always shows warmth and friendliness

Comments: ______________________________
____

______Subtotal—Page 1 (Add up the circled numbers on page 1)

The Service Quality Institute employs this evaluation form for front-line customer service employees. The form is four pages long.

PERFORMANCE STANDARDS

Page 2

Punctuality:
1 Frequently late
2 Usually on time
3 Always prompt

Comments: ______________________________
____

Sickness/Lost Work Time: (per 30 day period)
1 5 or more days gone
2 2-4 days gone
3 0-1 days gone

Comments: (authorized/unauthorized) ______
____

Reliability:
1 Requires constant supervision
2 Requires little supervision
3 Requires no supervision

Comments: ______________________________
____

Attitude at Work to Supervisor and Co-workers:
1 Resentful, aloof or indifferent
2 Helpful and cordial
3 Motivated

Comments: ______________________________
____

Instructions:
1 Can't follow instructions
2 Does okay when instructions are repeated
3 Follows instructions well

Comments: ______________________________
____

Work Habits:
1 Poor work habits, does less than what is required
2 Does only what is required
3 Does more than required

Comments: ______________________________
____

Team Work:
1 Does not contribute to team effort
2 Has some ability, offers suggestions
3 Talented and team motivated

Comments: ______________________________
____

Personal Appearance, Dress, and Uniform:
1 Dress and personal appearance is not business acclimated
2 Usually neat/tidy, needs to be more business acclimated
3 Dresses appropriately and has good appearance

Comments: ______________________________
____

Personal Cleanliness and Hygiene:
1 Poor, needs to improve
2 Usually okay but needs to be more consistent
3 Excellent habits

Comments: ______________________________
____

Initiative:
1 Does only what is specifically outlined
2 Requires supervisory guidance to be motivated
3 Self-motivated—little or no supervision required

Comments: ______________________________
____

Product or Job Skills Knowledge:
1 Has limited knowledge and shows little interest
2 Has some knowledge and is interested in knowing more
3 Knowledgeable

Comments: ______________________________
____

______Subtotal—Page 2

PERFORMANCE STANDARDS

Page 3

Listening Skills:

1 Does not pay attention to the needs of customers
2 Occasionally pays attention but needs improvement
3 Asks good questions and pays attention to customer needs

Comments: ______________________________

____

Keeping Promises to Customers:

1 Lacks follow-through on promises
2 Usually remembers but needs improvement
3 Good follow-through on promises

Comments: ______________________________

____

Positive Communication to Customers on a Daily Basis:

1 Pays little attention to customers and avoids compliments
2 Gives compliments but needs to be more sincere
3 Generous with genuine and sincere compliments

Comments: ______________________________

____

Positive Communication to Co-workers on a Daily Basis:

1 Pays little attention to co-workers and avoids compliments
2 Gives compliments but needs to be more sincere
3 Generous with genuine and sincere compliments

Comments: ______________________________

____

Negative Communication to Customers:

1 Poor attitude, performance, and feedback
2 Communication is normally good but needs to be more consistent
3 Rarely gives negative communication

Comments: ______________________________

____

Negative Communication to Co-workers:

1 Poor attitude, performance, and feedback
2 Communication is normally good but needs to be more consistent
3 Rarely uses negative feedback

Comments: ______________________________

____

Ignores Customers/Absense of Quality Service Techniques:

1 Very poor, frequently ignores customers
2 Pays attention but needs to use techniques daily
3 Pays attention; never ignores customers

Comments: ______________________________

____

Plastic Insincere Communication to Customers:

1 Communication is insincere and phony
2 Tries to be genuine but is often perceived as being plastic
3 Rarely plastic—usually very sincere and genuine with customers

Comments: ______________________________

____

Handling Irate Customers by Using the Six Keys to Cooling Down an Irate Customer

1 Seldom; needs improvement
2 Usually—but needs more practice
3 Very good; usually turns customers around

Comments: ______________________________

____

______Subtotal—Page 3

PERFORMANCE STANDARDS

Page 4

Ability to see Potential Problems and Stop Them Before Customer Becomes Irate:

1 Ignores obvious problem
2 Uses the techniques but not often enough
3 Uses the skills for defusing problems

Comments: ______________________________

____

Takes Responsibility for Legitimate Problems/Complaints:

1 Defensive, tries to avoid blame
2 Tries to use the techniques but clumsy and inconsistent
3 Effective at taking responsibility for legitimate complaints and turning the situation around

Comments: ______________________________

____

Accuracy of Performance:

1 Very careless and sloppy performance
2 Tends to be inaccurate and occasionally makes mistakes
3 Careful and consistently accurate

Comments: ______________________________

____

Quality of Work Performance:

1 Poor and deficient quality of work
2 Performs at average level of quality
3 Places a high value on the quality of his/her work

Comments: ______________________________

____

Job Commitment:

1 Shows lack of real job commitment
2 Does an average job but lacks commitment for superior job performance
3 Dedicated commitment to work and does a thorough job

Comments: ______________________________

____

Doing More Than the Minimum for Others:

1 Not helpful; tends to be rude and impatient
2 Friendly but needs to develop "put customers first" attitude
3 Consistently gives more than the minimum to customers with pride and pleasure

Comments: ______________________________

____

Minimum Standards of Excellence with Customers and Co-workers:

1 Inconsistent and unreliable at meeting personal standards of excellence
2 Sets high standards but is not consistent in meeting these standards with customers
3 Sets high standards of excellence and has consistent habits of positive communication

Comments: ______________________________

____

Feels Good About Self:

1 Suspicious, distrustful and unresponsive to receiving positive feedback
2 Likes self but needs to feel more comforable and receptive to receiving positive feedback
3 Likes self and is good at receiving and giving positive communication

Comments: ______________________________

____

______Subtotal—Page 4

______Total Score (pages 1, 2, 3 and 4)

It's vital that organizational service objectives are incorporated into the personal objectives of all employees. Forty-two percent of companies with customer service programs that responded to an American Management Association survey include consumer affairs objectives as part of their performance appraisal systems.

At IBM, *every* employee's job description is related to the corporation's goal of providing customers, prospects, and vendors with the best service.

It is, after all, individuals, one at a time, who make the decisions and provide the follow-through to achieve organizational objectives.

Employees Implementing Objectives

The next step should be involvement of front-line employees in implementing policy. All across an organization front-line employees should help develop specifications for their own performance. When they have a hand in establishing personal objectives, they are more likely to identify with them and to fully understand them.

Senior managers of British Airways run Customer First Workshops to develop specific criteria for service quality on the front line. A typical service specification begins by explaining the customer's expectations for a particular service, such as baggage handling, telephone reservations, or food service aboard a plane. The second part of a specification describes what staff people must do to meet those expectations.

The idea behind "Customer First" teams in the United Kingdom and in other countries is to provide a forum for line people to develop and to experiment with new approaches to service management.

When British Airways management wanted to develop new service standards, it gave the matter to Customer First teams instead of imposing procedures and measures from on high. The teams generated several thousand service improvement suggestions.

Empowering Employees

If customer-contact employees do not deliver service with intelligence, enthusiasm, and good judgment, the service plan and the organizational structure might as well not exist. Even an elaborate, sophisticated plan would function like a long irrigation pipe in which water flows freely until it reaches a plug in the end of the pipe. No water reaches the field. No service (or very little of it) reaches customers when employees' hands are tied by strict rules and penalties for deviating from rules.

When employees are afraid to make any decision that has not been preapproved by written policy, there's a plug in the pipe. They must have the authority to do what's necessary to achieve customer satisfaction. They must be *empowered*.

We want to touch on this point to emphasize its place in the organizational structure, though it is discussed in detail in Chapter 6.

Ever hear of Disney World's reputation for exceptional service? Empowerment is a religion there. Employees are thoroughly trained and then told that they have the authority—it has been delegated to them—to do whatever is necessary to deal with problems on the spot in order to make customers happy.

Said James Poisant when he was manager of business seminars at Walt Disney World: "If a supervisor notices a front line person giving away the store, he'll usually wait and talk it over with him later." He'll wait instead of intervening.

Cast members (as front-line employees are called) don't say, "That's not my job, I'll get a supervisor." When people with problems call a number at Disney World, the first employee who answers the phone makes an effort—a heroic effort, if necessary—to solve the problem. The employee doesn't send the caller all over the company.

When you walk up to a guest relations window at EPCOT Center, register a complaint, and ask for return of your money, the employee at the window will more than likely act in your favor immediately and send you away happy. Management interference is discouraged.

The Disney philosophy is reflected in a statement that every organization in America with a desire for customer loyalty should mount on the board room wall: "Management Must Not Only Support the Front Line but It Must TRUST It as Well."

Disney World believes that front-line employees should be the first—and the last—contact for customers. These employees and *all Disney employees* are treated with respect.

Disney realizes great financial benefit for its quality service standards. Because clients are willing to pay for helpfulness and friendliness, for cleanliness, and for fun, Disney facilities are able to charge admissions that are about 20 percent higher than admission charges at any other major entertainment center in Florida or California. Stock prices are high. Executives receive significant bonuses.

One-Stop Shopping

Dow Chemical has the same philosophy. Mitchell Kern, manager of customer service resources, says: "We view the customer service department as one-stop shopping. We want our customers to have a single Dow contact—someone who can handle order taking, credit, delivery, and so on. The last thing we want when a customer calls is to tell him that we'll get back to him or to refer him or her to somebody else."

I believe that this *empowerment* of customer contact employees is a valuable "new dimension" in customer service.

Empowerment definitely was not the order of the day at a ski shop in Reno, Nevada, where I negotiated a reduced price on a pair of after-ski boots with an employee. My wife had stopped in three times, but the salesperson failed to close the sale.

Unfortunately for the employee, the transaction was overheard and vetoed by the fiance of the store owner. Red faced with anger she denounced the employee in our presence and threatened to fire him. To be sure, this was not an "empowered" employee, and the shoe store certainly has suffered for the dictatorial, distrustful management style of the owner's fiance.

SERVICE IS EVERY EMPLOYEE'S PRIORITY

Service, we've said, should be part of everyone's job description. Service should be the umbrella over your corporate organization plan for service delivery. Avoid pigeonholing customer service in a customer service "department." That's a fine way to sabotage a service plan that's ostensibly aimed at achieving total customer satisfaction.

The trouble is that having a department for being helpful to customers engenders a "That's not *my* job" mentality. One trademark of the late comedian, Freddie Prinz, was saying "That's not *my* job" to every request from "Please pass the salt" to "Do you have the time?"

What is needed is a *whole company* customer service mentality. But American business managers have tended to leave the matter of giving the customer what she or he wants to the customer service department. Out of sight, out of mind. They typically *assume* that someone "in customer service" will take care of the customer.

The problem with specialization such as this is that everybody else in an organization begins to depend upon the specialists whose function becomes absolving everybody else from service responsibility.

Some organizations, in fact, even have created special senior management positions dedicated, in practice, to making it unnecessary for anybody else in a company to be concerned with customer satisfaction.

Service at the Source

More effective is the kind of service provided by Hartford's Travelers Insurance Company where claims clerks no longer just type endless claim forms and pass them along for approval by someone else. Instead, they settle an increasing number of minor claims on the spot with a few deft punches on their computer keyboards. Now, says Bob Fenn, director of training at Travelers: "Entry-level clerks have to be capable of using information and making decisions."

Large and increasingly automated organizations normally do not promote sensitivity to customers among employees when the immediacy of customer needs is segregated into the customer service/support area or when it is a "function" assigned to the sales area.

Instead of pushing customer service into a closely kept little department, it is far better that every department does its bit in the customer service effort.

The consumer affairs department can answer inquiries and field complaints. The sales force can make sales calls. Market researchers conduct focus groups. The R&D staff conducts value analysis attaching dollar benefits to product *and service* features. Shipping pushes finished goods out the door on schedule.

But one function all these departments should have in common is—you know—*service to customers.*

Integration of Service

The American Management Association noted that "successful, high-growth companies . . . integrate all these parts into strategic business plans that run on a good deal more than slogans."

Achieving and maintaining a high level of customer satisfaction is related to everything that anyone in the organization does. This is true because every management and nonmanagement function—from the janitor's job to the CEO's job—affects customer buying decisions.

"It's not just the sales force but everyone in the organization—from the people in the back rooms to those answering the telephones—who have an effect upon the customer," says John Guaspari, lecturer and author of the book *I Know It When I See It,* a title that refers to quality.

Says Richard Gamgort, director of Quality Assurance and Customer Affairs for Armstrong World Industries: "We preach that customer service is everyone's responsibility, from salesman in the field to R and D and technical personnel to marketing people who handle products and revisions and changes in products."

Don't allow yourself the luxury of expecting that your employee newsletter pronouncements about service quality will be enough to spread the service doctrine throughout the company and to keep it alive and lively. Remember that most employees probably don't know what good service is, if your company does not have a long-standing service culture. So telling them to provide service is like telling a high school student to draw a map of the United States.

Employees must be told what service is, shown what service is, led through a period of actually providing service, and then remotivated and retrained periodically.

When employees have never been told that they have customer service responsibilities, the majority of them lose the sense of working for the customer and end up working for personal or departmental objectives. Those objectives easily can conflict with organizational service objectives.

SPREADING CUSTOMER SERVICE AWARENESS

To promote strong service-mindedness among employees, one leading company routinely rotates people between staff and line positions. The theory behind this practice is that line employees who deal directly with customers are more customer conscious. So sending staff people to spend time in line jobs raises their customer consciousness and also elevates customer awareness among their peers and, thence, throughout the company.

Whole company service is important because customers perceive the company as a whole. They don't make allowances and comment, "Oh, he (she) is in a staff job. He (she) doesn't know what customers want."

A foul-up in one department that's low on the customer consciousness scale affects customer perception of the entire company.

Long-Term Benefit

Rotation of employees between staff and line positions is not always convenient for the company or for employees. But a strong service-minded organization should be so important that management is willing to accept short-term disruption to achieve long-term benefit.

In training sessions, every single employee should be taught that he or she becomes part of the company's sales effort through the service they provide. Every employee should be trained to assume that every person they meet on the job is a customer or a prospective customer and to treat them as if his or her job depends upon that person's satisfaction. The internal customer is just as important as the external customer. The Scandinavian Airlines System spread service consciousness throughout the company, said Jan Carlzon, president, by declaring that "we would turn a profit by becoming a service-oriented airline." He continued: "We ignited a radical change in the culture at SAS."

"Traditionally," said Carlzon, "executives deal with investments, management, and administration. Service was . . . the province of employees located way out on the periphery of the company. Now, the *entire* company—from the executive suite to the most remote check-in terminal—was focused on service."

Share Customer Service Facilities

Share customer service awareness with dealers, distributors, and franchisees in a companywide product and service delivery system. Tell them that they have full access to the company's sales and service operations. That should include on-line programs that track service and parts, to ensure customer satisfaction. Enhance awareness of service facilities also by discussing with resellers a division of service responsibilities. Which service problems they should handle themselves and which ones they should pass on to the marketer should be a topic that's discussed long before need arises.

Most marketers, however, are reluctant to establish policies that deal with these issues. They're reluctant to allow dealers and distributors access to their communication systems. So service consciousness tends to die like a flower after the first frost somewhere between manufacturer and manufacturer's representatives.

But a dealer, distributor, or franchisee *is* the manufacturer to customers. Actions taken by them reflect upon the manufacturer. A chain is only as strong as its weakest link.

Tom Peters and Nancy Austin expressed the need for customer service awareness when they said in *Passion for Excellence*: "Attention to quality can become the organization's mind-set only if all of its managers—indeed, all of its people—live it."

MONITORING SERVICE

Automobile driving consists of a series of adjustments in steering that keep you in your lane and on the road. Similarly, to maintain a level of service that retains customers, you need a mechanism for monitoring service performance.

Do it by periodically reevaluating all service support systems to make certain that they really do support the service strategy. Be aware that support systems can block or weaken a strategy.

Evaluate by answering these questions with *current* information:

- Does recruiting and hiring turn up people who are *capable* of learning to practice professional customer service?
- Do orientation programs for new employees instill them with an awareness of service strategy from the beginning?
- Does the company newsletter preach the same gospel as the chief executive?
- Do training programs advance the cause of effective service?
- Does the performance appraisal system provide feedback to employees about effectiveness of their customer service efforts?

Gamgort of Armstrong says: "We in customer affairs have taken on responsibility to design the methods and to manage the systems that provide constant monitoring and feedback as to how well we're doing in terms of meeting customer expectations."

Responsibility for responding to that feedback and making sure that any area of weakness is strengthened is assumed by the various support functions, says Gamgort.

The Technical Assistance Research Corporation (TARP) developed two statistical models that monitor service by documenting value of a service system (by measuring its performance) and by determining how to improve service in a cost-effective manner. The TARP models also project results of a service system before it is implemented and provides a way to prove that contemplated service will achieve bottom-line results.

Market Impact of Service

"The Market Impact of Service Model" determines effect of reaching people who are dissatisfied and of concluding such contacts satisfactorily, a common activity.

This service model quantifies economic impact of various levels of service for corporate executives. It indicates, too, which service should be changed to achieve optimum bottom-line impact.

Assume that sales support/customer service staff takes on most of the after-sales support that salespeople formerly did for themselves such as handling terms, exchanges, and adjustments. This frequently makes a sales force *5 percent more productive,* the TARP model has determined.

Normally this amounts to the equivalent of one more field sales call per week. In the typical situation, that's a profit contribution of more than $65 per salesperson per week, the recent average cost of a field sales call. With, say, 50 people on the sales force you're talking about $170,000 in added productivity resulting from sales support/customer service staff taking on after-sales support. This added productivity costs almost nothing to achieve.

When salespeople become more productive, they are able to make more calls and more sales. If those sales are significant, as they often are in heavy industry and supplier categories (chemical sales average more than $40,000), you're talking about an estimated $10 million increase in sales per year at no added cost to the company if productivity increases 10 percent. This is the kind of information turned up in careful monitoring of a service system with statistical models like TARP's.

"The Market Impact of Service Model" also enables executives to determine the amount of profit and return on investment increase for increments of decrease in "unarticulated dissatisfaction." That's dissatisfaction that a customer hasn't told you about but which is likely to motivate him or her to patronize your competitor.

The model also yields amount saved when the number of service contacts per customer are reduced (because more customers are more often satisfied) and when the number of satisfied customers increases.

Documenting Service Value

The model is salvation for executives charged with overseeing a service system. It enables them to document their contention that service is a profit center generating substantial additional sales.

In summary, "The Market Impact of Service Model" reveals

1. Increased sales and return on investment from better service. Service gets better as a result of improvements made to prevent dissatisfaction of customers.
2. Amount of reduction in service costs through prevention of dissatisfaction.
3. Positive market impact by the satisfaction that good service causes among a larger proportion of customers.

The Service Model estimates increased service-generated sales and return on investment by combining company-provided data and data obtained from customer surveys. The result is calculations such as these:

New purchases resulting from complaint satisfaction.
New purchases resulting from positive word of mouth. That is, recommendations resulting from effective complaint handling.
Sales resulting from positive word of mouth recommendation by satisfied customers.
Profit on sales from complaint handling and resultant word-of-mouth recommendation.
ROI from money invested in service.

Primary use of the second model, the "Sensitivity to Profits Model," is to postulate impact of various expenditures upon customer satisfaction *before expenditures are made*. The model equips executives to make educated decisions about priorities.

Monitoring your service system also makes it possible to determine degree of customer satisfaction needed to retain the customer's brand loyalty or company loyalty.

This is vital data. Research has documented the importance of satisfaction in establishing brand loyalty. Brand loyalty, by the way, determines a company's ability to retain or to increase market share.

MIDDLE MANAGER BACKLASH

A new service structure might sustain major damage from "sabotage," if you do not take preventive steps. The unintentioned "saboteurs" are managers reacting with apathy, neglect, or even with hostility to seeming "devaluation" of their managerial role.

Managers may feel that a companywide customer service concept diminishes their authority because, typically, front-line employees are given more authority to make decisions in achieving customer satisfaction. Their job requirements, they feel, consist mostly of mere coaching, informing, criticizing, praising, and educating.

Accountable for Profit and Service

To cope with managerial backlash, make managers accountable for customer service as much as they are accountable for profit, and base bonuses and evaluation scores upon how well they succeed in achieving service objectives through their people.

The degree to which objectives are achieved should be determined by continuing impartial evaluation. It is advisable that an unbiased outside organization does the evaluating and that the organization prepares a "customer service index."

Tie appraisals to meaningful customer service measures. Appraisals should be based upon customer surveys and direct observation instead of upon guesswork. Failure to develop realistic appraisal methods contributes to weak service motivation and cynicism.

When managers realize that achieving customer service objectives, expressed as their personal objectives, can help them become successful in their careers, they are likely to abandon any hostility to them.

Carlzon of Scandinavian Airlines had something to say about managerial cynicism and hostility in his book, *Moments of Truth*: "the middle managers, who were understandably confused by their new role within the organization (after front-line employees were given more responsibility) became hostile and counterproductive. We had put them in a completely unfamiliar situation where they were squeezed from both directions. Directives came shooting down from above that conflicted with their expectations and experience. They heard what we said but didn't know how to translate it into practical actions. From below came demands for responsibility and power to make decisions, which they viewed as threats to their own position.

> We had directed middle managers to go out and listen to the people on the front line—to find out what they needed to do their jobs. The managers, however, were not accustomed to thinking of themselves as filling a support function, especially if they were supporting people previously considered subordinates.

> The word "support" conjures up an image of attending to needs, not administering. At SAS, like at other companies, support and service always had been relegated to a low status. Every promotion had moved people away from serving the customer and toward administration.
>
> When people on the front lines "broke the rule" to help the customers, naturally the middle managers responded by reining them in. This infuriated the front line.

Keeping Managers Happy

To solve the problem of offended managers, SAS made them responsible for breaking down broad company objectives into smaller objectives that the front-line people could accomplish.

Communicate to managers *before* a new or expanded service program begins. Tell them that their roles will change but that their authority will go unchanged. Work with them to achieve the understanding that now the organization depends more than ever upon their proficiency at coaching, informing, criticizing, praising, and educating.

The authority of managers will be broadened in a total company service strategy to include translating overall strategies into practical guidelines that the front line can follow. Managers also mobilize resources that the front line needs to achieve objectives.

Point out to middle managers that all this requires hard-nosed business planning and healthy doses of creativity and resourcefulness.

Change in managerial responsibilities when an organization becomes customer oriented are significant. Ascending hierarchical tiers of responsibility must be flattened so that customer contact employees respond directly and quickly to customer needs. Front-line people who deal personally with customers become managers, too—managers of their own situations vis-à-vis customers, one at a time.

In an advanced service system, employees have the authority to select appropriate action and to supervise implementation to achieve customer satisfaction.

However, before employees actually have this authority, people occupying higher levels of the old management "pyramid" must understand that their roles have changed greatly. They are now leaders, making it possible for those out front to make operational decisions. Nevertheless, it is they (the middle managers) who have total responsibility for achieving stated service results.

REPORTING STRUCTURE

Views still differ about who ought to have authority over the service function. Some feel that sales and service will cooperate only if a sale manager controls both functions. Others say that the service function needs a separate management structure to keep service reps focused on customer satisfaction instead of on quotas and other sales issues.

In the most profitable service organizations, the head of service reports either to the chairman or to the president of a division. That's proper because they make profit decisions.

In the most customer-oriented organizations, marketing, sales, and service all report to one person, usually the chairman or the president, who is accountable for all customer interactions.

But often you'll find that customer service is located in the marketing, accounting, production, or distribution department. Sometimes it's called the "complaint department," and it ranks low on the organization chart.

The function called "consumer affairs" more often is a staff position reporting directly to the top. In many cases, customer relations is the company's main mouthpiece, as it should be when the company doesn't have a customer service function. For instance, in retail chains, consumer affairs must have the full force of the company behind it when dealing with vendors in regard to warranty work.

Customers Come First

Actually, the organization chart for a corporation ought to show the customer at the top instead of the CEO. Xerox Canada expressed the idea graphically. The company built a six-foot metallic pyramid inscribed with the names of 4,500 Canadian employees. The corporate silver and blue pyramid was designed to tell the world that a Xerox customer, at the apex of the pyramid, is supported by every employee in the organization, listed below "customer."

Mansour's, a family-owned department and specialty store in Columbus and LaGrange, Georgia, is built "from the sales associates on up," says Fred Mansour, president. Each associate is vital to the operation, he says, and is made to feel very much a part of it.

This attitude has spread throughout the business world. For instance, Peter Burwash, president of a management and consulting firm in the hospitality industry, says: "Clubs (exercise clubs, social clubs, spas) see the employee as being their most important asset. The reason most clubs fail is because owners, presidents, and general managers think they are the most important people in the club. They create a huge communication gap that results in employee resentment and lack of effort toward both management and members."

Now, let's take a look at how a large corporation that has an exceptional customer service reputation, Dow Chemical USA, organizes its service function.

Centralized Customer Service

Until 1983, there was no such thing as a customer service department in Dow. Service was handled by an inside sales force. This work, in many respects, was considered to be training for outside sales.

In 1983 the company eliminated the inside sales force and created six regional professional customer service centers. To retain even better control over the service effort and to professionalize it further, Dow centralized the function into a single Customer Service Center in Midland, Michigan, by late 1988.

Now, with customer service a separate entity reporting directly to the president of Dow USA, service employees know that their function is valued for the important role it plays.

The Dow customer service organization has more than 270 employees who handle traditional and advanced account management activity. This runs the gamut from order entry to managing an inquiry center where the focus is availability to answer technical and business questions for customers.

Six job levels make up the customer service organization. Employees are given opportunities to grow and to advance professionally in a long-term career.

The six job levels are

1. *Customer Service Representative, two levels.* CSRs are required to have a four-year degree in business, marketing, or a related field. They are responsible for:

   Assuring excellent customer service.

   Supporting the field sales organization by handling order handling, credit and collections, adjustments, sales leads, and up-to-date business activity.

   Maintaining technical expertise in order entry, products, and applications to provide fast and accurate information to customers.

   Preserving effective relationships with functional support groups such as production, distribution, and customer financial service to implement policies and procedures of each group.

   Anticipating customer needs by taking a proactive rather than a reactive role and dealing with issues before they become problems.

2. *Customer Service Specialist, three levels.* CSSs are responsible for:

   Exercising more individual problem-solving activity than CSRs.

   Supporting the field sales organization on key accounts through order handling, credit and collections, adjustments, sales leads, customer visits, and other functions.

CONSOLIDATION UPDATE

News on the customer service Organization

Management Team sets announcement deadlines

The Customer Service Management Team met in Chicago November 19 and 20 to plan for the consolidation next year. The hot topics were outlining the organization, defining job descriptions, and starting to define when groups will move to Midland. During eleven hours of meetings the team produced an organizational structure and made tentative deadlines for personnel assignments.

Reporting to the previously named customer service managers (CSM) will be operations managers. They will be responsible for the daily management of the assigned business unit(s). They'll take the leading role in performance appraisal and will be responsible for management in the CSM's absence.

Reporting to each operations manager will be team leaders. Team leaders will be the key players in training high performance customer service teams, with approximately1/3 of their job dedicated to handling key accounts and 2/3 devoted to team training and coaching.

December 31 is the tentative deadline for announcing the operations managers and team leaders.

On the moving schedule side, the team plans to announce group moving dates by mid-January.

According to Phil Rathburn, Director of Customer Service, the meeting was designed to answer the key questions people had about the consolidation. "We started by discussing how to take care of our people — by answering the questions they were concerned about. Then we moved on to other topics such as a smooth transition, communications programs, and systems updates. I hope we answered a few of the key questions people have been asking."

The team split the meeting into four topics: people, transition, communications, and systems. Under each topic they discussed a number of concerns.

Under people the team outlined programs to handle training, hiring, performance appraisals, and clerical support. They also discussed outcounseling for non-moving employees and motivating and retaining personnel until the businesses move.

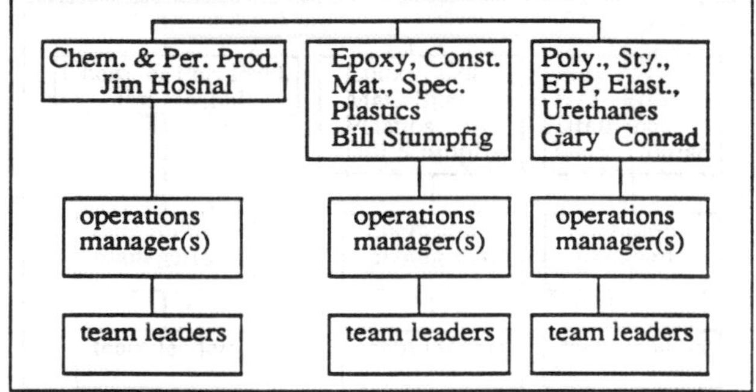

The main discussions under the transition topic centered around scheduling moves to Midland and maintaining quality service during that transition. The team delayed the scheduling decision until early January to make certain CS plans and strategies matched those of the new Dow U.S.A. business units.

Under communication, the team decided to continue and strengthen the role of *Consolidation Update* as the source of customer service information. Overnight delivery will ensure future issues reach the Regional Centers as quickly as they reach the Dow Center.

Systems will play a big part in the new organization. Mitch Kern, Manager of Customer Service Resources, updated the team on topics including IDS integration, C.L.A.S.S. prototyping, and consistent CS policy. All C.L.A.S.S. information can be found in *C.L.A.S.S. NOTES*, a monthly publication scheduled to begin in December.

As each of these areas becomes more clearly defined, they'll be reported in *Consolidation Update*. "We created a good basic plan for many areas during this meeting," said Rathburn. "We also created someting else — a lot of work. Pursuing what we outlined will keep everyone busy for the next several weeks. The next meeting will be around the end of December to finish personnel assignments and finalize that consolidation schedule. We know that's important to our people, so we're going all-out to meet our deadlines."

Communications Department, The Dow Chemical Company, Midland, Michigan 48674

*Trademark of The Dow Chemical Company

A newsletter, *Consolidation Update,* kept all concerned people well informed during planning and implementation of a consolidation of six Dow Chemical USA regional service centers into a single Customer Service Center in Midland, Michigan. (Reprinted courtesy of Dow Chemical USA.)

Maintaining excellent relationships with internal functional support groups such as schedulers, customer financial services, product departments, marketing administration, and distribution.

Maintaining technical expertise; providing leadership in order entry, computer capabilities, inquiry handling, and product knowledge; and facilitating fast and helpful service.

Participating in production department activities, inventory management, order solicitation, special projects, training, and customer calls, with minimal supervision.

Providing backup support in the team leader's absence.

Assisting in interviewing potential CSRs and helping to train new CSRs and field salespeople.

3. *Team Leaders, one level,* are responsible for:

   Supervising daily team performance.

   Helping the manager evaluate team performance.

   Developing performance standards for the team.

   Acting as a team resource.

   Providing training and initial personnel selection.

   Accounting to the manager for team performance.

THE RIGHT LEADER

A thoroughly committed company needs a respected and motivated leader to drive and to manage the service function for the company in the same way that a corporate counsel or senior vice president of finance manage their functions.

A senior executive assigned to customer service must be viewed as the occupant of a key position. So he or she must hold the rank of senior vice president or vice president of customer service.

Especially in industrial companies the vice president of customer service should be in charge of service *and product quality.*

He or she should be an innovative and creative person who is willing to take chances and able to recognize an end result benefit when it presents itself.

The top customer service position holder and also executives who report to her or him must be ready to endure and even to thrive on criticism directed at them for ruffling feathers in the process of achieving goals.

To attract executives with these qualities, rewards for success must be great. But attracting them is easier than it once was. In years past, if you were sent to work in customer service, obviously you had done something wrong. But now, customer service has become a tour of duty for people on the fast track.

4

Let Me Introduce You to . . . Your Customer

SERVICE IS WHAT YOUR CUSTOMER SAYS IT IS

Give the lady what she wants.

—Marshall Field, pioneering merchant

My first message is: Listen, listen, listen to the people who do the work.

—H. Ross Perot, chairman, Perot Systems, Inc.

"High-growth companies stay in touch with their markets—and willingly spend the money to do so. They know their customers and they keep their knowledge fresh," says the American Management Association (AMA) stated in its "Research Report on Consumer Affairs."

It's important to know your customers' wants and needs before you try to sell them a service or a product. If you don't know, you're guessing. And guesswork makes dissatisfaction inevitable.

Yes, knowing your customers so you can give them what they want and keep them as customers costs money. But spending money on something that pays off in profit has never been a problem for a company.

When dissatisfied customers complain to you—or, as more often happens, they switch their business to your competitors without complaining—you learn what they *don't like*, all right. But you'll wish that you'd known that and also what they like before you alienated them. You'll wish you'd practiced proactive, research-based customer service instead of reactive service.

The Sometimes Fatal Assumption

You might have been good at predicting customer behavior in the past, but remember that it isn't what you think you know that's important. It's what customers think that matters, even if they are illogical, uninformed, or witless. Good service has nothing to do with what the provider of services believes it to be, unless these beliefs coincide with the attitudes of customers.

Good service only has to do with what customers believe it to be. Few executives truly understand what good service is, nor are they close enough to their own employees to understand how bad and inconsistent service is.

Manufacturers and service firms need to realize that dealers, distributors and franchisees are a reflection of their company. Service standards should be emphasized and enforced. A chain, remember, is only as strong as its weakest link.

Never assume what customers want instead of spending time or money asking them. Remember that opinions and needs change over time, so what you knew in the past about your customers may well have changed. What's more, the information you have may be too general to apply to specific business projects you have in mind.

A company that sold package tours to retired people felt that it knew the market well. But inferences based upon generalizations about the market proved faulty. The president of the company said: "We had decided that they would want to stay in hotels with other older persons, would want nurses with them, would like American food no matter where they were, and would enjoy only brief excursions that wouldn't tire them."

The company was wrong. Sales plummeted after an initial surge.

"Then," the president said, "we talked to the oldsters. We found that they wanted to see new places, mix with the young and the old and with people who live in the areas they visit. They also wanted to eat new food, and they weren't overly worried about their health. They thought our program was a bore."

"[Service] is in the eye of the beholder," says Jack G. Lowenstein, director of administration for FMC Corporation's Chemical Research and Development Center in Princeton, New Jersey. "The customer decides whether one organization is better. If the customer rates you excellent then, by George, you've got it."

Says Lowenstein: "Ultimately the key words are 'customer perception.' It matters not whether all the specs are met, whether all dimensions are perfect. If the customer doesn't like the product, that's the ultimate reality. Only when we deliver a product on time and it truly meets the customer's expectations of quality, usefulness, and price worthiness can we expect the customer to heap superlatives upon us."

Whether or not customers like the product and the service is something you ought to know early in the game.

Perception of Customers Is Reality for You

Lowenstein thinks that a wall in every office should bear this sign: "Perception Is Reality When It Comes to Being Judged by Others."

The first step toward learning what customers consider reality should be to decide exactly what business you're in, from a customer point of view, if you haven't done so already. Usually you'll conclude that you are in the business of providing customers with a variety of "services," even if you are not a service business, strictly speaking. Make a list. You might surprise yourself.

Many service firms still do not realize that they are in the service business. My company is engaged in a joint venture with a Soviet organization to help the Soviet Union develop and train employees in customer service. We hope to help them understand what they must do to become service driven and to improve their reputation.

In the Soviet Union, it is common for an organization to be uncertain about the business they are in. Customs agents believe that they are in security, for instance, so two-hour waits for airline passengers are common. At supermarkets consumers stand in line to make selections. Then they move to another line and wait to pay for the selections. After that they take the "paid" receipt to yet another line where they wait to obtain their purchases.

We hope to help the Soviets understand at all levels of management what they must do to be service driven and to improve their image.

The second step is to identify *all* market segments—all customer groups. It's important to determine needs and wants of all customers.

The third step is to set up the systems you'll need for *listening* to customers. The way to find out what customers want is to ask them. And to allow them to tell you. Make it easy for customers to communicate with the company.

Print an 800 phone number on billings, for instance.

Provide customers with postcards that they can use to convey their opinions. Make sure that employees know how customers should contact the company so they can tell them.

Factor the advantages of voice mail into your telephone system. Computer networking is becoming more effective as more home computers are purchased. You may wish to retain a communications consultant to design a system that streamlines communications among departments so they can speedily and accurately exchange information needed to respond to customer needs.

Collect data and then analyze it for generalizations and trends. Hyatt Hotels & Resorts does this. Its "In Touch for the 90's" quality assurance program includes a customer rating system that rewards individual hotels for the most favorable customer comment cards. Follow-up is done by focus groups of hotel general managers who discuss service results and philosophy, according to Darryl Hartley-Leonard, president of Hyatt.

Consider a continuing evaluation of the ups and downs of service quality and on the basis of it prepare a "customer service index." The index could become the universal scale of your performance in the customer service area.

SURVEY TOOLS

Informal Surveys

One informal survey format is a simple discussion of recent customer reactions at a monthly or weekly staff meeting. Use findings from these discussions as guides to action needed to improve or to expand service.

Managers and supervisors who attend these staff meetings come prepared with results of surveys of front-line employees. They've asked them what customers are saying about service, good and bad.

Jim Kowalski and his wife, owners of several supermarkets in the St. Paul, Minnesota, area, have a fine informal survey format that could be used by an organization of any size. Each quarter they rent a conference room somewhere near each of their stores. They meet at each store with an invited group of 8 to 12 customers.

"Nothing formal," says Kowalski. "We just order out for pizza and ask them a lot of questions about what they like and—more important—what they don't like about our stores. They talk. We listen."

Out of these meetings have come decisions to stock more low-calorie foods for older customers, to offer smaller meat cuts to accommodate people who live alone, and so on.

Formal Surveys

The basic formal survey form is focus groups in which a leader asks questions and motivates response. The group should consist of customers and also employees from all functions and from all seniority levels. Conduct formal customer surveys every 60 to 90 days. Less frequency than 90 days is risky because you're likely to miss a development that mandates a change in service.

The best companies survey customers *and* employees. Usually both company staff and an outside consulting organization conduct surveys. The inside survey of sales and marketing people asks questions designed to determine whether they believe that the company is doing a good job of satisfying customers.

Employee Surveys

When employees are queried by an outside consultant they are not told that their employer is sponsoring the survey. Reason: Greater candor by employees. They'll make statements that they would suppress if they thought that the assertions would reach their bosses. A significant percentage of these statements make revelations that, followed up, lead to significant improvements in service.

Professor Michael LeBoeuf of the University of New Orleans suggests questions that are variants, customized to a company's business, of what he calls "the platinum questions," to indicate their value. They are

- "How are we doing?"
- "How can we get better?"

When surveying former customers, ask a different question: Why did you stop buying? Applying professional surveying standards, fashion questions that ferret out answers to these general queries, too:

"What do customers want that we can profitably make?"
"What kind of information do our customers need to have from *their* perspective?"

A survey called the Customer Satisfaction Audit is a prepackaged direct-mail survey of customers. It can be tailored to fit the needs of most service companies. Its results determine how customers rate a service company's performance. Designed for computer tabulation, the survey provides quantitative scores for basic elements of customer satisfaction and compares them with average scores of similar service businesses.

The University of Minnesota developed the Customer Satisfaction Audit with input from polling techniques expert Douglas R. Berdie. It is available from W. J. Lynott Associates, Dept. ASN, 614 N. Easton Rd., Suite 200, Glenside, Pennsylvania 19038.

An Effective Focus Group

One effective focus group is the Consumer Advisory Panel of Puget Sound Power & Light Company of Bellevue, Washington.

Chief Executive Officer John W. Ellis says about the Consumer Panel Program: "We are convinced that direct dialogue helps Puget Power make better decisions in tune with real customer interests and concerns. We found that one excellent, if obvious, way to find what customers want is to ask them."

Nearly 1,500 customers have served one-year terms in 57 advisory groups since Puget Power established a network of customer advisory panels. Purposes of the panels are

1. To involve customers more actively in Puget Power's planning and decision-making process.
2. To improve management's awareness of and responsiveness to community expectations of the company.

Panel members are recruited from every community, and they serve annual terms. They are not "blue ribbon" panels. Members are mainly "just plain folks," say Puget Power executives. Some are opinion leaders, and some are not. Some represent groups, and some represent themselves or their families. Each local panel contains a mixture of people with opinions largely representative of people who live in their communities.

In the first seven years of the program, Puget Power management agreed in whole or in substantial part with more than 75 percent of 1,018 recommendations for changes or initiations of everything from sweeping policy issues to project details.

Northwest Airlines began drawing upon employee ideas for new service action in 1989. Two management teams were formed to poll employees about service needs and to determine which improvements are likely to be most cost effective. The teams, headed by senior management, conducted interviews with focus groups of front-line employees. Employees were asked what tools could be used to achieve greater customer satisfaction. Northwest planned to ask all 35,000 employees for suggestions.

Another focus group format is the Consumer Advisory Board of Land O' Lakes, Inc., Minneapolis, food processor. Arlene Stansfield, customer service manager, reports that 16 people from all walks of life assemble at corporate headquarters. The company submits subjects for their consideration. The same people are used for blind taste tests and other research.

800 Numbers

Incoming WATS lines are widely used to make it easy for consumers to contact a company.

An AMA study found that in a recent year average expenditure for 800 number operations by organizations using them was well over $250,000. Some large companies spent more than a million dollars a year.

Chesebrough Ponds spent $800,000 during one recent year. Other companies that spend a great deal on 800 number systems are General Electric (GE Answer Center) and Whirlpool (Cool Line).

One midsized chemical processor spent $350,000 to install and to operate an 800 number to put its salespeople in touch by direct line with customers without going through retailers. Result: Sales increased by 20 percent.

A billion-dollar chain of convenience stores—a business that does all its selling over the local counter and that takes no phone orders at national headquarters—spent $200,000 on an 800 line to field customer queries and complaints. Result: Sales revenues increased by 19 percent.

Incoming WATS lines to facilitate customer comment, inquiry, and complaint pay off.

Mervyn's, said to be the largest department store chain in the United States, strongly encourages contact by both wholesale and retail customers over its 800 number. Some 70 to 75 percent of calls received deal with technical information. About 25 percent of them clearly deal with merchandise-related problems.

Mervyn's has named its system Field Intelligence. It gives management a continuous reading on whether Mervyn's is satisfying customer needs and requirements.

K-Mart has its toll-free Customer Care Network. Service deficiencies cited in calls are promptly corrected. In analyzing calls and letters received in one quarter, the company found that the number of complaints dropped significantly in certain areas and customer compliments improved 120 percent. Calls and letters were compared with corresponding communications received during the previous quarter.

"Thank You" Customer Calls

The Royal Bank of Canada uses its WATS line for proactive instead of reactive customer service. In a continuous program, reps call existing customers and say little more than "Thank you for being our customer. We appreciate your business and we want to know if you are having any problems."

The project works so well that what was expected to be just a justifiable business expense actually paid for itself with more business within the first year, not even considering the financial benefits of saving accounts that would have been lost without such a program. Increased income came from referrals, up-grades, and cross-selling.

Stephen Higgins, manager of Direct Marketing Services for the Ontario District of the Royal Bank, says: "Our system centers on uncovering customer needs. But people don't tell you what their needs really are if they think you're trying to sell them something. So we call just to touch base with them and to learn about each unique situation.

"Of course, when we uncover needs that we can satisfy, we make recommendations. That generates more business from each customer. And because our customers feel that they have been treated fairly, they are more than willing to make referrals that generate new customers."

The initial objective of the Royal Bank program was to drive new business into the branch office network. But more and more customers asked to finalize business over the phone, so the bank moved toward completing more transactions on the phone.

Lloyd Warren
Vice President, In-flight Services
NORTHWEST

Welcome

WE VALUE YOUR COMMENTS

Northwest is committed to providing quality service. You are the best qualified to assess our services, so we ask that you help us by taking a moment to rate your experiences with today's flight. After you have completed the comment card, just drop it in the mail. We value your business and appreciate your comments.

Bienvenue

NOUS APPRECIONS VOS COMMENTAIRES

Vos commentaires tient à offrir un service de qualité. Comme vous êtes les mieux qualifiés pour évaluer nos services, nous vous demandons de nous aider en prenant quelques minutes pour donner votre opinion sur les expériences du vol d'aujourd'hui. Après avoir completé la carte de commentaires, mettez-la simplement dans une boîte aux lettres. Vos affaires nous importent et nous apprécions vos commentaires.

Willkommen

WIR LEGEN WERT AUF IHRE MEINUNG

Es ist unser Ziel bei Northwest einen qualitätsgerechten Service zu bieten. Sie können unsere Leistungen am besten einschätzen, darum bitten wir Sie uns zu helfen, indem Sie sich einen Moment Zeit nehmen, um Ihre Eindrücke des heutigen Fluges zu bewerten. Wenn Sie Ihren Bewertungsbogen fertig ausgefüllt haben, brauchen Sie ihn nur mit der Post abzuschicken. Wir rechnen Ihnen Ihre Bemühung hoch an und schätzen Ihre Meinung.

FLIGHT INFORMATION — INFORMATION DU VOL — FLUG INFORMATION

Your flight number	From	To	Date of flight
Numéro de votre vol Ihre Flugnummer	De von	A nach	Date du vol Abflugsdatum

Your seat number

Numéro de votre siège
Ihre Platznummer

Your seat class		Classe de votre siège	Ihre Sitzklasse
First Class	☐	Première Classe	Erste Klasse
Executive Class/Main Deck	☐	Affaires/Etage principal	Businessklasse/Hauptdeck
Executive Class/Upper Deck	☐	Affaires/Etage supérieur	Businessklasse/Vorderdeck
Main Cabin	☐	Cabine principale	Hauptkabine

PRIOR TO YOUR FLIGHT — AVANT VOTRE VOL — VOR IHREM ABFLUG

Ticket Counter Staff	EXCELLENT EXCELLENT AUSGEZEICHNET	GOOD BON GUT	FAIR PASSABLE MITTELMÄSSIG	POOR MEDIOCRE SCHLECHT	Personnel Au Guichet	Personal am Ticketschalter
Speed and efficiency of service	☐	☐	☐	☐	Rapidité et efficacité du service	Schnelligkeit und Tüchtigkeit des Services
Courtesy and helpfulness to you	☐	☐	☐	☐	Politesses et obligeance envers vous	Höflichkeit und Hilfsbereitschaft Ihnen gegenüber
Professional appearance	☐	☐	☐	☐	Apparence professionelle	Professionelles Auftreten
Boarding Gate Staff					**Personnel à la Porte d'Embarcation**	**Personal am Flugschalter**
Speed and efficiency of service	☐	☐	☐	☐	Rapidité et efficacité du service	Schnelligkeit und Tüchtigkeit des Services
Courtesy and helpfulness to you	☐	☐	☐	☐	Politesses et obligeance envers vous	Höflichkeit und Hilfsbereitschaft Ihnen gegenüber
Professional appearance	☐	☐	☐	☐	Apparence professionelle	Professionelles Auftreten

(over please) (suite au verso) (bitte wenden) (moisten entire panel and fold to seal)

Northwest Airlines furnishes a comment form in its inflight magazine for passengers to convey their service experience. (Reprinted courtesy of Northwest Airlines.)

Automated Response Systems

Messages received from consumers via 800 phone lines, by letter, or by other means often are answered by the use of automated response systems. Large consumer goods companies with high-capacity computers can generate customized, apparently personal responses by the thousands. It's the only practical way to respond to *everyone* who contacts a huge company.

General Mills has a rather advanced system. As far back as 1978 the company was doing paragraph assembly. The system consists of a word processing package tied into a mainframe computer. Operators can do many things not available on word processing software alone.

The company has about 1,500 paragraph responses that are "sequentialized" to form individual letters. Operators key in customer name and address and product name.

Data is stored in the computer. At end of every month and at the end of the current recording cycle information such as comments, compliments, and complaints by product are compiled in a report.

With its computerized system General Mills responds to about 300,000 customers each year.

Mail/Phone Questionnaires

General Electric calls or sends a postcard to everyone who receives a GE service call and asks customers to assign a satisfaction rating to the call. The company mailed 700,000 postcards in a recent year and received a customer-satisfied rating of more than 90 percent. GE contacts dissatisfied customers and asks them what they would like the company to do differently.

Northern Telecom Co., manufacturer of telecommunications equipment, mails questionnaires to customers. The objective is to determine reasons for any customer dissatisfaction and to take appropriate action. But Northern Telecom and other companies that conduct surveys also benefit in terms of positive impression upon customers that's made by the company's evident interest in them.

Northern Telecom also sends out engineering questionnaires tailored to each type of customer and to business cycles. This is done just after installations, 30 days after installation, and six months after installation.

If the company waited to send out questionnaires until, say, a year after installation, "a cancer may have killed the patient," says Jack Shaw, director of Quality Assurance and Field Operations.

Questionnaire Results Influence Compensation

Everyone who uses a Humana Hospital (Humana Health Care Corp.) receives a mailer asking for an evaluation of care and service. About one-third of 300,000 surveys Humana sends out monthly are returned. Results influence employee compensation and are used to identify areas that will be improved throughout the organization.

Renex, the computer interconnectivity products company, uses mail and phone surveys to solicit customer evaluations. Questionnaires employ a scale of 1 to 10 to rate tech reps on courtesy, responsiveness, and clarity of instructions.

Questionnaires also ask for ratings of corporate strengths and weaknesses with questions such as:

> Do we work your problems through until they're resolved?
> How well do the things we sell work?

A small firm that sells software to *Fortune* 500 companies spent $110,000 on mail/phone questionnaires, $100,000 on consumer education materials, and $300,000 to educate its own employees in customer relations—and grew by 30 percent as a result.

Timothy W. Firnstahl, founder and CEO of Satisfaction Guaranteed Eateries, Inc., in the Seattle area, says that once a month groups of his employees call several hundred customers and ask them to rate their experiences. They obtain names from reservations lists and credit card charges.

Says Firnstahl: "Most people are amazed and delighted that we take the trouble to phone them. Many develop enormous loyalty to our restaurants."

Customer Comment Cards

You see them everywhere. They take many forms, but most are postcards or similar card formats that are deposited in collection boxes.

Target stores' "Customer Comment Card" bears a color photo of George Hite, vice president of Consumer Affairs, saying "I'm reading your mail." Store managers personally call customers within 24 hours when they request a call. Accentuating the positive, the card claims that Target receives more than 50,000 letters and cards from "helpful" customers and, in a suggestive vein, headlines: "We accept praise for a job well done."

Foley's department stores uses customer survey forms inserted in customers' bills. The forms are placed beside cash register and near doors, and packed into shopping bags. Foley's receives 5,000 to 7,000 replies and summarizes them every month.

Mervyn's has customer comment response cards in two or three plastic holders at every service counter. About 10,000 are filled out by customers every month. Seventy to 80 percent convey positive messages, the company reports.

Every person who writes a comment in a space at the bottom of a Mervyn's card or who requests a reply by checking a box receives a written response or personal phone call from a store or corporate manager.

Dear St. Paul Book & Stationery Customer,

To us you are #1. Our commitment to you, our customer, is to be recognized as your best performing supplier of quality products and service.

We'd like to take this opportunity to thank you for doing business with St. Paul Book & Stationery. We are proud of our company and the service we provide our customers.

Each of us realizes the ongoing commitment that is necessary to provide you with the most responsible, competent service available. It is with that in mind that I ask you to fill out this comment card. If you've had a good experience I'd like to hear about it, if you've had a bad experience I <u>need</u> to hear about it.

Charles Holm,
President

HEY CHUCK!

I'm ...

Very Impressed. ☐
Pleasantly Surprised. ☐
Satisfied. ☐
Mildly Irritated. ☐
Very Annoyed. ☐

COMMENTS ____________________

____

____

____

____

____

NAME AND
PHONE (OPTIONAL) ____________________

A large business reply card is provided to customers by St. Paul Book & Stationery. A message from Charles Holm, president, includes this: "If you've had a good experience I'd like to hear about it. If you've had a bad experience I NEED to hear about it." (Reprinted courtesy of St. Paul Book & Stationery.)

THE LAWS OF CUSTOMER SERVICE.

Yes, there are laws that govern and affect customer service, and those laws are just as immutable and constant as the laws of gravity or aerodynamic lift.

The laws of gravity and lift are working all the time...for or against you.

You may not know those laws; you may not understand them, but they affect you none the less.

Ignorance of the laws of gravity and lift does not exempt you from their consequences.

And that's the way it is with the laws of customer service. Customer service laws are always at work, and you will certainly experience the consequences of the laws.
Let's look at these laws of customer service and then decide to make the laws work for us rather than suffer the consequences when they work against us.

The Law of First Impression.

This is best explained by stating the following: How people perceive you determines how they tend to react to you.

It's simple. You put out bad vibes, scowls and glaring hostility, and you'll be perceived as an unfriendly person and one to be avoided if at all possible. And all this happens within 20-30 seconds. Consequences? Scarcity of sales and loss of repeat customers.

The Law of Harvest.

Or, "What you plant is what you get." Most everyone realizes that if you plant corn, you get corn. If you plant beans, you get beans. And, if you plant weeds, you get weeds. It's that way with customer service...Plant friendly, courteous and prompt service, and you get a harvest of respect, loyalty and prosperity. The law of HARVEST also involves ABUNDANCE. One seed can produce 3 or 4 ears of corn with many kernels on each ear. That's abundance. The same holds true for customer service. Plant seeds of friendly, courteous and prompt service, reap a harvest of respect, loyalty and prosperity.

The 2nd Law of Thermodynamics.

This is a very technical law requiring a pretty sophisticated explanation. However, in layman's terms it simply means, "Anything left to itself goes to pot," or deteriorates. Your house is a good example. Never paint it, roof it, or caulk it, and in a few years it will be in shambles.

Customer service is like that too. Do nothing positive about it in your place of business, and it won't get better, but will instead become a problem through lack of attention. We have to make positive efforts to keep things in shape!

"The laws of customer service" amount to a personal philosophy recommended for anyone dedicated to satisfying customers. (Reprinted courtesy of the Service Quality Institute.)

Getting the law on your side.

Knowing the laws and the fixed consequences of those laws gives us an opportunity to make the laws work for us.

Three simple steps can help you establish the laws of customer service in your organization so that they are always working for you.

FIRST. Establish customer service as a philosophy, policy and standard operating procedure. Never "leave it alone". Always be applying some pressure to keep it looking alive, sharp and attractive. Make customer service training a habit in your organization and decide to measure your efforts and the results.

SECOND. Plant seeds of friendly, courteous and prompt service every day as often as you possibly can. Remember...the law of harvest includes abundance. Make that work for you by planting many seeds of customer service each day. Plan to reap big harvests.

THIRD. Check your attitude...and that of all your employees. Don't let them get before your customers until they've taken charge of their attitudes. Check them out...smiles, pleasant voice, knowledge of their jobs and a willingness to be of service. Teach your staff, "The customer IS my job".....not an interruption of the job. The customer is the REASON for our jobs. Get the point nailed down in the minds and hearts of every employee! Then, FIRST IMPRESSIONS by customers will be positive, favorable and profitable to you.

IS THE LAW ON YOUR SIDE? Are these laws working for or against you?

For more help with customer service and the law, write or call:

Service Quality Institute
9201 East Bloomington Freeway
Bloomington, MN 55420
Tel. (612) 884 3311

In general, though, I am surprised at how few organizations respond to written complaints. Hotels seem to have been best at responding immediately to customer complaints. The reason for my surprise is that research shows that if a complaint is resolved quickly, a company can *retain* 82 to 95 percent of complaining customers.

Advertising dollars are so plentiful that businesses are committed to the process of acquiring *new* customers. Business managers often believe that there are enough potential customers out there that they don't need to do anything to *keep* present customers.

It's a shame that many firms don't understand the economic value of keeping present customers.

Creative Approaches

Some means of staying in touch with customer wants and complaints are quite imaginative.

Lost sale follow-up programs

Companies follow up lost customers or lost sales by finding out exactly why customers took their business elsewhere. They ask them. Then they make adjustments to prevent further losses for the same reasons.

Key account reviews

Some companies refer to key account reviews as "debriefings." Everyone involved in an account from product managers to customer service supervisors conduct open-ended discussions. Problems, upcoming special needs, and recognition of competent activity, all are topics for discussion.

Key accounts are worth preventive action such as this.

Armstrong World Industries executives ask key customers for both criticism and compliments. Customers are given the opportunity to comment as they wish about Armstrong products. Calls are made every month to key accounts and to other customers selected at random.

Customer visits

Some companies visit their customers' premises now and then. They observe their products being used, and they talk with their customers' employees to find out if they have any insights and observations that might help in product design, delivery, or service. There's no better way to get an insight into your customers' needs and how you can meet them than by watching them and communicating with them while they are working. You'll make a powerful positive impression upon the employees and their managers, too.

In some companies, one of the job objectives of all middle managers is a specific number of customer visits such as this each year.

CLIENTELE RECORD

LAST NAME	FIRST NAME	DATE
MARITAL STATUS	☐ CASH ☐ CHARGE	ACCOUNT #
CARD #, CLOSE DATE	OTHER CARD #, EXP. DATE	
ADDRESS		
CITY	STATE	ZIP
SECOND ADDRESS		
CITY	STATE	ZIP
HOME PHONE	BUSINESS PHONE	OCCUPATION
SIZE INFORMATION		
BIRTHDAY(S)	ANNIVERSARY(S)	

CUSTOMER CONTACT PREFERENCE: _____ PHONE ______ MAIL

VENDOR PREFERENCE(S) ____________________

COLOR AND STYLE ____________________

PERSONAL INFORMATION ____________________

REFERENCES/SWATCHES/BUSINESS CARD/MISC. ____________________

A "Clientele Record" is kept by retail salespeople in a three-ring binder. It enables salespeople to establish rapport with customers by being knowledgeable about their personal preferences. Information in the "Clientele Record" is helpful during phone calls to customers, suggested for salespeople in specialty retail stores. The concept is described by Stanley Marcus, chairman emeritus of Neiman Marcus, in a quality selling and service education program entitled "Quest for the Best" that he narrates. Produced by Marcus and the Service Quality Institute.

PURCHASES					
MO/YR	DEPT	ARTICLE DESCRIPTION	COLOR	SIZE	PRICE

CONTACT RECORD					
MO/YR	CODE	MO/YR	CODE	MO/YR	CODE
1		1		1	
2		2		2	
3		3		3	
4		4		4	
5		5		5	
6		6		6	
7		7		7	
8		8		8	
9		9		9	
10		10		10	

Code: TY = Thank You S = Sale M = Merchandise INV = Invitation P = Phone Call

(Reprinted courtesy of the Service Quality Institute.)

The vice president of a company that offers drilling services to the oil and gas industry reports a variation on the customer visit practice. He says that the sales force visits buyers before every job begins. The salespeople review data and interpret it for clients' chief engineers. Then they report back to the home office and make recommendations for service that should be provided, based on their interpretations at job sites.

Complaint correspondence summaries

Summaries of customer complaint correspondence are routinely circulated in some companies to senior management, middle management, and front-line people who work in areas referred to in correspondence.

Service expenses

Look for tips to customer needs and wants in repair costs, field service costs, liability costs, high warranty costs, and returns/refunds. Include counts and amounts in regular management reports.

Mervyn's compiles information on product returns under warranty by product line.

Videotape focus group meetings

Make the topic for a meeting "What is it like to do business with us?" and videotape the meeting. Show the video to every employee. Run it continually in employee lounges, perhaps, and show it as part of most routine training sessions.

Respondents in an American Management Association survey selected these as the most successful tactics in assessing customer needs and wants:

800 numbers
Focus groups
Mail/phone questionnaires

The least effective methods, according to the AMA survey, were

Point-of-purchase surveys
Assigning nonsales personnel to point-of-purchase stations to conduct surveys
Comment cards enclosed with merchandise

SO WHAT *DO* CUSTOMERS WANT?

Here's a genuine shortcut that saves time and money for you: Take our word for what you'll find when you ask customers what they want. Just ask employees what they think customers want—then skip the surveys! Employees are quite perceptive about customer opinion.

But—please—do not take our advice! Conduct your own surveys. Debrief customers, talk to customers who call in on 800 lines, make it convenient for customers to contact you, and so on. *Your* customers differ from everybody else's customers in very discernible ways.

More Service

You'll find that customers want more service today than in the self-serve 1970s. One reason is that they have less time for buying, so they want the buying process to be fast and efficient. Even industrial customers are caught up in the hurry-hurry syndrome.

A parody on this desire for more service was part of the movie, *Back to the Future*. Michael J. Fox's character, who was traveling backward in time, walks past a 1950s-era filling station and is flabbergasted (not realizing yet that he's traveled back in time) to see four cheery attendants in neatly pressed coveralls rushing around to service a car. Like a pit crew at the Indianapolis 500 race, they dash up to the customer's car, fill the gas tank, check the oil, clean the windows, and polish the chrome.

Service. People want and expect more of it.

The *Journal of Marketing* reported results of a survey under the heading "What Customers Care About." They care about

Product Quality, 100%
Customer Service, 97%
Price, 92%
Vendor/franchise management, 86%
Location, 65%

A *Chain Store Age* magazine survey found that 80 percent of shoppers said that the prime reason for choosing a retailer was ability to get their money back with no hassle.

Most major retailers excel at providing money-back guarantees. Unfortunately, millions of small businesses can't afford money-back guarantees. (So the big keep getting bigger.)

The Marketing Science Institute of Cambridge, Massachusetts, asked customers of a wide range of service businesses such as banking and appliance repair what factors they considered most important in assuring their satisfaction with a product or a service. Researchers found that these were the most important characteristics of quality service:

Reliability. Customers want companies to perform desired service dependably, accurately, and consistently. A major source of customer dissatisfaction is unkept promises, it turned out.

Responsiveness. Companies should be helpful and provide prompt service. A business that answers or responds to telephone calls quickly meets this expectation.

Assurance. Employees should be knowledgeable and courteous, customers say, and should convey confidence in the service they provide.
Tangibles. Physical facilities and equipment should be attractive and clean, and employees should be well groomed.
Empathy. Customers want companies to provide individualized attention and to listen to them. The Marketing Sciences survey indicates that people want to be treated as individuals. They want to be noticed.

That want is confirmed by a Rockefeller Foundation study that discovered that an astonishing 68 percent of all customers stopped buying from companies because of the indifferent way they were treated. Not only does the disgruntled person stop buying, but she or he usually tells 8 to 10 people *why* she or he stopped buying, the study found. And 1 in 5 of them broadcast the bad news to as many as 20 others.

Nevertheless, companies are reluctant to finance training for employees to teach them superior customer service skills and to motivate them to replace indifference with enthusiasm. They assume a native ability to provide service. Or they assume that employees are too dumb to learn or that they expect turnover to be so great that training would be a waste of money.

Of course, managers who think this way are encouraging a self-fulfilling prophecy.

Managers of World Series and Super Bowl teams usually attribute their teams' success to a mastery of "the basics." Their players make very few mistakes, they say.

But companies that pay employees $4 to $10 per hour feel that training them to excel at the "basics" is unnecessary. That's funny. They sorely need training.

Professional athletes train constantly to maintain *consistently* top performance. (Can you imagine Joe Montana, all-star quarterback of the San Francisco '49ers, being a no-show for training camp and giving his reason as "I'm already good enough"?) But it's a rare employee in American business who ever receives more than two hours of training in quality customer service practices.

"The evidence is overwhelming that people, not machines, are the driving force behind economic growth," according to a special report on human capital in a 1988 issue of *Business Week*. Yet it is quite rare for companies to provide customer contact employees who actually *convey service* with more than one to two hours of training.

Customer dissatisfaction damages a business because it takes a dozen positive contacts to dispel one negative incident, according to research. Your surveys probably will reveal, too, that customer loyalty begins to fade quickly as the level of service declines below *expectation*.

The customer wants and expects service to be at a suitable level all the time. When the level of service no longer meets his or her expectations, the customer exercises other options like buying elsewhere.

Customers begin to wander away, the Better Business Bureaus of the United States found, when they are faced with *too large a selection*—an incomprehensibly wide range of product/merchandise choices coupled with little information on which to base intelligent decisions.

Customers also lose interest in the face of unclarified complexity and advanced technology such as complicated product design and inadequate or complicated instructions. Whatever the reason, lack of consumer understanding translates into unrealistic and unreliable consumer expectations. This is a worst-case scenario, in a marketing sense.

It's sometimes very enlightening and even a little disturbing to see the results of customer surveys.

A poll of its readers by *The Atlanta Journal* and *The Atlanta Constitution* asked readers for their conclusions about its causes. These are the responses that were listed by 610 respondents:

Greed.
Lack of pride in their work by service people.
Low pay.
Lack of training.
Automation.

SO YOU KNOW WHAT CUSTOMERS THINK. NOW WHAT?

Once known, customer needs and expectations should be translated into specific activities and procedures that add value to basic products and services and that intensify customer loyalty.

First, tell every employee what you found. Make them aware of what customers are saying about service. One company prints customers' comments and questions, matched with responses, and circulates them every week to every employee.

Inform all employees, but take the greatest care to communicate the information to front-line sales and service people who do the real customer-contact work. They should be especially well acquainted with results of surveys of customer needs, wants, and dislikes. The American Management Association suggests that front-line people receive all consumer comment/complaint reports.

Tell Employees

So, let customer contact employees and also all other employees know the results of 800 number phone calls and focus group studies, for instance.

Let everyone in on results of mail/phone questionnaires. Post results throughout the company for everyone—including customers—to see.

Also submit customer comments to a Customer Service Task Force for discussion, if it exists. American Express does it, says Peggy Haney, vice president of consumer affairs. The task force is made up of key people from each section's customer service division. It's a clearinghouse where problems that come up in departments are discussed.

"In this way," says Haney, "people get involved with the whole company in the process of discussing problems and creating solutions."

Report to Management

Gamgort, director of Quality Assurance and Customer Affairs at Armstrong World Industries, says that customer survey information is presented formally at monthly executive staff meetings attended by the president and his entire staff. The information also is issued in report form to key appropriate management in the company—vice presidents of marketing and sales, of manufacturing, and of finance. It is sent to the employee relations director too.

"We have brought on some very loyal customers whose original contacts with our company resulted from their 'concern' with the product," says Gamgort.

Not surprisingly, Armstrong's official view of complaints is that they are opportunities—opportunities to improve customer satisfaction level and, thereby, to increase sales and profit.

Every four weeks Marriott Corporation circulates a report that goes to Bill Marriott, board chairman and president, to hotel general managers, and to everyone in between.

Satisfaction Index

Marriott develops a Guest Satisfaction Index from the customer surveys. It is one of the factors that determines bonuses for hotel managers. Hourly employees are hooked into this index. It's their report card every four weeks.

The Consumer Council of Land O' Lakes, Inc., meets every month to discuss results of consumer surveys and other issues that pertain to the business. What emerges are recommendations that go directly to the CEO.

At Zayre Corporation, reports on customer contact go to senior management, including the CEO, as well as to people on the front lines, merchandisers, department managers, and store managers. They review the reports with employees, says Stan Berkovitz, vice president and director of consumer/community affairs. "We put up no barriers . . . shield no one in the company from what the customers think."

"If there's a problem of some proportion," Berkovitz adds, "the person in charge hears from us daily until it's straightened out. Company policy has been changed by one letter from a customer."

Isn't that the way it ought to be?

5

Don't Hire Employees Who Hate Customers

THEY ARE UNTRAINABLE

> Incompetent people can't render good service, so the best companies tend to recruit meticulously.
>
> — *Fortune magazine, December, 1987*

A dynamic service economy must be staffed by employees who are anxious to provide service. And they should not be allergic to work.

A motivated work force begins with the hiring process. Hire people who want to be friendly and helpful; then make good service part of their job descriptions.

Hire people it is possible to motivate. Hire people-oriented employees and teach them how to implement your professional service program. Hire people who are naturally endowed with positive service attitudes and values. They can be trained in service techniques.

Customer contact employees must possess and practice the right "attitude" toward people before they can convey positive communication skills that make customers feel "important" and that induce them to return.

People who skulk behind a barely suppressed sneer are largely untrainable with resources available to most organizations.

Don't hire people who are embarrassed to provide service. They won't be trainable either.

The editors of *Fortune* magazine continued the statement that begins this chapter with: "They make outlandish efforts to hire only the right people, to train and to motivate them, and to give them the authority necessary to serve customers well."

Motivation is the subject of Chapter 6. Training is the subject of Chapter 12.

Mark Roeder, public affairs coordinator for Giant Food, Inc., of Landover, Maryland, expressed the concept of hiring people with a tendency for service when he said: "You can't train people to be friendly. We hire friendly people from the start." (Note: Friendly people are trained in service technique, however.)

Frank Draeger, owner of Draeger's, a grocery store in Menlo Park, California, says that the store maintains its reputation for service with careful selection of managers: "If a manager doesn't have an inner conviction about excellent service, we find that we can't always instill it, so we have to choose service-minded people."

That's the secret: find people with good service potential and train them.

You can't expect to change the basic personalities of employees who sneer at the world in general and at customers in particular. It is still true that you can't make a silk purse out of a sow's ear, as the saying goes.

Yet it is common for businesspeople to believe that "everybody knows" how to provide quality service, that somehow employees just soak up knowledge of service techniques so all you need to do is to put them in a service job, and they will quickly "evolve" into skilled service pros.

Some service industry managers today complain that many people who apply for work dislike working and aren't anxious to provide service. It's not as difficult to find "warm bodies" as it is to find qualified service professionals.

SHORTAGE OF SERVICE EMPLOYEES

According to the U.S. Bureau of Labor Statistics, the population of 16- to 24-year-olds began declining by half a million per year in 1980. The decline is expected to continue at a rate of about 20 percent through 1995. Meanwhile, the Bureau forecast that the U.S. economy would develop 21 million new jobs between 1988 and 2000 with 20 million of those jobs in the service sector.

The 1960s gave us birth-control pills, women's liberation, and zero population growth. People born during those years are members of the baby *bust* generation when fewer births occurred.

A worst-case scenario projects millions of ill-trained and semiliterate workers moving into the high-tech workplace of talking cash registers and smart typewriters. Fast food becomes slow food as lines trail out the door, and hospitals close emergency wards for lack of skilled nurses. Heavy manufacturing continues to move abroad because of a lack of skilled machinists and engineers.

The best-case scenario is that maybe, somehow, the number of qualified employees available will correspond to the number needed, and one of the only remaining problems will be training employees to provide service competently and willingly.

Service. Servile?

But, for the time being, says Thomas Kelly, assistant professor at Cornell University's School of Hotel Administration, "The American service economy is burdened with people who frequently view service as 'servile' work. In our culture, [service] jobs are not considered a worthwhile occupation. When workers view giving service as beneath them, it shows."

Indeed, "The customer is always right," the motto of the early American merchant class, is likely to be the punch line in a joke among service employees today.

The younger generation of individualistic workers would much rather be "in command" than "in service."

Ask a passing waiter for a glass of water, and you're informed that it's not his table. Seek the attention of an idle clerk, and he or she acts as though you're interrupting. Watch the office worker sit within arm's reach of a ringing telephone and ignore it because it's not his or her time to answer.

Do service workers act this way because they are unmotivated? Is business partly responsible for their lack of motivation? There's evidence that the answer to both questions is "Yes."

In a cover story on service, *Time* magazine reported: "many sales clerks, delivery-truck drivers, and other service workers are unmotivated because of the low pay and lack of career path in their jobs." Says Journalist David Halberstam, whose best-seller, *The Reckoning*, chronicled the decline of America's auto industry: "The main questions are, 'Does this job lead to anything? Does it have any dignity?' No."

But we've got to believe that people still are "educable" to the service life, once they've been hired.

HOW TO FIND EMPLOYEES

Some suggested courses of action are presented in the discussions that follow.

1. Ask Present Employees for References

Employees can be your best recruiters and best source of referrals. Some employers ask new employees for recommendations their first week on the job.

CONSOLIDATION UPDATE

News on the customer service Organization Issue 2

Many will make the move to the new CSC

By the October deadline, 46 employees opted for the move to Midland

The new Customer Service Center in Midland will have a strong nucleus of current Customer Service Center employees when it begins operating in 1988. A total of 46 current CSC employees will move to Midland during the transition to one Center next year.

According to Phil Rathburn, Director of Customer Service, those moving to Midland represent 32% of current CSC employees. "We're glad these people decided to be a part of the new organization. They'll be the core of a top-notch group. I would have liked 100% coming to Midland, but I know there were many personal reasons why more people were unable to make the move. We'll try to help those who aren't moving to Midland just as much as those who are."

Those opting for the move are:

Atlanta: Atkinson, Cadieu, Hickey, Ray, Sanders, Spires, Spitz, Stumpfig and Zondlak.

Chicago: Browning, Lundberg, Sudholt and Sunderland.

Cleveland: Greywitt, Kerr, Kissel, Otis, Schaefer, Smith, Vargas and Varner.

Houston: Banks, D. Brown, I. Brown, Bullard, Conrad, Goff, Hirsch, Hogan, Holloway, Kirk, Noles, Phillips, Pollard, Smith, Walker and Walkowiak.

Philadelphia: Breneman, Filipiak, Glawe, Hoshal and Woodson.

San Francisco: Archibald, Bulter, Francis and Keister.

Recruiters look for best both inside and outside Dow

The transfer of 46 employees to Midland still leaves the new CSO with a deficit of nearly 90 people. To make up that difference, Dow is recruiting heavily inside Dow, in the local area and on campus. Twenty-five Dow people have already been interviewed and recruiters are now on campus screening candidates. The recruiting process is similar for both groups.

Dow employees first contact Gail Griggs in the Personnel Department. Griggs reviews employee information and makes certain the employee's supervisor is aware of the process. If the candidate possesses the appropriate skills, they move on to the interview stage. According to Phil Rathburn, "We're trying to give Dow people as much opportunity as possible. If current Dow people qualify, we're very interested in hiring them. Our main problem is that many people in Dow find it difficult to move for 6-9 months to a regional Customer Service Center for training."

Candidates outside Dow but not on campus send a resume and application. With a sound resume and a successful telephone interview, candidates are invited for interviews.

Candidates on ten campuses Dow will visit register with their Placement Office for 20-25 minute interviews. The top candidates from these inter-

Continued on back

Fall 1987 Recruiting Schedule

School	Dates	Recruiter
Wayne State University	**Oct. 7-8**	**Joe Monroe, Midland**
Saginaw Valley	**Oct. 14-15**	**Gail Griggs, Midland**
University of Illinois	**Oct. 19-20**	**Rich Sunderland, Chicago**
Indiana University	**Oct. 19-20**	**Jill Plotkin, Chicago**
Michigan State University	**Oct. 20-21**	**John Barber, Midland**
Youngstown State University	**Oct. 20-21**	**Len Azzaro, Midland**
University of Akron	**Oct. 20-21**	**Joe Monroe, Midland**
Western Michigan University	**Oct. 21-22**	**Jim Hoshal, Philadelphia**
Central Michigan University	**Nov. 4-5**	**Jerry Walkowiak, Houston**
The Ohio State University	**Nov. 9-10**	**John Barber, Midland**

Communications Department, The Dow Chemical Company, Midland, Michigan 48674

When Dow Chemical USA consolidated six regional service centers into one headquarters-based service center, a newsletter entitled *Consolidation Update* was instituted. One of its functions was to help in recruiting new customer service employees to replace those who could not transfer to headquarters. (Reprinted courtesy of Dow Chemical USA.)

Burger King pays employees $500 for referral of a person who is hired as a manager and pays Burger "bucks" for referral of entry-level workers. Employees get 1 buck if a friend turns in an application, 5 bucks if the friend is interviewed, and 25 more bucks if the friend is hired. Bucks are redeemable for gift certificates at retail stores.

Great Adventure Theme Park in New Jersey pays $50 to the referring employee and $50 to the new hire.

Existing employees get a "referral fee" for introducing successful new hires at University National Bank & Trust Co. They are asked to refer people they worked with elsewhere who were outstanding employees. "Our goal," says Vice President Ann Sonnenberg, "is to hire genuinely nice people who are very capable and who enjoy helping others." She realizes that it is impossible to fabricate a "genuinely nice" person.

In-house ad promotions, grand prize drawings for vacations and other awards also are used to induce employees to suggest applicants.

But remember that employees are unlikely to help you find new people if they don't enjoy working for you, so pleasant working conditions and high morale are fundamental to success of any effort to find new employees through present employees.

One bit of good news is that once you begin a customer service program, it can be a great help in finding employees. That's because a service environment that produces satisfied and complimentary customers is a climate that employees want to continue to be part of. On the other hand, without a good working environment, malaise sets in. Employees feel that they are victims of their job environment.

In an enlightened approach to hiring courteous people, Disney World uses its best "cast members" (employees) to select employees. They pull the best employees out of the departments for which the company is hiring—the potential peers of the new employees—and give them three weeks of intensive training in applicable labor law. Then they let them select final candidates during 45-minute interview sessions.

"It's human nature," says James Poisant, former manager of business seminars at Disney World who was in charge of this process, "to recruit in your own image. We put them in a room and say, 'Pick the person that most reflects your values.' In 45 minutes cast members pick up on who's fooling and who is genuine."

2. Adopt Creative Techniques

A supermarket chain in the East parks a well-marked Winnebago camper in shopping center and school parking lots to solicit job applications. Potential employees enter the camper to fill out applications and are interviewed on the spot.

Builders supply stores in the south are advised by their industry association to offer tools and scrap lumber to high school shop teachers in exchange for student workers.

A Connecticut restaurant chain imported 75 French students to work during summer school break. The students paid their own way to America and home again and also found their own housing. Restaurants reported that the French students motivated local young people to apply for jobs, too.

McDonald's and Pizza Hut began offering tuition assistance in low-employment areas. Burger King offered scholarships.

Restaurant, hotel, grocery, and other retail managers are visiting high school counselors in person now instead of phoning in job openings. Also, they speak to classes about their industries and about long-term opportunities.

White Castle restaurant representatives attend job fairs to talk to parents about the work experience and benefits that they provide students.

All over the country businesses are reaching out to younger students to begin building early interest in jobs. Many organizations offer tours of their facilities to grade schoolers.

Finally, companies have recognized that customers, too, are potential employees. One retail chain began a recruitment campaign based on the motto: "Our customers make some of our best employees." Store signs displayed the message.

Pizza Hut employees told management, when asked, that one of two main reasons they applied to Pizza Hut was that they had been customers and liked the atmosphere. The other reason for applying was that their friends who worked at Pizza Hut encouraged them to apply.

The Pizza Hut employees also liked flexible hours and a teamwork style that made the job fun.

3. Hire the Handicapped

Prudential Insurance Co. employs the deaf in computer operations. Pizza Hut employs 500 handicapped workers in 38 states, at last report. Marriott and Radisson hotels use both physically and mentally handicapped workers.

Thirty-six million Americans have disabilities. Two-thirds of disabled adult men and even a greater proportion of disabled adult women are unemployed. The handicapped constitute a valuable pool of potential employees, considering that new and affordable technology makes the workplace far more accessible to them than ever before.

For example, now that computer data can be encoded into speech or braille, blind persons are employed effectively as computer programmers, telephone operators, customer service reps, and staff writers, to name but a few occupations open to them.

Recognizing this, IBM Corporation created a national support center for people with disabilities. Located in Atlanta, the center's purpose is to spread information about the hundreds of computer-aided products that improve the productivity—and the quality of life—of people with disabilities. The Center's staff is knowledgeable and experienced in informing employers about technologies available to help people with various disabilities to function in the workplace. Nearly 20,000 inquiries were handled in a recent year. Many of them were generated by network TV commercials.

But misconceptions continue to deter employers from even considering the handicapped. One prevalent fallacy is that the cost of remodeling and adding facilities to accommodate the handicapped is very high. Not true. The U.S. Labor Department asked 367 federal contractors to estimate cost of physical accommodations for the disabled in the workplace. Seventy percent of the accommodations on the Labor Department's list cost $100 or less to construct.

Another fact that ought to break down mental barriers to hiring the handicapped, in the face of continuing shortage of service workers, is aid available from state and local agencies. Many state vocational rehabilitation departments loan adaptive devices for use by disabled employees who are blind or disabled in other ways. Many also assist with supervision and training of more severely disabled workers and also provide job coaches.

4. Hire the Elderly

Charles McIntyre, manager of Stebbins-Anderson home center store in Baltimore, may have an idea that many commercial, governmental, and private organizations can use. He says: "Older workers who've been in this business feel very comfortable offering service. They don't feel that it's demeaning to be polite and to rush to a customer's aid. That's not necessarily the life-style of younger people. I don't want to put them down; it's just that the older people grew up in a different time." Building Supply Home Centers, March, 1988.

McDonald's was a pioneer in targeting the elderly employment group when the fast-food chain introduced its McMasters Program in 1986. The program trains seniors who want to return to the work force but lack confidence. It increased the percentage of older workers in McDonald's labor force to more than 13 percent at last report.

Kentucky Fried Chicken, Marriott, and Pizza Hut are other hospitality industry companies that are leaders in training and employing seniors.

Day's Inns National Reservation Center in Atlanta has employed more than 50 older workers through senior citizen job fairs. Seniors usually don't read help wanted ads, so contact senior centers and churches to list available jobs. Specify "seniors welcome" on help wanted signs in stores.

Most firms that employ seniors caution that it's important to pay attention to the relations between older and younger workers. Problems can arise if a senior employee feels that he or she doesn't fit in.

Recognizing this difficulty, Kentucky Fried Chicken tells older workers that they are not compared with younger workers in evaluations. The chain also teaches managers how to deal with seniors and to recognize their talents. Many a young manager feels awkward being the boss of a senior employee.

MOTIVATING JOB SEEKERS TO TAKE YOUR JOB

Today service workers enjoy a sellers' job market. They can and do pick and choose where they want to work. So you must make your workplace and your jobs as appealing as your budget allows.

Consider flexibility in work hours. It's a requirement for today's service jobs. Radisson Hotels no longer tell potential new hires when shifts are available. They *ask* interviewees when *they* are available and arrange schedules to meet their wishes. Other employers do the same.

Commissions

Commission systems at Radisson Hotels entice more applicants from whom the best can be chosen. The chain also offers better wages, full-time positions with time flexibility, health benefits, discounts on merchandise, bonuses, and strong sales training.

At First Service Bank in Massachusetts a commission and bonus system motivates and rewards employees for practicing their product knowledge and sales referral skills. Cash, trips, or event tickets are awarded. And new employee perks include birthday gifts and luncheons and one-year service awards.

Offers of free training attract employees too. First Service Bank offers a 36-month, three-level training and certification program. Most of the training was developed and is delivered in-house by staff members. Once "cast members" (employees, from costumed characters to sanitation workers) at Disney World in Orlando, Florida, have been hired they go through three days of orientation at Disney University. Orientation begins with two days of traditional courses that include Disney World history, achievement, and philosophy (company culture) and discussion of cast responsibilities. On the third day, cast members are introduced to company policies, procedures, and benefits and familiarized with their work areas. This orientation is followed by 1 to 14 days of on-the-job training.

Disney World has 1,100 job categories filled by more than 25,000 full-time and part-time employees.

CHOOSING SERVICE-MINDED EMPLOYEES

Nordstrom's department stores ran "now hiring" ads that sketched a fine profile of a desirable customer service employee. The copy read:

"We are looking for experienced people who want to learn, grow and expand with us. People who genuinely like people; who find satisfaction in helping others; in going out of their way to be of service. We need people to make things go smoothly. People with ideas."

Screening

The recruitment screening process should be directed at assessing behavioral characteristics that influence service-delivery ability. A list includes oral communication skills, cooperation and teamwork, problem-solving and decision-making skills, sensitivity and concern for others, dependability, judgment, enthusiasm, high energy level, flexibility, and adaptability.

To assist you in screening applicants for service potential, buy or develop tools such as

Structured interview tools
Realistic job previews
Job-related personality tests
Ability tests
Simulation exercises

Some of the most common personality tests are offered by Profiles International. Other widely used tests are the Minnesota Multiphasic Personality Inventory, Jackson Personality Inventory, Predictive Index, and California Personality Inventory. Cost is about $50 to $250 each.

Stanton Corporation, a psychological testing and evaluation company, developed a personnel selection inventory that gives prospective employers a snapshot of an applicant's work attitudes. It is designed to evaluate a job seeker's reactions to supervision, orientation toward customer service, and attitudes toward work values, safety, and drugs. The test can be analyzed instantly on an IBM-compatible computer or scored remotely by telephone.

Tests that measure characteristics similar to those rated by Stanton are marketed by London House. In screening job candidates, look for evidence of the traits you want in that person's prior behavior. Or set up scenarios and ask candidates how they would respond in various common and revealing situations.

Dennis Clark of Jim Cathcart, Inc., personnel consultants feels that it is important to determine if candidates are coachable and eager to enhance their knowledge.

If a person isn't interested in improving, chances are that the person doesn't care much about helping the company provide good service to customers, says Clark.

He offers these interviewing tips:

1. Find out what applicants are good at and look for themes. Find out what they believe in, what stands they take, and what they defend.
2. In testing prospects with tasks, beware of general impressions that create a halo effect that blurs meaningful details about a prospect's qualifications.

People Skills

Employees who deal with customers need people skills—the interpersonal know-how to handle a universe of customer attitudes and diverse situations and to uncover and to address needs. Employees must leave customers with the feeling they are in good hands.

As a result of their people skills, employees derive more satisfaction from their work and have more respect for themselves, for the work they do, and for their employer. Their people skills, by the way, should be applied to peers and subordinates because it will increase the cooperativeness needed to obtain good service for customers.

Anne Pinkerton, director of customer service at Bio-Lab Incorporated, expresses it this way: "We want our employees to be friendly, outgoing, and professional."

Including Managers

Hervey Feldman, president of Embassy Suites, looks most closely at general manager candidates' interpersonal skills, especially the way they treat low-pay employees who deliver service. Feldman believes that they should be treated as competent workers so they will be motivated to deliver competent service. "With training and experience," says Feldman, "they [employees] all have the curiosity and intelligence to go beyond making beds."

Clark of Jim Cathcart, Inc., suggests listing characteristics you are looking for in new employees—loyalty, enthusiasm, initiative, integrity, whatever. Then divide traits into "critical" and "desirable" categories. One of the "critical" traits ought to be favorable personality, he suggests. You ought to like the person yourself. If you don't, chances are that your clients or customers won't, either.

Handwriting Analysis

Indications are that handwriting analysis might even be an effective screening method. Sue Blair, president of Grapho-Dynamics, Inc., of Edina, Minnesota, documents 72 percent accuracy in predicting success in insurance sales positions on the basis of an analysis of candidates' handwriting.

She says that a customer service personality is revealed in handwriting, too.

"Your handwriting is a psychomotor expression of who you really are," says Blair. "People project their mental processes into their writing. They subconsciously shape and organize their letters, words, and lines in a way that directly reflects personality."

In France, and in many other European countries, nearly 80 percent of large companies employ handwriting analysts to help them hire the right people.

Grapho Analysis isn't exactly rare in the United States, either. According to *Industry Week* magazine, "More than 5,000 American companies have hired handwriting analysts for use in personnel selection."

When screening for desirable customer service employees, University National Bank & Trust Co. of Palo Alto, California, looks for experienced people with a record of providing good service happily.

Other Desirable Service Characteristics

Thinkers

You want people who know how to think. If someone is solving the same problem three times, then they don't belong in customer service. Employees should be able to get to the root of problems.

Education

Donlyn Turmaine, director of worldwide customer operations at The Timberland Co., a footwear manufacturer in Hampton, New Hampshire, says that she looks for bright, well-educated people because of their tendency to be aware of the value of customer service.

To be considered for a position in Dow Chemical Co.'s customer service department applicants must usually have a college degree (in anything from art history to engineering) and fit the company's profile—"proactive, a communicator, and a problem solver."

Communication Ability

To gauge communication abilities Dow telephones candidates for customer service employment instead of writing a letter. After all, they will be doing much of their work by phone, so their employer should be aware of the impression they convey by phone.

Structured Work

In customer service employees Dow looks for some of the same qualities found in good salespeople, but with a slight difference, says Kern, manager of customer service resources. Along with the aggressiveness of successful salesmen, Dow looks for customer service employees who can work well in a structured environment.

"Salespeople often are free spirits, which may not be perfect for this job," says Kern.

But in other characteristics, good customer service employees are very similar to salespeople. Jim Marxhausen, Minneapolis retailing executive, says: "The best associates are secure, enjoy life, think highly of others and are motivated by strokes."

Identification with Company Values

Recruitment efforts must be aimed at hiring people who share corporate customer service values. Those values must be continually reinforced from the first day on the job to the retirement party.

Steve Riley, account manager for EDS Corp., says that his company has a strict code of ethics that is part of the corporation's customer service philosophy.

TRAINING

Customer service pros are made, not born, even if they are cordial and *willing* to provide service. They rarely learn by experience, either, because role models are rare. If employees practice what they see and experience as customers, then they are more likely to be rude and neglectful than they are to be considerate and helpful.

Delta Air Lines accepts only 40 to 48 of more than 20,000 applicants for flight attendant jobs who apply each month. Then the company conducts months of rigorous training for those lucky enough to be hired.

Even after training, aspiring stewards and stewardesses are not assigned to in-flight jobs where they work with customers. They labor in the back-office ranks before they get their wings. Here they learn the right answers to questions and the means of satisfying requests. Only if they perform well do they get their wings.

The recruitment philosophy at Disney World is: You can't teach courtesy, but you can hire people with that quality. After hiring courteous employees Disney trains them in the *expression* of their courtesy.

Disney World hires only 1 of 60 people that it invites for interviews.

Because Disney's employee management methods are widely admired, the organization conducts intensive three-day courses for companies that want to duplicate the Disney method. Representatives of hospitality and other service companies from hundreds of countries attend the course entitled "The Disney Approach to People Management."

An important lesson here, especially for small businesses or for companies far removed from entertainment or hospitality, is that Disney built an appealing company culture on indoctrination of employees in its history, its philosophy, respect for employees, and the realities of public perceptions of the company. This culture gives Disney a big edge over other service companies in attracting desirable employees. Any company can do the same thing in its own way.

Low-Budget Training

Many small businesses, however, do not have sufficient resources to train employees. They can consult the Small Business Administration (SBA) and the U.S. Department of Education that joined forces to prepare a manual outlining on-the-job training options for small businesses. Up-to-date information can be obtained by calling the SBA's Office of Advocacy (202) 634-6115.

Your industry's national or state trade association also may be a source of guidance and materials helpful in providing employee education and training.

For example, the National Restaurant Association's Educational Foundation developed videos, training seminars, textbooks, and specialized programs including customized in-house programs for small and medium-sized chains. They also bought more than a dozen home study courses from Cornell University that they offer to members.

We customized a service program for Miller Brewing Co. to offer to "waitpeople." The company knows that service-driven employees who feel good about themselves sell more Miller beer.

A few convenience stores make extensive use of video programs on customer service. The Pantry, a 460-unit chain based in North Carolina, produces videos on customer service and on company history and philosophy. Other Pantry videos convey news and announcements and information about marketing programs. Finished production cost for each tape is about $10,000.

The Pantry credits its videos with cutting the employee turnover rate in half.

The National Association of Convenience Stores produces videos for members.

Real-World Training

The best kind of training is practical, real-world training depicting situations that employees recognize and identify with.

One specific example of real-world training is that provided by Poppy Rossano, in Williamsville, New York, for repair technicians who work for her office machine business. She teaches them to "leave the client's place neat and clean."

Employees of the Meridian banking group (180 branches in Pennsylvania and Delaware) take a course in professional customer relations that includes filling out deposit slips while wearing glasses smeared with Vaseline —and counting money while three fingers on each hand are taped together. The purpose is to give employees better understanding of the difficulty faced by older customers with glaucoma or arthritis when they do business in the bank.

KEEPING EMPLOYEES ONCE YOU'VE GOT 'EM

After you've attracted applicants, induced them to apply, hired them, and then "trained them in," you still don't have a stable work force in a day when service industry employees probably have more employment options than any other workers in history. You must develop and then you must maintain loyalty and commitment.

You must let minimum-wage employees know how much you appreciate them and how important they are to the organization. Appreciation and recognition through training are important, considering the fact that service employees often quit because they feel unappreciated and unwanted.

When we find people willing to work for $4 to $10 an hour, we should counsel ourselves: "I am lucky to find this individual. I'm going to treat her right. I will do everything I can to let this person know how much I appreciate her and how important she is to this organization."

I am repeatedly amazed at the minimal respect accorded low-pay employees by their managers (except in the glowing words of the annual report). Don't they know that the cost of replacing them approaches $1,000?

If your service training is effective, you can expect an immediate impact upon employee retention. A work force that's dominating in its service delivery can be self-perpetuating because employees will enjoy their jobs.

It works this way: once you reach a point where the "customer satisfaction index" is high, then employees will be far more likely to stay than they were when customers viewed them as adversaries and sought revenge by being "difficult."

So after you have trained employees to treat customers as friends instead of as antagonists and interruptions in their busy schedules, then customers begin smiling and calling them by name. As a result, employees become enthusiastic about their jobs, thereby earning even more applause from customers. They begin working even harder. And better. Self image improves. Morale runs high. Pride and team spirit take over and raise retention rate.

People-oriented employees who derive personal satisfaction from dealing with customers are more likely to enjoy their work. So your turnover will be low, and that's no small benefit at a time when good employees are hard to find and hard to keep.

Poor Service Causes Turnover

A Forum Corporation study found that staff turnover is inversely proportional to employee perceptions of service quality: turnover drops when employees feel that the company is providing high-quality service. On the other hand, when a company has poor service, not only do consumers not like to patronize your firm, but also employees don't like to work for you. Turnover rises.

Quoting the Forum report on its study: "The highest turnover rates are associated with companies possessing the lowest employee ratings of service quality. . . . Factors such as length of service with the company, job function, and frequency of contact with customers demonstrate little influence (upon turnover rate)."

Recognizing the influence of quality customer service upon turnover is Peter Gregerson, Sr., chairman and president of Warehouse Groceries Management of Gadsden, Alabama. One purpose of the company's service program, he says, is "to increase the employee's value and worth to the company and to himself. We want to develop skills our competitors don't have in customer relations," says Gregerson. "We hope, with these things in mind, to increase our sales and our profit with repeat business and fewer customer complaints. We feel it will help our employee turnover as well."

When employees learn to enjoy their jobs thoroughly and turnover rate drops, you've achieved a great deal, considering the high cost of hiring and training. Now you are *keeping* employees so you don't have to find new ones.

The Team Concept

Both small business and large corporations are learning that fostering a team concept (employee involvement) and a partner relationship with employees pays big dividends.

The Disney company attributes its enviable achievements in employee commitment and customer service to "pixie dust." The formula for pixie dust is not secret. It is *training* plus *communication* plus *care* equals *pride*.

Texas Instruments' "Total Quality Culture" program involves all 77,000 of its employees at more than 50 locations. The program is built upon a team concept and seeks to maximize involvement and commitment. Productivity and product quality improved after the program began.

Three types of employee teams at Texas Instruments are:

- Quality improvement teams. They meet once a month, identify and address broad problems within assigned product areas, and examine issues such as productivity and waste reduction.

- Corrective action teams. Made up of workers from a number of disciplines, they work on solving specific problems including any uncovered by quality improvement teams. These teams are short-term and disband after completing a project.
- Effectiveness teams. They meet one hour per week, addressing employee concerns. Participation in this team is voluntary. Management selects and trains team leaders. As with similar efforts in other companies, recognition, team spirit, and identity are key elements in the program.

Each team designs its own logo that is displayed on jackets, T-shirts, and plaques.

Employee Communication

Disney management believes that 90 percent of all organization problems are caused by poor communication. Forms of Disney employee communication are weekly divisional newsletters, a companywide weekly newsletter, management forums, employee opinion polls, exit interviews, and the "I Have an Idea" program. Cast members (employees) can win up to $10,000 for submitting original suggestions to management.

Kindercare operates three Disney World day care centers for employee child care needs.

Disney has an entire department devoted to maximizing the employee work experience. The Activities Department coordinates a full range of clubs and travel, instructional and community services, and the employees' Little Lake Bryan Recreation Area where picnics and parties are held.

In the Hardees fast-food chain, district rallies attended by hundreds kicked off a retention program called "Serve with Pride." Unit crews performed skits with program themes. Prizes were awarded and T-shirts, mugs, and visors bearing the "Serve with Pride" message were given to everyone.

The retention program includes broad-based employee training and expansion of a fast-track development program from managers only to hourly workers.

Hardees built a 1989 national TV campaign on employee recruitment and retention themes.

Public Relations

Employees often decide to apply for work with a particular organization and decide to continue working there because they enjoy the distinction of working for a company that has a good reputation and high recognition value among their friends. The "image" of an organization can help reduce turnover. Image, of course, is greatly influenced by the quality of service.

A top public relations priority for the national association serving the restaurant and hotel industries is to upgrade the public image of jobs in the industries. The association tells anyone who listens that it is not necessary for employees to be available for work 120 hours a week to work in a hotel. And fast food and restaurant support jobs are not dead-end employment.

Preventive Action

Conduct exit interviews to find out why employees leave, then eliminate the causes.

Employee surveys and exit interviews frequently point to poor supervision as the reason for quitting a job. Supervisors who treat people like chess pieces are an even more common reason for employee discontent than low pay. So many service companies are training and motivating supervisors in employee retention technique.

Many managers are now being graded as much on their employee retention rate as on their sales and customer counts, in fact. At Burger King, 25 percent of the bonuses of top managers is based upon performance in developing and retaining personnel. Rax of Indiana requires district managers to document turnover in their reports.

Consider testing skills training for a few groups of new hires and then evaluating effectiveness. Is it reducing turnover? If it is, this is a program you'll want to continue.

Incentive Programs

Incentive programs, long restricted to sales staff, are increasingly being used to motivate hourly employees and to reduce turnover. There are, however, conflicting schools of thought regarding incentives for nonsales workers. Should employees be set up to compete with each other for achievement awards? Or should incentives be offered in an open-ended fashion to all? My experience leads me to sanction the latter alternative: each employee should be given opportunity to achieve her or his highest potential—no matter how that potential compares with overachievers on the staff.

But note this: Because the purpose of incentives typically is to motivate employees to improve performance and productivity, a poorly conceived incentive program might be considered insulting if employees already feel that they are working hard and productively.

First: Sincere Recognition

Most employees prefer rewards that are "icing on the cake" instead of the primary motive for performance. Sincere recognition by supervisors and by peers and then positive reinforcement for good work seems to be a very effective employee motivation system.

Increasingly, employers reward employees who simply meet acceptable service standards and then provide additional incentives to those who exceed them. That's one effective way to motivate and to maintain employee loyalty to the employer. But as with other types of incentives, "pay for performance" requires careful planning and implementation as well as a valid means of measuring employee performance and productivity.

My experience tells me that the 19" color TV sets given to each of 21,000 employees by Stone Container Corp. of Chicago one year as a reward for record sales the previous year probably was not very effective as a turnover preventive action. But the company may have seen the TV sets as no more than an earned reward.

Certain rules should be followed in administering pay-for-performance incentive systems.

1. Timeliness

Present awards as soon as possible after the desired behavior takes place. Instant or spot rewards can be cash, a dinner, or a gift certificate. Tokens or other currency awarded for superior performance can be redeemable for premiums or applied toward company lotteries or drawings. Offer special parking privileges. Post a framed photo of the employee in the lobby for a month. All these forms of recognition are effective and provide instant feedback.

The Grand Hyatt Hotel in New York recognizes outstanding employee performance by awarding wooden coins redeemable for free haircuts, facials, manicures, or valet and laundry privileges for a month. Twenty-five coins earn a one-week vacation in Hawaii. By the way, incentives are even more effective when they contain an element of fun.

2. Public presentation

The second rule is to present the awards publicly whenever possible. Status and prestige conveyed by awards often is equal to or greater than monetary value in motivational terms.

Stew Leonard's, the very successful Norwalk, Connecticut, dairy store famous for its customer service, may have defined the essential nature of such awards. The store bestows the Superstar of the Month Award upon one employee in each department who is selected for overall superior performance. Selection is based upon criteria such as attendance, attitude, achievement, and safety.

At presentation time costumed animal characters—cows, animals, and ducks—bring balloons to winners. Fellow workers gather around and a plaque is presented right there on the sales floor. A picture is taken and featured in Stew's News, the company newsletter.

The picture also is mounted on a walnut plaque and is hung in the "Avenue of the Stars," an entire picture-covered store wall. "Ladder of

Success" charts are mounted at cash registers. They display to customers each employee's progress at the store.

The ABCD (Above and Beyond the Call of Duty) Award goes to employees who do something for a customer that's not called for in their job descriptions. Recipients receive polo shirts featuring the ABCD award imprint.

Then there's the "Hall of Fame" program that honors employees for career achievement, and, finally, there are "Stewie Awards," determined by employee balloting. The "Stewie" is presented annually to top manager, top supervisor, top employee, and rookie of the year.

3. Employee selection of the incentive system

Solicit input from employees on the type of system that's meaningful to them. (Allowing greater employee involvement in decisions affecting them is itself a turnover reduction strategy.) Employees often are more conservative than managers in the size of awards they recommend, by the way. Often employees have valuable insight into means of measuring and improving performance. For instance, it reportedly was an employee suggestion that began the system of immediate awards to employees by mystery customers when they discover superior service. Banks, restaurants, hotels, and other retailers, particularly, use mystery customers who score employees against a checklist of required customer service and procedural items. Employees who rate a perfect score receive immediate awards, usually cash, a gift certificate, or redeemable tokens.

Many companies, such as fast-food outlets, achieve the same recognition results by simply awarding achievement pins or certificates. But some companies use extra paid vacation days as incentive awards.

4. Tenure bonuses

Reducing turnover among hourly employees is the sole objective of another type of incentive program, tenure or longevity bonuses.

With some businesses such as seasonal resorts and amusement and food service operations, longevity is a relative term and cash bonuses may be paid for as few as 30 days on the job. The principle is the same, however, whether the payoff comes at 90 days, 6 months, a year, or later. Most businesses that use this system structure it on a graduated scale according to the seriousness of the turnover situation and the supply of replacement workers.

Employee Dignity

Many savings and loans and banks such as First Service Bank in Massachusetts have changed the teller position to "Bank Service Representative" (BSR). The BSR position incorporates broader duties and greater responsibility, an example of changing traditional positions and internal structure to utilize the skills of employees more fully and effectively.

First Service reports that the current staff of 81 BSRs in no way resembles the underutilized and underpaid tellers of the past. Turnover dropped immediately by 50 percent. Productivity rose 25 percent. Even uniform design influences employees' feelings of dignity. Both Burger King and Rax of Indiana have designed more stylish uniforms, in line with employe preferences.

Job Sharing

Job sharing is flourishing in restaurants, retail operations, and elsewhere. Working in five or six jobs over a period of time instead of in one job gives employees a greater overall understanding of and appreciation for the business they're in and reduces the boredom that often is the result of working in one job. Result: Reduced turnover.

COST

What means are available for controlling costs of incentive awards? Most leading consumer products manufacturers sell their products for incentive or recognition purposes at wholesale prices. Many can provide drop shipping services as well.

Co-op It

It's not difficult to find other service employers in your community that are having the same problems attracting and keeping employees. Many of them have or would like to have incentive and recognition award programs. So propose to them that you form a reciprocal gift certificate exchange. Each place of business—a movie theater, restaurants, retailers, or a convenience store that sells gas, for instance—contributes something free to all the other businesses.

Since 1985, the Arlington, Texas, Convention and Visitors Bureau, has sponsored incentive awards for employees of their visitor-oriented businesses that are based on such a system. The "Arlington Loves Company" promotion, tent cards in restaurants, and posters encourage visitors to provide the bureau with names of employees who are especially friendly and helpful. Drawings determine weekly winners who receive free passes to area amusement parks or to Texas Rangers baseball games.

In a grand prize drawing at the end of the summer, one employee and the visitor who made the winning nomination earn free trips for two. One year, four-day stays in Hawaii were awarded.

Managers can no longer merely be spectators to turnover, hoping that employees will stay and that they will continue to be content, productive, and docile. They must practice leadership. They must accept responsibility for confronting turnover, practicing retention strategies, and strengthening their abilities to provide positive support and encouragement to employees.

During the 1990s trainable employees with good social skills are even more difficult to find than they were in the 1980s. So it makes survival sense to exert strenuous effort to retain the employee already working for you. Given the often-poor qualifications of new employees, you'd be better off with present employees.

These strategies, combined with aggressive and creative employee "prospecting" techniques are likely to solve the employee shortage problem for a service business.

6
Carrots Are Motivational for Employees

BREAK YOUR STICK

"The dollar bills the customer gets from the tellers in four banks are the same. What is different are the tellers."

—*Stanley Marcus*
Chairman Emeritus, Neiman-Marcus Department Stores

The only way to motivate employees is to pay them more. Some managers still believe this outdated management maxim.

The next bit of logic out of the mouths of uninformed managers often is: "So, since we can't afford a larger payroll I guess we're stuck with poor service. We'll just have to make the most of what we've got."

Not so, Mr. Executive. Not so.

It's as if some managers never heard of the hundreds of studies in human motivation that prove that job satisfaction, self-respect, and other intangible values usually motivate better than money.

Studies inevitably rank "more money" anywhere from third to tenth on a list of employee motivators.

More Important than Money

The Hay Group, a leading management research firm that specializes in tracking employee attitudes, has found that for employees of any industry's high-performing companies, as measured by asset and profit growth, "money is important, but not an end-all," says Edmund A. Pinelli, a vice president of research. This is true, says Pinelli, "as long as they understand why they get paid what they get paid."

In 1976 I released my first program called "Better than Money." Its basic theme was that employees are motivated by recognition and praise. Positive reinforcement can substantially outperform salaries and bonuses as an employee motivation tool.

Wal-Mart has over 200,000 people working only marginally above minimum wage who greet customers every day and ask enthusiastically, "How may I help you?" Workers are "associates" rather than "the staff" or "the crew," and they are *treated* like associates. Incentive programs generously reward exceptional service. Closed-circuit telecasts to each store transmit pep talks from the company's notable founder, Sam Walton.

Wal-Mart is the most admired retail store chain in America, according to an early 1990 report.

Motivation Is Money

Consider the financial value of motivated employees. Employees deliver the service that satisfies the customers who buy the products and services. It is employees (not their supervisors) who deal face to face or phone to phone with customers or who communicate in other ways directly with customers. Employees create impressions about a company and its products and services. The truth is that what employees learned about service before they came to you more often is inconsiderateness and disinterest in any avoidable effort in behalf of customers. They learned it from other service employees while they (your employees) were customers.

MOTIVATION IS VITAL

Motivation of employees to provide service to customers certainly is important. After all, it isn't the president or the vice presidents who have continuous contact with customers and who convey an impression of the company to them. It is employees who deal directly with customers, so it is employees who bear primary responsibility for making a positive service impression."

"The Customer Is Always Right" is a useless slogan without employees who are motivated to believe it and enthusiastic about customer satisfaction.

Companies that don't know how to motivate employees or that don't care about motivation overvalue money as motivation and they usually think that negative reinforcement and close supervision are great motivators.

Certainly it is usually possible to force employees to go through the motions of being eager, helpful, and friendly. But customer service by rote turns off customers as often as poor service itself.

Service by Rote

Service by rote is what's happening when a zombielike employee says, for the 576th time in a day, "Have-a-nice-day, next," as if the employee's mouth is wired to a continuous loop tape recorder. Sometimes the absurdity of the vapid phrase is so evident that employees speak the words so quietly or mumble so badly that it's difficult to hear them.

Where's the customer service in that?

Isn't it much better for employees to make friendly conversation with customers because they feel like doing so instead of because the boss told them to do so?

A reader wrote to Ann Landers, the newspaper advice columnist, asking: "Where did that brainless line come from—'Have a nice day'?

"You go to a restaurant. The service is lousy, the food is awful and the prices are out of this world. You pay the bill and the waitress says, 'Have a nice day.'

"You go to the variety store. There aren't enough cashiers. You see no one around to help you so you paw through the merchandise on your own. By the time you find what you want you can't get anyone who will take your money. You are mad as hell. Finally a cashier shows up, takes your money and says, 'Have a nice day.'

"You go to the drug store for some medicine. You feel rotten and look like death warmed over. The pharmacist has four people ahead of you. He is smiling and talking to a pretty customer while the three people ahead of you are glaring. By the time he gets to you, you are ready to wring his neck. After he finally fills the prescription he hands it to you and says, you guessed it, 'Have a nice day.'"

NINE MOTIVATORS

Discard the belief that high-quality customer service can be achieved just by ordering employees to be friendly to customers, to provide assistance, to be reliable and trustworthy, to become acquainted with product features, to handle complaints immediately, and so on.

Innocuous, mock-friendly phrases don't forge close ties with customers or encourage them to return again and again.

Management Commitment

Clear and obvious commitment by top management and also by every supervisor in the company to quality service by every employee is the most motivational condition that can exist there. When the boss believes in service and proves it by the way he or she treats employees and peers in the department and in other departments, then an employee begins to see personal benefit in service. It becomes clear that providing service will improve likelihood of raises and promotions, especially when service performance is a standard in formal job reviews. So employees find satisfaction in delivering service because they realize that they are building their own future.

In some companies such as Hertz, middle and senior managers actually serve customers now and then for days at a time, standing side by side with employees. The effect of that kind of demonstrated commitment is powerful.

Employees are proud to work for an organization that is committed to excellence in service to people, some of them friends and acquaintances. Performance improves. Turnover drops.

Service Culture

Best of all, management commitment gives rise to a service "culture" that in itself engenders pride, productivity, and work quality.

For a company to shine in customer service—for employees to feel motivated to deliver service—every manager must get "the service religion."

Motivating employees through management commitment, you see, is a two-tier process. The top executive occupies the first tier. Middle-management executives and all other supervisors occupy the second tier.

First, the top executive must perform as a true leader does and lead by example. He or she must, for example, be able to excite the eager participation of middle management in his or her strategies. He or she must communicate with his or her employees, imparting the company's vision. But he or she must also listen to what employees say they need in the way of resources to convert that vision into reality.

To succeed, a CEO no longer can be an isolated and autocratic decision maker. She must be a visionary, a strategist, an informer, a teacher, and an inspirer.

On the second tier, managers must also lead by example if changes in employee behavior are expected. Never can they get caught in the middle between "Do as I say," on one side and "Don't do as I do" on the other side.

Instead, in leading by example, supervisors say "Do as I do" and they are fair, consistent, and competent in dealing with the people who report to them.

Supervisors also must help employees to see connections between their performance and organizational objectives. Employees must notice that their quality service performance is furthering the objectives of top management and of their immediate superiors.

A final note: The call to quality customer service performance must not be viewed as a quick fix that will have a perpetual impact. Continuous management commitment and employee enthusiasm are needed if quality service is to survive and work its magic on customer loyalty.

Training

How-to-do-it training is essential to good customer service. When an employee knows how to do the job, he or she is far more likely to do it.

Training should include not just the skills needed to deliver quality service but to obtain it from internal suppliers—fellow employees.

But training carries a bonus with it. "Training tends to make salespeople feel special," says Charles W. Jackson, marketing and management consultant in the Princeton, New Jersey, office of Right Associates, outplacement specialists. He is the former senior vice president of human resources for Philadelphia-based John Wanamaker's department stores.

That training makes employees feel "special" was borne out in a training program for all 22,000 employees of Zellers, the Canadian department store giant, in 215 stores. A Zellers spokesperson reported that a strong team spirit developed after the training with our "Feelings" program. Team spirit was a result of the fact that "Feelings" is both a personal improvement program *and* a customer relations program.

The spokesperson commented: "When employees feel good about themselves after the personal improvement program, they like their jobs and derive more personal satisfaction from their work. They also are more eager to acknowledge and to compliment customers."

Clearly, the mere act of providing training is motivational. Training makes employees feel important.

The same effect often occurs after a service program has begun. Employee morale and motivation skyrocket. This is sometimes called the Hawthorne effect. A study of employee motivation at the Hawthorne Works of Western Electric (an electrical generating plant) near Chicago found that motivation increased during the study even before action had been taken to enhance motivation. Just "paying attention" to employees increased their desire to work. It's a development worth noting.

Unfortunately, front-line employees are never trained in some companies because managers consider individual contributions to be insignificantly small. Respect for employees and appreciation for their contributions seem to decline in direct proportion to rank of executive in the corporate hierarchy.

Time magazine noted in a special service issue: "Business spends too little time training and motivating their front-line employees whom they treat as the lowest workers on the ladder."

Often it is difficult to get management to admit that their service employees are important enough to train. A company will readily spend the bank on management training but hardly a piggy bank for employee training.

But you *must* train the bottom 95 percent of the work force in the actions that constitute service to customers. You can train their supervisors and managers at the same time, but train them differently. Train them as facilitators. It is their important job to *drive* a service strategy but not to deliver the service.

Another mistake that some companies make is to believe that training employees for two hours trains them for a lifetime. If, then, the training doesn't stick, well, obviously, a dumb employee was inadvertently hired. (Some companies, unfortunately, consider two hours to be an excessive investment in an employee.)

That's unfair. Training must be comprehensive for all employees. It must apply visual techniques—video, film, slides—to be effective in this visual age. It must employ educational tactics that have proven to be effective—role playing, modeling, repetition, and more.

Remember, too, that training must be reinforced. And it must be repeated periodically.

The competition for customers ultimately is won or lost on the front lines whenever they come in contact with any member of a firm. The front-line team *is* the firm in the customer's eyes. Therefore, the front-line team must be treated as the heroes they genuinely are—and supported with tools (training systems) that allow them to serve customers.

Praise and Recognition

In some companies, the only time employees get attention is when they make a mistake. No one comments on their good work. There is foundation for an assertion that the almost total absence of positive reinforcement for employees who deliver service is the foremost service problem. Most employees go year after year without getting a word of praise.

When employees labor anonymously with no way to determine how the company values their work, they are likely to wonder, even speaking aloud to coworkers, "It doesn't make any difference if I screw up or not? So why should I exert myself?"

Employees in service businesses need to feel that their contributions are noticed because recognition influences self-esteem—and self-esteem gives a person the assurance and buoyancy that impresses customers and wins their loyalty. So supervisors, remember that a word of well-deserved praise can do more than any management system to set the quality of service.

Deliver your "thank yous" personally as often as possible. It's a good idea to spend some time with employees, too. The mere presence of the boss is a form of recognition.

Praise puts employees in a frame of mind to *want to* do service right. Without a positive attitude, any training will be mostly wasted. That's why a significant part of the Service Quality Institute's leading customer service training course, "Feelings," deals with how to enhance self-concept, thereby increasing enthusiasm and job satisfaction.

Means of Administering Praise and Recognition

You may adopt one of the following programs:

1. Service Employee of the Month Award and a tangible prize
2. Reference to employee in company journals
3. Acknowledgment at company functions

American Express Travel Related Services Company has an annual Great Performers Award for employees who provide customers with high levels of service.

Federal Express's Golden Falcon Award is the highest honor that FedEx bestows upon nonmanagement employees "for service above and beyond their customary line of duty." The award includes a pin bearing the company's Gold Falcon emblem and ten shares of FedEx stock.

Delta Air Lines awards a golden lapel pin to employees who go above and beyond duty in providing service to passengers.

At Precision LensCrafters, a variety of incentive programs tie into the quality of its products. Through a "Horizon Club" program that honors customer service performance, managers nominate "associates" who have gone beyond the call of duty to service customers. For 1989, a total of 89 associates were nominated. Eighty of them received $100 and 9 received $1,000 each in addition to a crystal memento.

Hyatt Hotels & Resorts has a quality assurance program it calls "In Touch for the 90's." It includes a President's Service Council that honors Hyatt employees who have gone above and beyond their job requirements to provide service to guests. It also includes a program called "Hyattalk" in which employees are encouraged to speak openly and frankly about their jobs, their hotels, and their company with all levels of management.

Celebration of Small Successes

Even small successes should be celebrated, thereby increasing the *frequency* of praise. Big bonuses are nice, but so are a pizza party, small gifts, a decorated cake, bouquets of balloons, humorous plaques, sincere handshakes, or a round of applause. This is the way it's done at Stew Leonard's "world's largest dairy store" referred to earlier.

Marshall's Department Store's "We All Win" program is based upon a point system. Employees receive points if they notice missing tickets on items, if they notice items are mismatched, or if a customer makes a positive comment about them. Points are written in a log book. After a specific number of points are accumulated, employees receive a $10 Marshall's merchandise certificate.

To increase concern for consumer comments by manufacturing plant employees, the Consumer Relations Department of Scott Paper Co. developed the Consumer Value Excellence Award. The award recognizes the manufacturing plant team that "demonstrated a unique obsession with creating value for consumers during the preceding year." It is based upon work done by manufacturing team employees responding to a problem referred by consumers.

Scott Paper's Consumer Value award is presented to employees during the company's National Business Meeting by the leader of the winning manufacturing team. Then a dinner is set up at the winning plant site and the vice president of marketing presents plaques to each team member.

As a secondary move to increase all employees' awareness of the value of consumer input, the Consumer Relations Department announces winner of the award during National Consumers Week. Other activities during the week are a video highlighting the winning team, buttons, display of consumer letters, display of free samples sent to consumers, posters, articles in employee publications, and a plant tour of the winning manufacturing facility.

Recognition

Giant Food, Inc., of Landover, Maryland, has a "Staffer of the Month" award. Says Mark Roeder, public affairs coordinator: "If we see employees being courteous toward customers, we give them a courtesy award."

The First National Bank of Chicago, that won the 1988 Award of Excellence from the International Customer Service Association, has a four-part quality strategy that includes performance measurement, employee involvement, decentralized customer service—and a variety of employee recognition programs. The bank is the largest bank holding company in the Midwest.

At Marriott Corporation bellhops and people in the reservation center have attention showered upon them whenever their work rises above the norm. Toshiba America made its service support phone operators into heroes. At Disney companies, even floor sweepers are "heroes."

Top mechanics at Sewell Village Cadillac are publicly praised. The best of them earn more than $100,000 per year. Training is the best available. They use computerized support systems.

At a financial services company, the Employee of the Month is given a day off with pay, has his or her picture displayed on bulletin boards, and receives a plaque.

A high-technology firm held a two-day, off-site meeting for distribution people to brainstorm new opportunities. The firm was careful to make the setting and trappings as lavish as those it provides for top management at similar affairs. This is a form of recognition.

By the way, if top sales performers earn sizable bonuses or expensive prizes, then top service performers should earn comparable rewards. If they don't then the unspoken message sent to employees is: "Service is less important than selling."

Employees as Entrepreneurs

John McCormack, who with his wife, Maryanne, owns 16 Visible Change salons, says that quality service is the secret of their success. A system of incentives and rewards is designed to make stylists at the salons, based in Houston, feel and act like entrepreneurs, each with his or her own clientele.

Those whose services are requested by repeat customers receive extra rewards. But at the same time, a stylist who doesn't achieve a 65 percent request rate within six months is asked to leave the firm.

Says McCormack: "The first step is setting standards. Then make sure everyone in the company understands those standards. If you reward your associates for superior performance, then your customers are going to get the service you want to deliver."

The company holds motivational classes that build employees' service-oriented attitudes and that enhance their self-confidence. McCormack comments: "If you take care of your employees, they will take care of your customers. There's not one company in America that has a problem as long as they have happy employees. If you don't have your people on your side, how can they help your business succeed?"

Team Spirit

Two stonecutters were chipping away at blocks of granite. A visitor asked, "What are you doing?" The first stone cutter grumbled, "I'm cutting this damned stone into a block." The second, who looked pleased with his work, replied, "I'm on a team that's building a cathedral." That's the spirit.

A worker who can envision "the whole cathedral" and who has been given responsibility for constructing his portion of it is far more satisfied and productive than the worker who sees only a granite stone and a long hard job staring him in the face.

Team spirit makes "Statement Day" at University National Bank & Trust Co. in Palo Alto, California, a big success for the bank and for its customers. Every employee, including the chairman, gathers around the big conference room table on the first day of each month to stuff statements into envelopes. This makes it possible to provide customers with a very special service among banks—a monthly statement that arrives within a couple days of the close of business.

Working together to accomplish a valued objective builds team spirit and a customer-oriented corporate culture.

University National Bank reports that its return-on-assets ratio is 75 percent higher than the state average. Executives credit customer service and team spirit for the record.

The Bank of San Francisco has developed a team framework for its client contact staff. Team leaders are given entrepreneurlike freedom and all team members are hand picked by the team leader. Furthermore, the market served by the team is one that the leader is thoroughly familiar and comfortable with. Team leaders know they have authority, and that they will receive the support necessary to build their business.

The rest of the bank—administration, operations, branches, credit—is designed to support the teams. All team leaders meet regularly with representatives of the other areas and with senior administration staff to assure reliable, high-quality support.

The authority of team leaders at the Bank of San Francisco cuts across the authority of organizational departments and middle managers, because it is critical that they be allowed to be flexible and innovative to meet individual client needs.

Pride

Pride is a powerful motivator. One source of pride is the return of customers. When a customer comes back, smiles at an employee, and buys something, that employee is motivated by the thought that he or she has been doing something right and is important to the company.

This kind of motivation often is far more effective in inspiring employees to provide good service than money is. It's called "job satisfaction."

There's no great mystery to employee motivation. We've known as much as we need to know about human motivation since the time of Alexander the Great: human beings are wanting animals. They commit their energies to the extent that doing so brings them what they want.

Rewards

Employees of Smith & Hawken, a mail order garden supply company, own stock in the company. Paul Hawken, president, says that employees are motivated to provide good service because they receive healthy stock dividends.

At Marshall Field Department Stores, when a manager observes a salesclerk being extra helpful to a customer, the employee receives a silver coin called a "Frangloon." Ten coins can be traded for a box of Field's Frango mint chocolates. One hundred Frangloons earn an extra day of paid vacation.

When Marshall Field stores began a service-improvement campaign, salespeople approached customers after only about 10 minutes. But thanks to changes such as the Frangloon incentive plan to motivate employees, and thanks also to a computer scheduling program that puts salespeople where they're needed most, Field lopped 8 minutes off average response time.

Incentive Compensation

Dow USA promotes customer service by adding incentive compensation, keyed to performance, to its tech service reps' salaries. But in determining amount of incentive, Dow combines the performance of tech service reps and salespeople in establishing performance ratings.

Says Kern: "If you say you want the customer service rep and the field seller to be part of an account retention team, reward them for their *joint* success."

It's an idea that would be endorsed by Michael LeBoeuf of the University of New Orleans. He favors bonuses both for service and for sales reps. "Most managers and people in charge don't reward service reps for taking care of the customer," he says.

This oversight fuels service reps' "attitude of indifference or even contempt" for customers, he adds.

Personal Benefit

Remember that the best of all motivation is personal benefit. Employees want to practice customer service when they recognize personal benefit in it.

The editors of *Electrical Contractor* magazine may have been somewhat harsh, but there's truth in a statement in a recent issue: "One of the first things (employees) should realize is how being customer oriented helps them secure their paychecks and also their security through the future growth and prosperity of their companies. They need to know why being customer oriented is critical to the success of the business. Then, they need to assess whether their behavior is helping to create and to maintain satisfied customers or to lose customers."

In a more constructive vein, Michael Barzelay, associate professor of public policy at Harvard University's Kennedy School, believes that a service quality campaign (in state and local government) can motivate career civil servants for several reasons. First, he says, it focuses on the value of what they do. Since the improvement process requires employees to solicit feedback from clients, they are reinforced when they learn that they've done something well.

Second, people are more enthusiastic and committed to *any* change project that they control themselves. In internally driven service-improvement projects, employees get a chance to voice their own ideas and strategies for change, rather than being subjected to the whims of outsiders or oversight groups.

Improved Relationships

When employees learn the value of friendly, helpful relationships with customers, they've also learned a lesson that will help them improve personal relationship both on and off the job.

On the job, smiles and friendly talk with customers and with an employee's peers create a pleasant working environment and ease the way through a day. When employees get along well with fellow employees and with customers, they feel good about themselves; so they are happier, more productive, and more effective.

Improved Self-worth

Off the job, when employees find their social lives improving, their feelings of self-worth improve, too. They have more self-esteem so they feel better about themselves, more confident, more hopeful about their lives, and more highly motivated. Employees in organizations known for stellar personal service experience enhanced personal popularity with peers and friends, a result of applying the same techniques that achieve customer satisfaction.

When relationships on and off the job are smoother, life gets better. A person feels as if he or she belongs.

Customer Applause Motivates

As a result of improved relationships with customers, employee performance is rewarded and reinforced with "applause" from customers. So being human, they continue what they've been doing and maybe even do it more often and with greater gusto. They may begin working harder, which leads to greater productivity and more sales per employee. Pride and team spirit take over and make inspired performance routine.

It's easy to understand why this happens. Customers are VIPs in a service employee's life. Employees are people and people respond emotionally to the attitudes of other people including customers.

Employees are much happier at work and after work when their customers are happy with them. It's far more pleasant for employees, you see, to deal with customers who aren't griping about the service all the time.

So encourage employees to apply customer service tactics in their personal lives on and off the job. Smile and compliment people, listen attentively, try to be helpful, and use friendly greetings and parting comments.

As a result, employees will often discover that their job, family, and social lives improve, so they stay motivated to continue applying the same service tactics.

One benefit, from the company's point of view, is improved internal communication, staff relations, and morale.

When personal benefit from application of customer service tactics becomes apparent to them, employees practice customer relations skills because they want to. They want to become customer relations professionals.

Because employees benefit from applying customer service techniques, they are likely to be motivated to learn, too, and to practice what they learn.

So motivate employees by pointing out how a service attitude and the friendly, helpful service techniques you are teaching them can help them *personally.*

When employees find their social lives improving, their feelings of self-worth improve. They have more self esteem, so they feel better about themselves, more confident, more hopeful about their lives, and more highly motivated to do well on the job. It all comes together.

As a result of practicing good customer service, employees earn more applause from customers, so they begin working still harder. And better. Pride and team spirit take over.

The objective of supervisors intent upon motivating employees to provide outstanding service should be to convince them that, personally, they're getting more out of their knowledge and practice of good service than the company is.

Employees are motivated by regular, reinforced training, by the belief that service attitude and practice help them in their personal lives—and by equitable, personal treatment by their supervisors.

Pride and Satisfaction

Employees should be encouraged to develop pride in their personal performance and also in the organization they work for that is more widely respected when customers are treated with respect and friendliness.

Andrew Adriance, manager of the Polo Club in Boca Raton, Florida, says: "We view service as a matter of pride among individuals because the service we offer is based on pride—pride in the facility, fellow employees, and management and pride in the membership. Once the pride is there, the peer pressure to provide service will be heavy and the person who isn't providing it becomes conspicuous.

"Pride means that service becomes the ultimate priority. If you don't serve, you lose members. If you lose members, you can't support the upkeep of the facility, and you lose the pride. It's a dangerous cycle."

Greater Self-respect

This feeling is a result of seeing customers return because they liked the way the employee treated them.

Optimism

Outlook becomes brighter. Hopes for professional advancement appear more realistic.

Control

Employees feel that they are in control of their lives. They are able to deal with customers and with job problems more easily and effectively.

Easier work

The job becomes less easier to handle as a result of teamwork and cooperation that friendly relationships engender. When one "gets along" with coworkers, work goes faster and easier.

Increased Self-confidence

When employees are secure in their relationships on and off the job they become more confident.

Job Enjoyment

Employees anticipate work with pleasure instead of with dread.

Employee Orientation and Information Literature

One of the most outstanding employee orientation programs I have ever seen is anchored by an 80-page, four-color booklet printed on expensive 8 1/2" X 11" glossy paper by Woolworth's of England for its new employees. The clearly high cost of this brochure signals the sincerity and commitment of the company to employee orientation and motivation.

The booklet looks like the fortunate result of collaboration between a star cartoonist and an inspired layout artist. Producers of the booklet used many color pictures, imaginative drawings and sketches, and copy that employs just enough words—no more than that—to excite, challenge, and motivate employees.

Service "Contract"

Inside the booklet is a "contract" with new employees that promises recognition and reward if they perform up to standards.

Supplementing the booklet are letters and stars on name badges signifying completion of various programs and achievement of specified knowledge and performance standards. After 12 months on the job, achievement of standards earns cash bonuses. One badge letter is "X," indicating that an employee has completed a training program in customer service.

Another fine piece of employee literature was a little red book entitled "Let's Get in There and Fight," distributed by SAS to every one of the airline's 20,000 employees and then to new employees. The book lays out information, in concise form, about the company's vision and goals—information that only the board of directors get to see in most companies.

Says Jan Carlzon, president of the Scandinavian Airlines System (SAS): "Beyond the attention to service, we were also able to stir new energy simply by ensuring that everyone connected with SAS—from board members to reservation clerks—knew about and understood our overall vision."

Ten Ways To Appreciate Customers

(From General Motors)

- Obey the golden rule ("Do unto others as you would have them do unto you")
- Use praise (Be generous and others will respond in a positive manner)
- Be sincere (A customer's trust depends on your sincerity)
- Use the customer's name (Everyone enjoys being recognized)
- Be a friend (It takes one to know one)
- Smile (It's the best way to hear what the customer is saying)
- Listen (It's the shortest distance between two people)
- Give (The customer will see and appreciate the value received)
- Think "you" instead of "I," (Consciously use the word and always retain your sense of humor)
- Care for the customers (Actions speak louder than words)

Customers: What They Want From Businesses

- Cleanliness
- To Feel Important
- Sincerity
- Integrity
- Honesty
- Trust
- Eye Pleasing Environment

To Help Customers, We Need To

- Believe in our product
- Be convinced of their needs
- Avoid showing anger
- Remain courteous
- Remember they want benefits
- Ask questions
- Give them full attention
- Say thank you

Many service employees intent on satisfying customers subscribe to the Golden Rule. Here are other guidelines for personal action with a list of customer service preferences and customer service action tips. (Reprinted courtesy of General Motors Corporation.)

Tools Needed to Provide Quality Service

Make sure that systems and technical support that "allow" employees to do their jobs as well as they can are in place. That may mean word processors instead of typewriters for employees or numerical control equipment on the production line.

One of Tom Peters's four major conclusions, published in his book, *Thriving on Chaos,* arose from ten years of poring over studies and observing companies. It was: "Workers in all parts of an organization will become energized by the opportunity to provide a top-quality product or service."

(Peters's other three conclusions from his ten years of study were the following: (1) The customer will pay a lot for better, and especially for best, quality. (2) Firms that provide that quality will thrive. (3) No product has a safe quality lead, since new entrants are constantly redefining, for the customer, what's possible.)

DOES MONEY ALSO MOTIVATE?

"Many service companies haven't realized that the person who delivers the service is the *most important* [in the company]," says Alden Clayton, head of the Marketing Science Institute of Cambridge, Massachusetts, a nonprofit business think tank.

Apparently certain that money is at least somewhat motivational, she suggests that people who deliver service should be paid very well instead of being pegged at the lowest position on the wage scale, a common practice.

Retailing companies using commission-based compensation systems are finding that the increased compensation that such systems pay is, indeed, motivational. The usual result of commission-based systems is better customer service.

Commissions

More and more often today the best customer service is found at companies where employees are on some kind of commission system whether you're buying a car or real estate, men's suits, or expensive women's clothing. Commission jobs pay more so they usually attract more capable people.

One specialty retailer, Bergdorf Goodman, has good results with an all-commission sales force. And the high-fashion Manhattan unit of Carter Hawley Hale of Los Angeles put all its sales associates on commission. Says Marita O'Dea, vice president and director of personnel: "We get people who are highly motivated, like to sell, and want to stay." But these people also must possess "the basics of good selling skills and knowledge of high fashion and high-priced merchandise," she adds.

Most employees of Nordstrom Department Stores work full time, unlike employees at most other department stores, and they all work on commission. They're encouraged to build long-term relationships with customers. They keep a "client book" on what each customer likes and doesn't like. Customers are then called when items that might interest them arrive or when preferred items are on sale. Competitors who've tried to imitate Nordstrom by putting more salespeople on commission—without building up the concept of long-term relationships and without using full-timers—have failed by driving away customers because the salespeople push too hard for a single sale.

Also on commission but at the opposite end of the service spectrum from Bergdorf Goodman and Carter Hawley Hale are the Mexican shops in border towns such as Juarez, across the border from El Paso, and Tijuana, near San Diego. Salespeople are extremely attentive. Too attentive, some people think. They are all on commission. Never is it necessary to go looking for a salesperson as often happens in U.S. stores. Of course, salespeople attentiveness is all the service you get.

Bloomingdale's, the department store chain, put all 1,500 sales personnel at its flagship store in Manhattan on commission instead of hourly wage. By the end of 1989 virtually all Bloomingdale stores had converted to commission selling.

The commission setup at Bloomingdale's is part of a plan to improve customer service by giving sales staff greater incentive to satisfy customers so they will buy more and return to buy again. When commission selling was established in the men's accessory department in December 1988, sales rose 22 percent as employee take-home pay grew.

A commission-based sales compensation system also has been successfully adopted by Stanley Korshak, the Dallas-based high-fashion retailer.

But commissions are not incentives for everybody.

Profit Sharing

Besides commissions, Maurice Maio, president of Maio Plumbing, the leading plumbing repair service in the San Diego area, offers money in the form of profit sharing and a 410-K retirement plan. He also has a very liberal vacation pay benefit program based on a year's total average earnings and several other attractive motivational perks.

Money may be motivational when it is a reward strictly for customer satisfaction. At Renex Corp., a Woodbridge, Virginia, company that sells computer interconnectivity products, customers help evaluate performance of tech reps who receive bonuses based on customer satisfaction. Tech reps who do outstanding work earn about 10 percent more than they would if they worked for competitive firms.

Renex Corp. treats technical service reps like salespeople. They want to make sure that tech reps really do reinforce sales. The company does not treat service reps like the bank manager in Chapter 2 did. He gave cash bonuses to high sales performers, you remember, but he dispensed lapel pins to high performers in the service area.

Bonuses

Allow customers to report good service, using response cards. Then reward with cash those employees who delivered the good service. The amount of financial reward they receive should increase in proportion to the number of good customer reports they receive.

Does money motivate? Certainly. But under many conditions money doesn't exert as much motivational impact as self-respect, opportunity to develop one's abilities (self-realization), and so on.

Here's a story about the motivational impact of money. In 1982, the airline industry was in turmoil, competition was increasing rapidly, and some carriers were not profitable. Delta was one of many companies whose profits nose-dived.

So what did the company do? Under the same financial conditions that led other carriers to furlough employees and to ask for wage concessions, Delta gave employees a pay raise, instead.

Delta management reasoned that the company's success up to that point was due largely to employees and that a successful effort to pull the company out of its economic problems would depend to a large extent upon the productivity and work quality of employees.

Did the tactic pay off? It paid off in employee enthusiasm, in productivity, and in what might be called "active gratitude." Employees got together and bought an airliner for the company! It was Delta's first Boeing 767. It was named "The Spirit of Delta."

EMPOWER EMPLOYEES; MOTIVATE WITH RESPONSIBILITY

You can motivate employees by trusting them with responsibility to make decisions about action needed to achieve customer satisfaction.

Indeed, workers who are willing to accept responsibility beyond the narrow confines of their authority (empowered) can be crucial to the success of an enterprise, as the economy becomes more service based.

This is true: customer satisfaction generally must be achieved by the first employee a customer deals with or customer satisfaction will be lost or lessened. This means that decisions should be made at the point of "discovery," not deferred to a decision point far up the corporate ladder.

Why? Because if a customer is forced to take her or his concern beyond the first personal contact, most of the time that customer will just give up. Often they will never return.

But I estimate that no more than 5 percent of companies train employees to deal with problems on the spot, though the practice is expanding. Yet, if customers are required to contact more than one person, most of them give up and many of them never return.

Barnett Banks of Florida has decentralized its retail operations, giving branch managers the power to make many decisions that once were passed on to headquarters. Many of the bank's tellers and credit officers now are authorized to make decisions and to solve problems that formerly were referred up the chain of command.

"Customers want responsible action, preferably from the first person they speak with," says Paul Hawken, president of a company introduced earlier in this chapter. No one should have to go "higher up" to get permission to be considerate, he says.

A good reason for encouraging employees to make customer satisfaction decisions was expressed by SAS president Jan Carlzon: ". . . those people out in the front lines . . . are the ones who most directly influence the customer's impression of the company."

Authority

Front-line employees must get more authority so they can respond to the needs and problems of individuals. They must be trained to respond to unique needs with speed and courtesy. Only in this way can companies multiply the number of happy, satisfied customers and build up an important competitive advantage.

When employees are empowered to pursue customer satisfaction, they are supercharged with enthusiasm.

An employee of L. L. Bean, Inc., drove a van 500 miles from Maine to New York to deliver a canoe to a customer leaving on a trip. Bean employees regularly meet vacation-bound customers at highway toll booths to deliver hiking or camping equipment.

An important reason for empowering employees is that doing so often maintains morale in difficult situations such as when a customer is angry. Employee morale is sorely damaged when employees aren't trained to handle irritated customers. They end up enduring unpleasant experiences and emotional strain. But, when employees have been empowered, given the authority to take action that, for example, defuses conflict situations, you will maintain morale and even reduce turnover.

Charles R. Day, editor of *Industry Week* magazine, reported that "A [Dollar Rent-A-Car] supervisor escorted me to my vehicle. My paperwork didn't indicate its location, and she didn't want to risk my wandering around a parking lot sticking keys in door locks like some crazed sweepstakes contestant. At 10 o'clock on a sweltering night in Tampa her concern was gratifying, and if anyone at Dollar ever wonders about overstaffing, don't. Such service lodges in the memory and helps heal wounds from future woes."

No policy book can cover contingencies such as the one the Dollar Rent-A-Car supervisor handled so well. Don't even try to concoct a policy. Just give employees responsibility to do what's right. It's being done throughout the economy.

A GTE phone company branch in Sun Prairie, Wisconsin, scrapped its computerized question-and-answer list normally asked of customers who need repairs. (Customers would try to say something that isn't a direct answer to a question and be cut off with a "Let's get back to the questions" retort by employees.) Now, service operators take down information as customers give it—and even chat a little if that's the customer's pleasure.

Service by Salespeople

Salespeople, definitely in the service business, are motivated with very-loose-reined supervision at Merck Sharp & Dohme, a U.S. pharmaceutical company. "They decide on their own how they will spend their time," says Jerry Keller, vice president.

"Salespeople can take off early if they want to. But, in return," says Keller, "they routinely give their home phone numbers to physicians and stand ready 24 hours a day to answer questions or to fill emergency orders. They pay us back in abundance."

Timothy W. Firnstahl, founder and CEO of Satisfaction Guaranteed Eateries, Inc., that owns four restaurants in the Seattle area, reported on success of his employee responsibility program.

The company's slogan had been "Your Enjoyment Guaranteed. Always." But says Firnstahl: "We had given employees responsibility (for good service) without giving them authority. The result was that they tried to bury mistakes or to blame others. I saw it every time we tried to track down a complaint. The food servers blamed the kitchen for late meals. The kitchen blamed the food servers for placing orders incorrectly."

The same things happen in other companies. Employees scurry about to avoid responsibility whenever a problem occurs.

"For our guarantee to be truly effective," says Firnstahl, "we needed to give workers themselves the power to make good on the promise of the guarantee—at once and on the spot. We decided to eliminate the hassle for customers and for ourselves. No forms to fill out, no phone calls to make, no 40 questions to answer, just immediate redress by the closest employee."

So Firnstahl instituted the idea that any employee could and should do anything to keep customers happy.

"In the event of an error or a delay, any employee right down to the busboy can provide complimentary wine or dessert or pick up an entire tab if necessary.

"Different guests respond in different ways, so we told our employees not to feel limited by the guidelines and to do whatever it took to make sure guests enjoyed themselves."

Authority Leads to Pride

It took a while for employees to get into the spirit. But soon they found that they liked working for a restaurant widely respected for its commitment to customer satisfaction.

Firnstahl expresses the philosophical basis for empowerment of employees. He says: "Preeminence in any field gives people feelings of self-worth that they could never get from just making a buck. Their power as company representatives increases their pride in the business and that, in turn, increases motivation."

The movement to give more decision-making responsibility to front-line employees, as a shortcut to customer satisfaction, was given impetus in the hospitality industry by a Quality Assurance Committee at an annual meeting of the American Hotel and Motel Association.

Beliefs Promoting Empowerment

The committee developed this list of beliefs that a manager must have to be successful in quality assurance responsibilities:

- The person doing the job knows best how the job can be done.
- Problem solving and decision making can be done at the lowest competent level in the organization.
- People are the greatest untapped resource in the organization.
- People rarely rise above the expectations set for them, but they will accomplish more than expected if empowered to do so.

Jan Carlzon, responding to executives who are afraid that employees who are empowered will "give away the store," said: "What's the danger of giving away too much? Are you worried about having an *over*satisfied customer? You can forget about an oversatisfied customer, but an *un*satisfied customer is one of the most expensive problems you can have."

Motivating employees by giving them more responsibility is a smart business move, considering the high cost of obtaining more business from a dissatisfied customer and the similarly high cost of attracting new customers.

"To get a satisfied customer back is just about free," says Carlzon. "On the other hand, it costs a small fortune to get dissatisfied customers back. So the danger is not that employees will give away too much. It's that they won't give away anything because they don't dare."

At Disney World, if a supervisor sees a front-line person "giving away the store," says James Poisant, former manager of business seminars, "he'll usually wait and talk it over with him later."

"It's okay if a guest gets away with something," says Poisant. "The alternative is that we could be wrong, and that could cost us a fortune. An aggrieved guest would tell everyone he knows that Disney is cheap. Occasionally, we'll take a hit, but that's okay."

Disney World feels sure that its outstanding training program justifies delegating authority to front-line "cast members." If you went out to a guest relations window today at EPCOT Center and told them that you didn't get value for your money and that you want your money back, the person in the window would most likely make a decision in your favor immediately.

"When you call a number at Disney World," says Poisant, "the people at the other end can solve your problem. They don't send you all over the company."

"Successful service organizations empower individuals to offer the best possible service they can, within reasonable limits," says Richard Whiteley, principal at The Forum Corporation, a Boston-based consulting firm that offers training, consulting, and research services in customer focus.

The way a missent or misaddressed check is handled illustrates the benefits of front-line decision making at one financial services company. In the past it took a management decision to air express a new check. Now, customer service reps have leeway to spend air express charges to get a new check out immediately."

Decision-making skills for sales associates is getting increasing attention by retailers. Instead of putting the customer through the aggravation of going to a supervisor with a complaint or a special request, many sales associates are given authority to make decisions in certain customer relations situations.

If a problem develops over a return or a credit, or if a customer is a day late for a big sale because she couldn't get in the day before, sales associates are trained to handle the situations immediately.

Imagine how good a customer feels when a clerk offers an immediate exchange of a purchase instead of fighting you all the way through to store management. Imagine the good opinion that a customer develops of a store when a salesperson says, "I know just how you feel. I want to apologize for the inconvenience" instead of saying "I'm sorry, that's our policy" or "I need to talk to my boss first."

At Johnson & Johnson in Racine, Wisconsin, customer service reps refund up to $50 without higher approval.

Motivation Through Responsibility

The benefits of motivation through responsibility can be spectacular. Consider how much Federal Express has benefited from word-of-mouth reporting of this incident: a courier's truck broke down while he was making deliveries. He called a tow truck, then persuaded the tow truck driver, pulling the courier's truck, to follow a route that just happened to coincide with his delivery route—and to stop at each delivery site! This Federal Express courier met his delivery deadline with a broken-down truck.

The policy of pushing decision-making responsibility as far down the line as possible resulted in an enlightened business decision that would not have been made had the courier felt constrained to follow the policy manual. Nowhere in the Federal Express policy manual, you see, are employees given permission to make deliveries from the end of a tow truck cable.

Implementing Empowerment

You might say that the first step in instituting an "employee responsibility system" is to outlaw the phrase "That's not my job" or its many malevolent or obscene variants. Then give sales and service people wide latitude to act as "the company" when they are in the field or on the phone, and especially when they are confronting a problem face to face. Turn them loose to make decisions instead of requiring them to perform by rote.

Remove the Shackles

Identify policy changes that will help employees serve customers better; then push for top management approval of them.

Identify Decision-Making Opportunities

Show employees the specific situations in which they can "bend the rules." And publicize rule benders.

Communicate Empowerment

Top management should tell employees, emphatically, that not only do they have freedom to do whatever is needed to keep a customer's business, but also they are expected to exercise that freedom. Tell them that they are being given responsibility *and authority* to do, immediately, whatever they think is right.

Flatten the Pyramid

Any business organization seeking to motivate employees to provide immediate, on-the-spot service must flatten the corporate pyramid. This means eliminating hierarchical tiers of responsibility in order to facilitate exercise of authority by front-line employees.

"Managing" is thus shifted from the executive suite to the operational level where everyone is now a manager of his or her own situation. When problems arise, each employee has authority to determine appropriate action and to see to it that the action is carried out by himself or herself or with the help of others.

I urge you to take a close, hard look at your organization. If you can flatten your pyramid, you will be creating a far more powerful and resilient organization that not only serves customers better but also unleashes the hidden energy within your employees. The results can be astounding.

Before this can be done successfully, though, upper levels of the old pyramid must understand that their roles are greatly changed. They are now leaders making it possible for those out front to make operational decisions. It's just that some of their decision-making authority has been transferred to front-line employees.

But make sure that supervisors understand that under the principle of greater responsibility for front-line employees they must come to terms with a seeming diminution of their authority.

When employees are "empowered," the boss's real role is to serve the employee, and the purpose of the employee becomes to serve the customer. When this happens, the bottom line takes care of itself.

Convey a Feeling of Security

Employees should know that they won't be fired if they make a mistake and that it's all right to make mistakes in the process of working to win customer satisfaction. Only then will they dare to use their new authority fully.

Having knowledge and information isn't enough if employees believe that a wrong decision may attract the fury of their bosses or even result in the loss of their jobs.

Security is the result of a heightened sense of self-worth that greater responsibility bestows.

"A good customer-service person must have the right to say, without fear, 'To heck with the company'" is the way Hawken expresses this concept.

Give Employees Justification for Making Decisions

A personal "reason" to change is needed. Unfortunately, most front-line employees have been following regulations for so long that few have the courage to try anything unusual. So emphasize this step.

One airline did it by communicating management's "vision" for the company to employees. (Company philosophy and goals are not shared with employees by very many companies. They should be.)

The company operated on the principle that anyone who is not given information about goals and philosophy cannot accept responsibility, while anyone who is given responsibility cannot avoid assuming it.

Once employees understood the company's "vision," they accepted responsibility with enthusiasm. The result was many beneficial developments in the company.

Mervyn's in Los Angeles, largest department store company in the country, at last report, does the same thing. The company keeps employees motivated by helping them understand company goals and objectives. Employees understand that they are management's partners in achieving goals.

Provide Guidelines for Employees

Give employees clear but just general guidelines so they have room to maneuver and to think creatively. Employees should operate under "shades-of-gray" decision-making guidelines that say, in effect: "These are the types of things you can do for the customer."

Rick Phillips, New Orleans business educator, recalls an incident in which an employee made an enlightened customer-satisfying decision on the basis of a general guideline. "A waitress serving the table behind me in a Washington, D.C., restaurant," said Phillips, "told her customers that there would be no charge for their meals since the restaurant did not have the wine the diner who was hosting the group had ordered. The manager told me that the waitress made the decision on her own because the paying customer was a regular. The wine was the one he ordered at least once a month to impress his clients.

"The manager said that every time a business diner leaves his restaurant disappointed, he risks losing up to $3,000 per year. 'I am a small businessman,' he said. 'I can't afford that.'"

Utilize the Knowledge and Experience of Front-Line Employees

Organizations of all kinds handcuff their employees with rules and policies instead of taking advantage of the motivational value of greater personal responsibility. They clearly tell employees: "Do what you're told. Follow the rules. We're not interested in what you think about the situation."

Instead, take the principle of greater front-line responsibility one step further by consulting the expertise of experienced employees.

For instance, ask employees for suggestions on changing rules that might be well intended but result in more customer hassles and turnoffs than is warranted by the low costs of rule changes.

After all, who knows more about an organization's products and customers than its front-line employees? Day after day they work right at the point where the business thrives or dies.

Summing up the values of employee empowerment, Whiteley of the Forum Corporation says: "You must give people authority far out on the line where the action is. . . . By giving them security, authority, and the right to make decisions based on current market conditions, you put yourself in the best position to gain a competitive edge."

MOTIVATE EMPLOYEES BY TREATING THEM RIGHT

A good case can be made for maintaining that an organization will not have employees who treat customers right if the company doesn't treat employees right. Equitable, individual treatment of employees is motivational.

"Show me a club whose employees don't serve people and I'll show you a club whose employees aren't being served," says Michael Scudder, vice president and general manager of The Club at Montrose in Montrose, New York.

Along with emphasis on guest relations, the Ramada Renaissance Hotels has set elimination of the "caste system" found in many hotels as one of its objectives.

Management promotes the view that every job is important, whether it's cleaning glassware or cleaning the floor, and that every employee's job is guest relations. While other hotels are busy constructing buildings that look beautiful, the Ramada Renaissance is staffed by beautiful *people*. Management is willing to bet that beautiful people will win out every time over beautiful buildings and appointments.

It's essential that employees "feel good" about their jobs because motivation is vital. You can't just order employees to do this or that and expect them to carry out your orders enthusiastically. That's like the drug program that suggests, "Just say 'No.'" Without enthusiasm and commitment, just saying "No" or just saying "Have a nice day" is not enough. Lack of enthusiasm will be painfully and embarrassingly clear.

Managers have a responsibility to treat their staffs with the same respect they should be showing their customers. This respect translates into motivation to work toward objectives established by management, including customer satisfaction.

Managers should look upon employees as *their* customers.

A management team must honestly respect, appreciate, and value employees. But many managers believe that a person working for $4 to $10 per hour couldn't possible have any real value.

If managers are not inclined by their own values to respect employees, they ought to consider the increasing difficulty of finding good employees as a reason for doing so no matter how they feel.

Treating employees like human beings will induce good employees to stay and motivate them to perform in the best interests of the company—that is, to give service to customers and to win their satisfaction.

Respectful Treatment

Econo Lodges of America, Inc., of Charlotte, North Carolina, found that respectful treatment of employees is one of the most effective means of reducing turnover. Larry Williams, director of training, said the company involves employees in decisions that affect their work. They ask their opinions and respond to them so that employees feel that they make a difference in the company's performance.

After instituting a quality service program, Econo Lodges tracked employee turnover and customer complaints. "We saw a significant improvement in both categories," says Williams.

At Marriott Corporation hotels, respect is demonstrated by calling employees "associates or "colleagues" instead of "customer service reps." And they are remarkably free to call on every part of the company in helping customers. They earn substantial bonuses, too, for extraordinary work.

The People Department

Wal-Mart's former "human resources" department now is called the People Department. The Army and Air Force Exchange Services also have People Departments now instead of personnel or human resources department.

Many companies are repudiating the antihuman attitude betrayed by reference to new employees as "new hires."

At Disney, management style comes down to this: in any business that depends on a front line of employees, management must not only support it but trust and respect it as well.

"There was a time when people were 'factors of production,' managed little differently from machines or capital. No more. The best people will not tolerate it," says Robert Waterman, in The Renewal Factor: " . . . if that way of managing ever generated productivity, it has the reverse effect today. While capital and machines . . . can be managed toward sameness, people are individuals. They must be managed (as individuals)," says Waterman.

A small business owner, Dale Boozer, president of Boozer Lumber Co. in Columbia, South Carolina, puts Waterman's views into practice. He says: "We treat employees as important parts of the organization. We don't make decisions involving them without their input. We try to structure vacations when they want to take them rather than when it's convenient for us. We try to help them with incentive programs to earn extra money." The payoff comes when, as Boozer says, "People want to work here."

There is power in a feeling of self-worth. Give employees a feeling of self-worth and you will have laid a solid foundation for your customer satisfaction program. As Elaine Grossinger-Etess, 1989 president of the American Hotel and Motel Association, said: "We need to instill self-worth in our employees. Employees need to be nurtured, trained, and motivated. I think that will do wonders for morale and motivation."

MOTIVATE THROUGH ORGANIZATIONAL COMMITMENT

When total commitment to customers becomes the culture of a company and when top managers continuously fortify the commitment with actions and words, then employees, too, become committed, motivated.

Commitment is not something that management can establish by edict. Instead, it is the result of extensive communication and management's ability to turn grand causes into small actions so that people throughout an organization can contribute to a central purpose.

The most motivating causes focus on quality products, service to the customer—making the work people do seem worth the effort—and on people quality, helping people believe in their individual worth.

Profit, alone, is not one of the causes that inspires much loyalty among the rank and file, unless company survival is at issue. Even then the profit motive, for the average employee, may not be enough to motivate them.

The best companies build a customer-oriented culture with a combination of cooperation, communication, and commitment.

MOTIVATE WITH EMPLOYEE INVOLVEMENT

We've said repeatedly that a customer service program will achieve its full flower only if every employee is enlisted in the cause. Scott Paper Company is just one of many companies that practices this policy. Customer commitment often is developed through listening: Lee Iacocca, chairman of Chrysler Corporation, says that Chrysler listens to what its employees have to say about customer service.

Elaborating upon "Team Spirit," listed earlier as one of "Ten Motivators," American Express's Customer Service Task Force, made up of key people from each section's customer service division, is a clearinghouse where employees meet to discuss service problems in their departments. Employees become involved with the entire company by discussing problems and creating solutions.

At CUNA Data employees in each customer service department meet with their supervisor and training coordinator every quarter. They discuss obstacles to fast and correct achievement of their objectives.

The result? Ideas. Ideas ranging in subject matter from changing procedures to changing forms design.

Forums and Service Teams

Employee involvement at Toshiba takes a different form. The company provides regular senior management forums in which sales, service, and support people express whatever is on their minds.

At Omni Hotels employees select the most service-oriented peer in their departments to serve as their representatives on a committee that attempts to correct interdepartmental service problems. Chosen employees can win prizes such as a vacation for the entire family at an Omni hotel.

The program paid off, says William Sheehan, president and CEO of Omni Hotels. Guest approval of check-in procedures rose 10.4 percent and restaurant service ratings climbed 12.4 percent.

Of all the various forms of "customer service teams," about half of them are in the United Kingdom. Their purpose is to provide a forum for line employees to develop and to experiment with new approaches to service management at the grass-roots level.

For example, when British Airways management contemplated the issue of developing new service standards, their decision was not to impose procedures and measures from on high, but to give the matter over to its Service First teams. Team suggestions range from extending office operating hours to provide better service to travelers to revamping lost-and-found procedures. Recommendations and suggestions that have system-wide implications or that might be expensive are bumped up to the head office for review and approval.

When the American Hotel & Motel Association held its first Quality Assurance Conference attendance exceeded all expectations. The Washington-based organization, an umbrella for more than 8,000 hotels, began studying and promoting service quality in 1982.

Satisfaction Standards

Hilton Hotels Corp. spent two years developing a chainwide quality assurance program for its 270-plus franchised properties. Out of initial research came a list of more than 300 guest satisfaction standards. The chain designed a video training program to communicate the standards to employees.

Hilton Hotel staffs form quality teams that meet once a week to discuss problems and look for solutions. Each department in a hotel, from housekeeping and engineering to management, has a team. Interdepartmental teams are made up of each unit's manager. Usually, each team is charged with determining performance and service standards, and employees often write their own job descriptions.

At weekly meetings, grievances are aired, and divisions of responsibility between departments are discussed and devised. Any recommendations for change made by a team are channeled through management, which will decide whether or not to take action.

The number of quality teams at a hotel can vary widely, depending on the hotel's size. Opryland Hotel, with 2,700 employees, has 26 teams. Smaller hotels might have only 2 or 3.

Some small hotels might put representatives from different departments, such as the front desk and housekeeping, on each team. Such interdepartmental representation has the advantage of allowing members to understand better what their coworkers' jobs entail.

At an annual conference of the National Retail Merchants Association, Leonard Berry, retail professor and consultant from Texas A&M University, implored several hundred retail executives to motivate employees to perform at their most enthusiastic and committed levels of customer service by inviting them to help establish performance standards and goals.

Berry asked the executives to train employees and to treat them well, to pay them enough so they can "sustain themselves," and to reward them for exemplary service.

"It should help bring customers back for more," said Professor Berry.

Involve Employees with Information

When employees are "in the know" about company objectives and programs, they identify with them. They are motivated to promote company interests, if communications to them stress their value in achieving objectives.

Treat employees as if they have a need to know how the company is faring in customer satisfaction. Actually, they do have a need to know. They're the ones who bear primary responsibility for providing service that satisfies customers.

In the forward to a publication, "Close to the Customer," the American Management Association calls for keeping the people who actually do the customer contact work—the front-line sales people—well informed. The AMA suggests that

- Employees should receive consumer comment/complaint reports.
- Everyone should be let in on the results of 800 number calls.
- Videotape meetings at which customer service is discussed and show the tape to everyone.
- Let everyone in on results of mail/phone questionnaire programs. Post results throughout the company for everyone—including customers—to see.

- Run focus groups on the topic, "what is it like to do business with us?"

Joy Schrage, general manager of the Appliance Information Service in the Consumer Affairs Division of the Whirlpool Corporation, lists these vehicles and methods by which the company keeps sales and service employees informed:

Education center.
Field training.
Factory educational and motivational training to show employees all the resources from which they can obtain information to pass on to consumers.

USE MOTIVATION TO REDUCE TURNOVER

When a work force is highly motivated, turnover and recruitment problems tend to solve themselves. You end up with more experienced employees who deliver better service, if you regularly reinforce motivation.

Once employees are delivering quality service, you will have a powerful restraint upon turnover.

When employees get into the swing of giving customers the best service they can—when they find themselves dealing with friendly, smiling customers who return often—then they enjoy their work. No more do customers assume that employees are going to be incompetent and surly and treat them as if they are ignorant and rude.

Customers as Friends

When customers become friends instead of antagonists as a result of pleasant, helpful, informed service a job is far more pleasant for an employee than a clock-watching job that's so boring it's hard to get up in the morning. This is the kind of job that employees try to keep. When turnover rate drops as a result of quality service so does the overall cost of labor including the cost of hiring and training.

Positions stay filled with competent people whose quality service skills continue to maintain customer loyalty—thereby reducing the amount you spend on marketing to replace customers who skip to competitors. No more standing "help wanted" ads. No more continual interviewing and reference checking. Far less paperwork all around.

Reducing Turnover

The most effective means of reducing employee turnover is not "pay them more." It is not "improve benefits." It is not creating a lot of "executive" janitors, "executive" receptionists, and "executive" housekeepers.

And it isn't sending them cards on their birthdays or a turkey at Christmas, either.

The most effective means of reducing turnover is motivating employees to high-quality performance from which they derive satisfaction that leads them to work hard to retain their jobs.

One of the major results of a customer service program at Kroger's, the largest supermarket chain in America, was reduced turnover and absenteeism.

Increased productivity is another significant benefit of quality service at Bio-Lab, Inc., in Decatur, Georgia. As a result of a service attitude, says Anne Pinkerton, director of customer service, "We processed $5 million more in orders in one recent year compared with the previous year—with the same number of employees."

Turnover Hints of Poor Service

Reduced turnover is such an established result of employee motivation as a result of quality service programs that its opposite—increased turnover—should be considered a warning that a company may not be customer focused.

This was one of the major findings in a survey of more than 700 companies throughout the world by the Forum Corporation. Turnover is directly associated with employee opinion of service quality. Some employees who leave, Forum found, do so because of dissatisfaction with their firm's poor internal and external service quality and the pall of negative attitude that hovers about the workplace.

So if your objective is quality service to customers and reduced turnover that yields a work force more capable of delivering quality service, consider the intangibles of respect for employees and value for their ideas. Consider giving them authority to make customer satisfaction decisions when customer satisfaction is their responsibility. Consider recognition, personal satisfaction, and opportunity for personal improvement. Consider keeping employees informed, and taking them into your confidence.

The times they are a-changin'. If you really want quality service, it's time to *commit* yourself to excellence in employee relations.

7

Knowledge Is Power—Profit Power

TACTICS, STRATEGY, AND QUALITY SERVICE

> Quality of service is more important than price. Price will bring shoppers but not customers . . . [But], give the customer something worthwhile and she or he will pay what it's worth.
>
> —*Tom Peters and Nancy Austin, A Passion for Excellence*

No business executive believes that she can build a successful career out of one-time sales, unless she sells the Brooklyn Bridge to an unsuspecting Arab oil sheik. Repeat sales are a necessity because customers always drop by the wayside if for no other reason than that they move or they die or, if the customer is a company, the employee who does the buying moves or dies.

Attrition is significant because few companies can depend upon a continuing flow of new customers to replace customers who stop buying.

So customer loyalty is very important to most companies.

And what's the best way to assure customer loyalty? Service. Service that earns satisfaction.

Customer satisfaction, to the extent that it retains customers, is a highly cost-effective strategy because it reduces the amount of new customer development that must be done. The cost of attracting new customers generally is five times greater than the cost of keeping the ones you already have, according to a rule-of-thumb standard that's been applied in the customer service field for years.

BASIC STRATEGIES

Certain basic strategies in the customer service field are essential to success. Consider them. Adopt some and discard others. But use them all to stimulate your creative instincts. First, let's consider strategies disclosed in findings of a 1989 *Chief Executive* magazine survey. Some 1,000 chief executives were asked for their views on how to improve customer satisfaction. The sample was slightly skewed toward larger companies and toward the manufacturing sector.

According to a report in *Chief Executive* magazine, "We expected some difference in what the improvers (companies that improved their customer service) would recommend to others as the place to start, or the place to devote the most resources. In fact, there is little difference in the rank ordering of priorities for recommended projects."

Starting Points

The most important places to start a customer service program, in declining order of frequency with which they were mentioned, are

1. Increase top management attention to customer satisfaction.
2. Improve product quality. This move received the highest number of votes in the "where to spend the most money" category.
3. Customer satisfaction training for employees. This move was second on "where to spend the most money."

Besides asking respondents for their recommendations of the place to start a customer service program and the place to devote most resources, *Chief Executive* analyzed responses to determine the most important differentiations between companies that improve service and those that don't improve. They are

1. Changes in customer handling policies and procedures by those that did improve service
2. Formal customer surveys
3. Formal internal reporting of performance
4. Customer satisfaction training
5. Top management action
6. Actual change in organizational structure. There's further guidance for your service program development in a consideration of strategies and tactics recommended in various other studies and reports. They employ similar language in recommending their agendas:

   a. Three basic characteristics

   (1) A written service strategy

   (2) Customer-friendly systems

(3) Customer-oriented front-line employees

b. Tactics used most often to achieve customer satisfaction

(1) Quality control and product assurance
(2) On-time delivery of product/service
(3) Ability to expedite special customer requests

c. Successful service organizations share these characteristics

(1) Strong vision
(2) They temper high-tech systems and methods with person-to-person dealings
(3) They hire and promote on the basis of success at providing service
(4) They communicate to customers the existence of service
(5) They measure service and make results available to employees

d. Strong similarities

(1) They make outlandish efforts to hire only the right people, to train and to motivate them, and to give them the authority needed to serve customers well
(2) They keep an especially sharp eye on the competition
(3) They ask customers to rate quality of service they receive
(4) They invest earlier and much more heavily than their competitors in technology to support customer service

Sandra Tuck, a principal in the management consulting firm of Booz, Allen & Hamilton, Inc., reports that only 47 of 101 service-oriented companies that the firm surveyed had effectively "leveraged technology" to deal with customers. Only 47 had provided employees with the technology they needed to service customers "exceptionally well."

"Customer service people should not just act as if they are staffing a complaint desk," says Ms. Tuck. "Customers must know you are thinking about them and acting in their behalf. She cited L. L. Bean, Inc., the Maine clothing and outdoor equipment retailer, that uses computers to determine whether items are in stock and to give telephone-order customers a quick idea of delivery dates.

Federal Express's ability to track packages is another example, she says. "Two packages we mailed from our office recently had their mailing labels switched by mistake. I called Federal Express and was able to track the packages and have the driver of the delivery truck change the labels."

Ms. Tuck suggests that customer service employees should be "less reactive and more proactive" in dealing with customers. For example, she says, sales personnel should not only listen and react to complaints about merchandise, but they should also go a step further by consulting a computer to determine whether the correct item was in stock and how soon it could be delivered, as L. L. Bean does.

A MATRIX: UNIVERSAL REALITIES

There are certain "great truths" about quality service that should overlay all action. Together they constitute a matrix of service that should guide the implementation of all service strategies.

1. Treat customers like life-long partners. Do it by listening to customers' expressions of needs and wants. Then help them obtain the service or product that serves those needs and wants best whether they're in your inventory or not. This is the proper procedure when you expect customers to return again and again over a long period.
2. Do not disappoint or anger customers. See Chapter 11 for guidance during occasions when you fail to achieve this objective.
3. See the business through customer eyes. Call it "empathy." At T.G.I. Friday restaurants, a chain of bistro-type restaurants, all managers are expected to sit (literally) in *every* chair. They see and experience the restaurant and its service from the point of view of all customers.
   Southland Corporation familiarizes employees with customer perceptions with reports from mystery shoppers who routinely check out store image, merchandise, and service from the customer point of view. Empathy is an important ingredient in the service business. How one handles a service problem, indeed, is as important to customers as the solution of the problem itself.
4. Deliver *more* service than you promise or than customers expect. This is a wonderful way to build customer loyalty upon their feeling that they got a "good deal."
   Practice the "and then some" principle. Your products do all you say they will, and then some. Service is prompt, reliable and courteous, and then some. If a customer needs help once a sale is complete, help the customer, and then some.
   Delivering more service than customers expect is a subtle competitive tactic that competitors usually don't notice. In the process of building volume you can confuse your competitors. They won't understand how you're doing it.
5. Try to get better. Imagine a mental fluorescent sign that flashes the questions: "How are we doing?" (Fine, but we can improve.) And "How can we get better?" (Apply the answers as if they were an action agenda.)

COMMON CHARACTERISTICS OF QUALITY SERVICE

In selecting programs and projects that will be most effective for *your* organization, consider what usually works well for most companies. Here are common characteristics of successful service programs. Their order in this presentation is not an implication of their relative effectiveness.

Customer-friendly Service Systems

A customer-friendly system is one whose basic design makes things easy for the customer, not primarily for the company. Such systems are a very noticeable contrast with the common practice of subordinating convenience for customers to convenience of employees and the cost advantage and "policies" of the company.

"We used to look for ways to make the work easier for us," says Chris Cox, chief of staff for the New Jersey Division of Motor Vehicles charged with improving service. "Now, when we redesign work, we do it to make things as easy as possible for the customer."

Suggesting methods used in developing an improved service system, Cox said: "If you are going to make real, lasting change for the customer, you have to make real, lasting change in the infrastructure of the organization."

Require Friendliness

Employees should be taught in no uncertain terms that friendliness is *expected,* not just encouraged. Follow the guidance of Mike Worsfold, managing director of Managerial Design Ltd, a Toronto management consulting firm, who says: "You don't smile just because the sun is shining and you had a good breakfast. You smile because it's your job to do so."

But some employees never smile. They are victims of "The Whatdoyawant Syndrome."

Bob Hynes, program manager in charge of training for American Hardware Supply Company, says salespeople in hardware stores sometimes are "almost curt in their role of 'skilled advisors.' They use housekeeping chores as an avoidance technique." They sweep the floor or stock shelves while talking out of the sides of their mouths to customers, he says.

These are customer-friendly systems: fast service, informational signing, convenient display, in-stock condition, check-out carts with wheels that actually *turn,* and employees who know what they're doing. A customer-friendly system also means honesty, good communication, and the golden rule.

But consistently high product quality is the most important feature of customer-friendly service, to some organizations. This is a very enlightened attitude. Al Braswell, vice president of Braswell Food Company, Inc., of Statesboro, Georgia, feels that prompt delivery and accuracy are important friendliness characteristics.

At Nordstrom's Department Stores employees are given carte blanche to fulfill the one overriding rule on the sales floor: The customer *must* leave satisfied.

Quality People

Hire people for whom it is not an unnatural act to be helpful and friendly. Then train them in additional, sophisticated service techniques and practices. Motivate them. And publicly recognize them and reward them.

Do these things and you are not likely to have employees who walk around with an expression that comedian George Carlin called DILLIGAD—"Do I look like I give a damn?" (The answer is "No.")

Review your personnel management system regularly to make sure you are still doing your best to find quality people and then to train them effectively. Answer these questions:

> Does our recruiting and hiring attract people who can fulfill service roles effectively?
>
> Does new employee orientation convey the service strategy? (Does the employee handbook, for example, have a section on service?)
>
> Do training programs advance the cause of effective service?
>
> Does the appraisal system provide feedback to employees about effectiveness of their customer service efforts? It's unlikely that employees will improve their service practices without constructive feedback. Tell them specifically the service performance that you expect of them.

Several years ago I introduced a very explicit four-page, 32-item customer service performance standards form. A performance standards scale is needed because employees must know specific behavior that you expect of them. Many performance standard forms are far too vague and general.

Committed Management

Management, particularly the CEO, must be committed in word *and* deed to service as a basic management principle. A quality service program probably won't get off the ground without management commitment that is genuine, continuous, and visible to every employee. Commitment leads to a corporate "culture" that favors, encourages, rewards, and, yes, *admires* quality service and the people who provide it. (Chapter 3 deals with management commitment.)

Availability of Service

Staffing level should be high enough to respond to customers promptly. If customers wait 10 to 15 minutes to complete a one-minute transaction, you'd better add employees at the problem point. When a customer sees a long line at a checkout counter and returns the product to the shelf (or to just drop it on the nearest shelf) rather than waiting to buy it, you might begin to have nightmares in which you see a janitor burning money.

Adequate staffing is just as important for mail order companies and for those that do much or all of their business by phone.

Sometimes adequate staffing is accomplished with a simple change in procedure. For instance, when an employee is servicing one customer and another customer calls on the phone, teach the employee to promise the caller politely that he or she will return to the phone as soon as the ongoing sale has been completed.

Renewal and Reinforcement of the Service Concept

Service programs *always* lose momentum beginning about a year to a year and a half following installation of a program, or sooner. The first round of training has ended several months earlier. All the easy-to-find solutions to problems have been applied. That leaves only the tougher problems, the ones that cause discouragement, and malaise. Service leaders practice reinforcement and renewal of service programs like a religion.

Original Research of Chicago, a company that has 350 "communicators" conducting customer satisfaction surveys by phone, keeps close tabs on their employees, but also recognizes good work. Says Denise Foy, senior vice president: "Our people get consistent feedback every day on performance. Every day they receive a grade in six areas of performance on the phone: listening skills, responsiveness, control of a conversation, adhering to the script, and so on.

"And when they do really good jobs, we have radio connection with supervisors from the control room where we are listening to employees on the phone. We might say 'Go tell Steve at station 21 that this was a really great way to handle that last call.' Or 'Tell Steve he needs to slow down. We're in no big hurry.'"

It's a serious error for the management of an organization to set a service program at the top of the hill, to give it a push to the accompaniment of *The Light Cavalry Overture*, and then to turn their backs and go on to other projects. Management must drive a service program with continuous attention manifested in active, personal commitment, in ongoing training, and standards that are regularly reinforced.

Ample Resources

Employees should not be pressed to do the normal work of two or more people if you want high quality service that wins customers and loyalty through reputation. Mechanics should have use of advanced electronic equipment to work on modern automobile engines. Office staff should not be using manual typewriters when competitors are using word processors. Warehouse workers should not be physically propelling pallets toward the loading dock when your competitors are using fancy new lift trucks.

Says Warren Blanding, president of the Customer Service Institute: "If a manager gets a complaint that a service giver has alienated a customer through poor performance or even through impoliteness, the first question that the manager should ask is whether the service giver was provided with resources needed to keep the customer satisfied."

Jerry Stead, CEO of Square D Company of Milwaukee, says: "You've got to get down and try to provide the resources, the priorities and the environment at all levels in the company so [the company] can be responsive [to its customers]. You've got to listen to what your people need." He refers to this management practice as "the revolution inside."

Good customer service often is a result of professional application and control of resources more than anything else. Poor service sometimes is not the fault of the person handling a transaction with a customer.

Communication with Customers

You know what they want. They know what to expect of you.

The American Management Association found in a survey that "high-growth companies" stay in touch with their markets and willingly spend the money to do so. They know their customers, and they keep their knowledge fresh.

Customer communication is important because from it you learn things that you cannot learn any other way.

- You learn whether they're satisfied.
- You learn what they bought and what they *didn't* buy, and why.
- You learn what they came in expecting to buy and to pay.
- You learn preferences and how they are changing over time.

The missing link in service often is intense awareness of the customer point of view.

Managers must be taught to realize that, from the customer point of view, dozens of things can go wrong—from improper recording at the outset of a transaction to late delivery and denial of service at the other end. A single mistake, from many possible errors in actions and decisions made, can alienate a customer. (It's enough to make you think, sometimes, that total customer satisfaction is a result of luck.)

In the Customer's Shoes

The best we can do is put ourselves in the customer's shoes: Do things for a customer the way that the customer would do them for himself or herself.

So two-way communication is vital to quality service delivery. If we're going to have a chance to win customer satisfaction, we need to know what the customer thinks—*our* customer, not the "average" customer who populates national economic statistics.

Bradley Printing Company invites representatives of client companies to watch their jobs being manufactured in the printing plant. They tell employees that clients are very interested in how their projects end up.

The company found that customer satisfaction went up leaps and bounds. One Bradley vice president said: "Our employees were capable of relating to what their customer wanted and took pride in what they were doing."

A fine example of two-way communication is noticeable in a company that offers drilling services to the oil and gas industry. A vice president of the company reports: "Our sales force visits the purchaser before every job. Salespeople review data and interpret it for the client's chief engineer. Then they return to the home office and make recommendations on the basis of their interpretations of the data obtained from the client."

Tragically (for the outlook of a company), some companies feel that talking with customers is a colossal waste of time.

Talk with Customers Slows Sales?

Jim Kowalski, co-owner with his wife of several very successful supermarkets in St. Paul, Minnesota, says: "Some food retailers don't even want their employees talking with customers because it interferes with sales per person-hour. "They forget that this is absolutely, positively a people business." So is any business that sells to people.

Generous Return Policy

I estimate that 90 percent or more of all claims and requests for adjustments are justified, in most industries. Most retailers estimate that dishonest customers who return items that they have already used or bought elsewhere account for fewer than 5 percent of returns. Therefore it makes no sense whatsoever to examine thoroughly the basis for every claim, thereby running up costs and reducing the profit margin on a sale or assuring a loss. Adopt a no-fault approach to claims and requests for refunds or returns unless the amount involved is very high. The result will be an overall savings in the cost of processing claims plus substantially improved customer goodwill.

Says Gwen Baum, director of customer satisfaction for the Neiman Marcus department store chain: "If you let profit protection or security rule the way you treat customers, satisfaction is bound to suffer."

Neiman Marcus is gracious with gripers and people who return merchandise. "We're not just looking for today's sale," says Baum. "We want a long-term relationship with our customers. If that means taking back a piece of Baccarat crystal that isn't from one of our stores we'll do it."

Hechinger Co., a Maryland-based retailer of hardware and home and gardening gear, accepts returns even when a customer obviously has abused them. The company also sends a dozen roses to any customer who becomes particularly perturbed.

Hechinger's return policies seem to have helped profits instead of hurting them. Earnings have compounded 29 percent annually since the company went public in 1971.

Guaranteed Service

Quill Corporation, a mail order office supply house in Lincolnshire, Illinois, that has 1,100 employees, offers a 90-day guarantee on every product. No questions. If you aren't satisfied with an item, return it, and your money will be refunded, the company tells customers. Quill has not gone broke.

Norrell Temporary Services of Atlanta promises clients that they won't have to pay if ever they are disappointed in the performance of Norrell's temporary employees—even if the reason for dissatisfaction doesn't surface for weeks.

Bea Ruffin, vice president of marketing, says that this guarantee of satisfaction is one reason that "our rate of sales growth outstripped the average rate of growth for the entire temporary employment industry."

Alvin L. Burger developed a number of businesses based upon a concept of service guarantees supported by these standards:

- Promises of *guaranteed* results cannot be a marketing tool alone. A no-holds-barred effort to achieve perfection must be built into operational structure.
- Guarantees must be self-punitive, making the cost of mistakes so high that producing promised results is the only viable option.

The successful businesses that Burger started are Hospitality Purchasing Corporation which provides furniture, fixtures, and equipment to hotels, offices, convention centers, and food service companies; GSG (Guest Satisfaction Guaranteed) Hotel Management Corporation; and Guaranteed Results, Inc., which accepts clients in any product or service area.

Attention to Detail

Leading customer service companies attend to the "little things" such as how long it takes their employees to answer the phone. They make sure they're one or two notches better than competitors.

These companies use only business forms that are crisply printed and clean. Their employees are well groomed and dressed tastefully.

Reports the American Management Association: "Successful companies have standards for response time, systems for monitoring customer complaints, and networks for moving information to people who can act upon it."

Very, Very Picky

Original Research II of Chicago is determined to be perfect at all times. So they are very, very picky. The company's business is conducting customer satisfaction surveys. Many of their clients are auto dealerships.

Says Denise Foy of Original Research: "Our people get consistent feedback on performance. Every day they receive a grade in six areas of performance on the phone such as listening skills, control of a conversation, responsiveness, and adhering to the script."

Once every 10 days all 350 "communicators" attend a seminar. Seminars cover topics such as

- How to handle an angry customer.
- How to use tone, pitch, and inflection to let a customer know that you care.
- How to be responsive.

In the spirit of being similarly detail oriented, take a look at your packaging some day. Is it, perhaps, so impenetrable that only martial arts experts with hands of steel can open it without using a machete?

Avoid food wraps that can't be opened without a scissors or sharp knife, blister packaging so tough that the item inside is endangered in the opening process, and packing tape that can only be cut with a very sharp instrument such as a razor blade.

Sensitivity to Customer Needs and Wants

Increased sensitivity has been showing up in the economy at an accelerating rate. Auto repair services such as The Mobile Wrench work on your car wherever it is, even if it just limped into a rest stop out on the Interstate. Banks such as the Wells Fargo Bank stay open on Saturdays. Glass companies replace your windshield while your car sits in the company parking lot. Convenience stores stay open 24 hours a day, 7 days a week.

Copy the spirit of these customer-sensitive strategies if you want to stay in step with modern needs such as those noted by Mike Ferraro, vice president of Mervyn's department stores who said: "Time is more valued today. Contrary to what we might have thought, people don't want to sit in line at Mervyn's."

Busy Consumers

"I think a lot of the impatience of consumers," Ferraro continued, "has to do with the fact that all the adults in many families are working. A wife doesn't have as much time as she used to have. She's committed to an 8 to 5 schedule because her income is vital to the financial survival of her family. But she also has a lot of house work and, often, child care to do once she gets home."

Spotting Changing Tastes

"People like this want to get in and out quickly, particularly if they are on their lunch hours. They don't want to commit an hour to shopping any more."

Benetton Group Spa, Italian manufacturer and seller of ready-made apparel, established a system for responding rapidly to customer preferences. The system spots consumer tastes and accelerates production pace to satisfy tastes within weeks.

When a sale is rung up at a Benetton store, type, color, and size of items are recorded along with a store code. This information from all stores is digested by a computer that announces hot products, hot colors, where they are hot geographically, and so on.

Computer printouts from all sales are sent to regional agents who create their own computer sheets and send them to the home office in Trevino, Italy. As soon as a pattern is clear, finishing is rushed through to shipping of fashions that are most favored by customers.

The company's Castrette operation features modern lasers and robotics that process and move orders to destinations. All merchandise is prelabeled for specific destinations. And it is tagged with correct price in the currency of its destination.

A Customer Service Growth Industry

Airlines began a period of greater sensitivity to customers after years of customer disdain following deregulation during the Reagan administration. American Airlines, for instance, increased the number of employees at gates and ticket counters during busy periods to reduce the duration of waiting periods for customers. For instance, when a departing wide-body airliner is expected to be at least 65 percent full—75 percent for a narrow-body plane—an extra agent is stationed at the gate. A second gate agent is routinely added 35 minutes before a flight.

This kind of treatment contrasts with that of organizations that allow managers to toy with customers just to make their own performance look better. A clever manager may decide that he's going to save the company some money by delaying the point at which his staff tells customers what their options are. He knows that by the time employees tell customers what their rights are, it'll be too late for customers to exercise them. Employees respond, in mock surprise: "Oh, didn't you know that you could . . .?" (You dummy, you.) This treatment was mentioned specifically among "most common gripes" in a list compiled by the American Society for Quality Control (ASQC).

The Transfer-and-Don't-Answer-Trick

Another common ASQC gripe was transferring customers, when they call, to other phones and then not answering the second phone. To counter this uncouth treatment, make sure switchboard operators monitor calls to see if the party to which a caller is transferred actually answers. Operators shouldn't allow phones to ring into perpetuity.

Sensitive to customer needs more than ever before, American corporations such as Chrysler Corporation are writing service policies. Chrysler calls one of its policies "The Car Buyer's Bill of Rights":

Every American has the right to a quality vehicle.
Every American has the right to long-term protection.
Every American has the right to friendly treatment, honest service, and competent repairs.
Every American has the right to a safe vehicle.
Every American has the right to redress grievances.

Total perfection in a vehicle is impossible, maintains Chairman Lee Iacocca. But an uncaring response is inexcusable. Chrysler has a Customer Arbitration Board that helps customers get satisfaction.

Personal Service

In the size of large corporations lies opportunity . . . for a corporation. Customers probably don't really expect personal service. So when you provide it, you are impressing them mightily, and they will remember.

Train your people to provide, in one-on-one transactions, the same personal, individual treatment they provide when they buy a used car from a neighbor for their child or a young relative.

There is hope for personal service in large organizations because every transaction involves one customer and one business representative at a time, even though many people may become involved. Promote the idea that a customer is not dealing with a multinational corporation but with one person who represents that multinational corporation.

Let's say that a consumer walks into an appliance store and buys a washing machine. The salesperson treats her respectfully and willingly spends all the time needed to satisfy her. That customer is going to feel good about this buying experience. She won't even think about the fact that the organization behind the salesperson employs half a million people.

The American Society for Quality Control suggests specific personal service:

> When equipment isn't working, do things for customers manually instead of not doing them at all. Tell employees in no uncertain terms that they are never to refuse an order or plead inability to answer questions just because "the computer isn't working." When an employee claims that he or she can't take an order because he'd have to write it, he's saying to customers: "I don't want to help you if it means that I have to work at it."
>
> When a fairly expensive product doesn't work, pick it up, don't put the customers to even greater inconvenience by requiring them to bring the product back themselves.

Train employees to say to customers: "If it doesn't work, give us a call and we'll pick it up and bring you a new one."

Employees should never say, with or without a smile: "If it doesn't work, just bring it back." Such behavior is another instance of arranging matters to suit the company, but the devil take the customer. Bringing back their purchases is a lot of trouble for customers, especially when a purchase is something they use every day such as a car or an appliance.

Some warranties, to the credit of business, state that the seller will pick up the product if it doesn't work, and repair it.

Take no customer for granted. Let them know how important they are.

Some businesses send a lot of thank you notes. Baron Hilton, for example, answered all complaint letters to his hotels with personal letters.

Commission selling, by the way, is a means of promoting personal service, if employees perceive the connection between friendly, informed, fast service and greater income.

Exceptional Service

The idea is catching on: make your service even better than your customers expect. That way they are sure to notice it, to react to it with commendations of it to friends and relatives, and to want more of it.

Colby Chandler, chairman of Eastman Kodak, expressed the concept when he addressed the National Quality Forum. He called for a new service strategy that reaches beyond "customer satisfaction" to "customer delight."

Delightful Experiences

Here are some delightful customer experiences: A mother put her baby on a Delta Air Lines plane that was to be met by her husband at the arrival point. The plane was leaving when she remembered that she'd forgotten to pack the baby's formula for the flight.

In a panic she asked a Delta attendant for help. The attendant contacted the pilot who radioed Operations. He asked them to pick up the formula and bring it to him on the taxi strip. An agent on a tug drove to the taxiway with the formula and tossed it up to the copilot leaning out his open window.

That's exceptional service.

New customers of Eastham's service station on Wisconsin Avenue in Bethesda, Maryland, including new members of Congress and employees in the Wisconsin Avenue embassies, are astounded by the exceptional service that they receive.

Here's an example of Eastham employees in action: It's already 90 degrees during morning rush hour, another day in a summer heat wave. A driver steers out of dense traffic and noses into Eastham's. Two attendants run toward the car. "Good morning!" they yell out to the driver who's barely cracking his window so his air conditioned air won't escape. The two attendants scurry about swiftly pumping gas, cleaning every inch of glass, and shouting for the driver to unlatch his hood. Hands fly among the hoses and belts checking oil and water levels.

A drop of sweat falls from one employee's forehead and lands on the front bumper. Quickly he bends over and wipes it off with a clean cloth.

The entire service process lasts about three minutes. The happy driver eases his car back into a crowded lane of traffic, wearing a smile. When was the last time this happened to you?

Eastham's, by the way, "does about twice as much business as the average service station in America," says Jerry Antosh, Washington, D.C., district manager for Exxon.

Can you tolerate a little more about Eastham's service? Bob Eastham, operator of the station, has plants hanging in his rest rooms. He rotates flowers in the flower beds nearly surrounding the station every season and trims the shrubbery weekly. Lying on end tables beside leather-covered furniture in his waiting room are current issues of *Vogue, Smithsonian,* and *National Geographic.*

Eastham pays his attendants an average of $35,000 per year.

Eastham's, to be sure, is an exception among service stations. Business is good because customers get product *and* service, unlike the situation in most full-service stations. The result of inferior service at "full-service" stations is that consumers buy their gas at self-service stations. I think that consumers don't want to pay a big premium for attendants to not smile, not remember their names, not check under the hood, not check the tire pressure, and not clean the windshield.

But even low-priced self-service stations leave a person dissatisfied. It would cost these stations no more for clerks to smile and to address consumers by name, recalling it from the last gas purchase—or, at least, noting names from credit cards or driver's licenses and using them.

Reliable Service

Promise what you can deliver: then deliver what you promise. But, remember, the higher you raise expectations the harder it is to meet them routinely.

In recognizing this fact, some service experts suggest that if you think that you can meet a service expectation in three days, promise it in five days. If you must provide an estimated bill, err on the high side so that you can surprise the customer.

But other service authorities warn about risking customer displeasure with a high time or price estimate. I agree. I think it's unwise to disappoint a customer initially by leading him or her to believe that your performance time is slower or your prices higher than your competitors'.

Keep Your Promises

But pull out all stops to keep your promises, whatever they are. When the inevitable happens (once a year or so) and you aren't able to meet a deadline, call the customer and set a new time instead of letting them show up at the appointed time, expecting delivery, says the American Society for Quality Control.

Graebel Van Lines intends to be reliable. Three of 11 points in its "Customer Service Guidelines" are

We will do it right the first time, every time.

We will treat every article as if it belongs to our mother.
Slogans, buzz words, rah rah, and a list of guidelines like these do not make superior customer service happen. Only our dedication, commitment, and professionalism will do that.

Three cheers for Graebel.

Reliability is important in advertising claims, too. This is a fact that escapes many who feel that customers overlook or cheerfully tolerate puffery. But loss-leader selling is not mere puffery. Exaggeration that leads prospects to believe that your service provides benefits that it does not provide is more than puffery.

You cannot add quality to a product or service with advertising claims. At best, advertising persuades a potential customer to try your product or service. But the first try is a trial. If the trial exposes unreliability, then the long-term sales that yield long-term success for your organization will not occur.

Fail to deliver what your advertising promises and you might not see a new customer a second time, warns Muriel G. Adamy, senior consultant for service quality and customer relations in the offices of Argyle Associates, Inc., and a former director of quality-consumer affairs for ITT Corporation.

Burger King, the chain of fast-food restaurants, discovered the truth in this assertion the hard way. Burger King had been a drag on Pillsbury's earnings for years, said an account executive at Piper, Jaffray and Hopwood, a brokerage firm that had researched Burger King and its parent company before and after Pillsbury was acquired by the British conglomerate, Grand Met.

A major reason for Burger King's poor performance, said the broker, was slippage between advertised claims of service and the reality of good service. He said that the company would spend a great deal of money making claims but that customers would discover that the claims were mere shams.

IMAGINARY SERVICE: COMMON CHARACTERISTICS

Some organizations seem to think that service is easy. They make a few pronouncements from Mount Olympus, run a few stories in the employee newsletter, retain a motivational speaker to 'wow' a middle management meeting, and then they go on to other work, confident that now they've "got" service.

These are the kinds of companies that fall into the trap of thinking that service is no more than

Positive thinking. So they emphasize motivational programs.
Telephone and courtesy skills. So they circulate a booklet.

Problem handling and listening. So they put up signs that say "Customer first. Listen. Assist."

These programs play a role in service, all right—a small role.

Positive Thinking

Motivational programs that promote positive thinking are particularly popular for nonexempt customer contact people. They learn to speak as if they are enthusiastic, eager to help, and very, very friendly. Often run by outside consultants, short motivational sessions are not designed to improve skills or knowledge but just to change behavior and short-term attitude.

Motivational sessions make employees feel good, but the good feeling dissipates quickly in the cauldron of daily give and take. After a few rounds of motivation, employees become cynical about the effectiveness of all training.

Motivational programs can have a positive effect. But they must be supported by skills training that equips employees to perpetuate that effect by repeating the basis for it. Employees must learn to take productive initiative that achieves positive outcome that, in itself, motivates.

Telephone and Courtesy Skills

Skills for handling telephone transactions, ranging from listening and probing to handling complaints, are combined in training programs with courtesy skills. Programs are designed to increase customer service representatives' efficiency and to present a positive, upbeat image to customers.

A courteous employee does tend to produce greater customer satisfaction. But employees must also take responsibility for resolving issues and assuring action. If the entire organization is not prepared to be responsive, then employees will have to deliver service in spite of the company. But this creates stress and frustration.

In the telephone courtesy category, it hardly needs saying, we hope, that answering machines ought to be "verboten" in any business that depends upon customers for economic survival.

Bernard Goldberg, CBS TV correspondent, posed a question about business's apparent unresponsiveness to consumers on the "Evening News": "How many times have you tried the customer service department and received the recorded massage 'At this time all of our representatives are busy'?"

After long experience with recorded messages like this customers might conclude that customer service departments consist entirely of answering machines grinding away in solitary obstinacy.

Problem Handling

Unfortunately, business's attitude too often is that the customer is the problem. Employees learn to handle "problem customers" instead of "customers' problems." Problem-handling programs focus on irate customers. They consist of skill-based training for customer contact workers, and they deal with managing personalities and identifying problems before they flare up.

Problem-handling and listening skills are useful, to be sure. Used properly they are part of everyday external and internal interactions. But never should they be viewed as the total substance of a customer service training program.

Internal Problems

When a customer has a problem, an employee may need to resolve the problem by requesting help, by clearly communicating the problem to others, by figuring out ways to prevent similar situations, and by keeping her or his boss informed.

Internal communications improve as a result of the annual national Hyatt In Touch Day, referred to earlier. According to Karen Rugen, assistant vice president for public relations, there were two goals for national Hyatt In Touch Day:

> To bring corporate and hotel staffs together so greater rapport will develop and so that they will work together to support each other in improving customer service.
>
> To give headquarters staff a better understanding of and appreciation for hotel employees "who really keep our company running."

Some employees, said Ms. Rugen, asked for a "reverse" Hyatt In Touch Day so they could work in the corporate offices.

External Problems

To resolve external customer problems, employees need skills to handle complex internal transactions. To maximize effectiveness of external customer problem solving, these skills should be the same ones taught for handling internal customer problems. External customers are no less human than coworkers and internal demands no less legitimate than the end users' needs.

Selling Skills: No Substitute for Service Skills

Sales and service definitely are blood brothers, but management should never demand an immediate and obvious financial payback for service. The benefits of service are substantial and long lasting; but they don't occur immediately.

Selling skills occasionally are taught to customer-contact employees to increase the amount of each sale—by plus-selling and by cross-selling. But customer satisfaction requires more than sales skills.

If a company calls selling skills "customer service," it's fooling itself.

Real quality service programs achieve increased customer satisfaction through awareness of all customer needs beyond successful completion of the current sale.

If the desired result of improved service quality is merely short-term business improvement from existing customers, sales skill training is appropriate. However, this kind of training is unlikely to address long-term customer satisfaction.

Selling in Sheep's Clothing

Sometimes "customer service" that's really selling in sheep's clothing is enhanced with incentives. It is true that without incentives, salaried and hourly workers are less likely to take initiative and cross sell. But, with incentives, care must be taken that sales do not take precedence over other critical job responsibilities such as sincerely friendly and helpful service.

Cross-selling is particularly popular among banks as a job responsibility for tellers.

Research by Barry Leeds & Associates found that 55 to 65 percent of banks pay incentives to "platform people" in an effort to spur them to cross sell. The percentage has been rising.

The Wrong Training

These are some of the shortcomings of customer service training:

For Front-line Only

Every employee should be tuned in the service program and turned on by it. If "support troops" do not recognize the need for service and its value to their organization, then customer contact people will have trouble consistently obtaining the help that they need from elsewhere in the company to service customers.

Too Short, No Follow-up

Training commonly occurs in a classroom and it lasts less than two hours, sometimes less than an hour. Often, the trainer introduces segments of the training, turns on the projector, lowers the light level, and leaves. Customer service training is treated like vaccination. Give 'em a shot and forget it.

Unfortunately, this kind of training is preferred by most companies. When employee skills show little or no improvement, management blames employees for not paying attention to training.

In Chapter 12 we explain why this kind of training is a waste of time and money.

Significance of Service Is Overlooked

Training isn't integrated with performance management systems, with management support or with anything else. Training is an island unto itself, floating in a large lake. Instead, training and the many elements of organizational success should all jump in the lake together.

External-Only Focus

Virtually all service quality training programs focus on resolving issues external to an organization. Very, very few of them deal with internal service issues or the relation between internal service quality and external customer satisfaction, as they should. When they do, they are held up as models and they are given awards.

SERVICE AND SALES: MARRIAGE OF CONVENIENCE

Customer service enhances the effectiveness of marketing strategies and wins greater sales and continuous business.

Marketing gets the customers and service keeps them.

What's more, after-sale service is essential in an organization that intends to stay in business. What you do for a customer after he or she has signed on the dotted line is just as important as what you did to earn the sale, as far as customer retention goes.

Neiman Marcus department stores send mailgrams to mail-order customers, during peak seasons, to inform them of order status. Service also sells. Consider order upgrading. Customer service employees working on phones can do it. Any customer-contact sales employee can do it. After taking on order for, say, 10,000 gallons of acetone, they might say, "If you buy 15,000 gallons, you know, you get a 10 percent discount." Or "If you buy 100 more computers I can give you 10 percent off on the entire purchase."

Federal Express is convinced that improved customer service skills made employees in its Business Service Centers more effective as salespeople. Says Kenneth R. Newell, former vice president of sales and operations and now vice president UK and Ireland, "Customer service has given the 'reorder' concept a new meaning in our Service Centers."

Easy to Buy

Customer service makes it much easier for prospects and customers to buy! Service assures positive attitudes toward the company, its products and services, and its employees. Service also is a slippery Teflon coating over the occasional problems and shortcomings that bedevil any organization's operations.

But sales and service must work in tandem, in full knowledge of what the other function is doing.

Coordination of Sales and Service

Jere A. Brown, Director of SLC Consultants, Inc., in Chicago, says that sales and service representatives must convey the same "messages and images" or customers become confused. For instance, if a service rep tells a customer that a certain model has been discontinued but the sales rep still tries to sell it, the buyer wonders whom to trust.

When service-minded employees provide service with the following characteristics they stimulate the buying motive:

Fast Service

In many families all the adults are working. None of them has as much time to shop as they did. In addition, women, whose income often is vital to the financial survival of their families, usually have housework to do when they get home and child care too. They love stores that get them in and out quickly.

With emphasis on efficiency and productivity in human resources management today, most employees seem to have more to do than ever. Any company's employee doing business with you appreciates your efficiency.

Reliable Service

Unless your customers can depend upon you, they may opt for self-service, when they can find it. When they do it themselves, they reason, they are more likely to be satisfied. It's a strategy that's being taken up with greater frequency.

Consumers may not be quite as turned off by service as John O'Shaughnessy, professor at Columbia Business School, but he has a point: "People want the personal element removed from their transactions in almost the same way that they would like to see cancer removed from cigarettes."

Says John Deighton, assistant professor of marketing at the University of Chicago: "There is a lot of unbundling of service and product going on as consumers become willing conspirators in the assumption of more responsibilities."

So it is that we see these things happening:

1. At transportation terminals, luggage carts are chosen over porters by people who want faster service, "less hassle," and no tip.
2. Buyers at appliance centers, shoe stores, and fast-food outlets have willingly turned into their own salespeople.

3. Robots are appearing in retail stores where, in response to keys punched by customers, they go get the merchandise and present it for check-out as in a video store in Minneapolis' Crystal Court.
4. Mervyn's, a chain of more than 200 moderately priced department stores owned by Dayton Hudson Corporation, installed a self-service system in its women's shoe department. Boxes of shoes in all sizes are displayed front and center. A sample shoe is displayed on top of each box. Only after a customer finds a shoe that she likes and that fits does she deal with a service worker—the cashier.
   Despite relatively high prices, sales in the Mervyn's revamped shoe department rose by a double-digit percentage the first year, more than any other Mervyn's department.
   "One reason for the sales increase," said William P. Condaxis, divisional merchandise manager, was that "customers no longer get frustrated standing on the floor waiting for a sales clerk."
   Is this "no service service" a legitimate way to circumvent bad service instead of training employees to provide quality service and, at the same time, a way to increase sales? Consumers seem to be saying "Yes."
5. At ARCO service stations customers pump their gas at high-speed pumps. Then, if they're hungry, they walk over to the adjacent AM/PM convenience store to make themselves a hamburger that's been kept on a warmer since it was made. They may extract a quart of milk from a cooler on the way to the check-out line where they meet their first service person.
   In 1974 only 9 percent of gas sold in this country came from self-service pumps. Today, 80 percent of gas is pumped by customers. Seventy-five percent of drivers buy self-service gas. We suspect that a major reason that customers avoid full-service stations is that they pay $2 to $5 more per tank of gas and still receive no service for their money. (Try to find a service station attendant who wipes your windshield and checks your oil.)
6. In 1979, 9,275 automated teller machines catered to the whims of bank customers. Now there are more than 70,000 of them. Fear of getting lost in velvet-rope labyrinths are not the only reason that bank customers prefer machines to tellers.
7. But even trips to the teller machine are too tedious for an increasing number of people. Unless they need cash in hand, they are transferring funds between accounts and checking their balances via touchpad telephone or home computer.
   Sears's and IBM's "Prodigy" service to home computer users had a fast start in 1989 providing check balance service and many

other services that eliminate services dispensed by live employees in the past.

8. Continental and Eastern airlines supplemented ticketing agents with ticketing machines on some routes.
9. Hotel guests increasingly review bills via closed-circuit TV and then pay with an automatic charge to their credit cards.
10. Rental car customers, armed with computer-generated rental agreements, move straight from airport terminal to waiting cars without so much as a "hello" to counter personnel.

Technology may increase the desire for self-service and, thereby, increase sales, too, because Americans are more comfortable with the technology of self-service than ever before.

Keep in mind the possibility that consumers might become disabused of the self-service concept, though, if it moves too far toward "high tech" on the high-touch–high-tech continuum. That people begin to miss the personal touch of personal service as more and more work is assumed by machines is a point made by John Naisbitt whose Naisbitt Group, Inc., of Washington, D.C., publishes a newsletter entitled *The Trend Letter*. So when a business offers self-service and cuts down on staffing, high quality of personal service by remaining employees and professional training is even more important than service is for full-service firms.

Nevertheless, I have seen many self-service firms abandon the service concept, reasoning that customers aren't paying for service so they shouldn't expect to receive it.

But service is here to stay, even if it's involved only in helping people serve themselves as a way to achieve the greatest reliability.

Service does not require huge outlays of money, but it does require long-term commitment, a fact understood by incomparable service firms such as Original Research II, Federal Express, and the Disney organization.

Benefits of service make the effort to provide it worthwhile. Zenger-Miller, the Cupertino, California, research and consulting firm, surveyed hundreds of companies, then drew conclusions about what they found: "Whenever we encountered head-to-head competition between companies on the basis of service quality, there seemed to be a recurring theme," the company reported. "The customer-focused organization was challenging or surpassing the transaction-focused company."

The Disney companies, Federal Express, Original Research II, and, yes, Eastham's service station—all know the secret that is "customer focus."

Focus doesn't require a lot of money—just commitment.

8

Little Things Make a Big Difference

CULTURE AND CONSENSUS IN SERVICE

Management commitment yields a nurturing corporate service culture as surely as a bulb planted in the fall yields a flower in the spring.

This corporate culture, this flower of management commitment, adorns and enhances service environment. In such an environment great service is routine, assumed. It is traditional.

A corporate culture that favors and rewards service is fundamental.

Once a company reaches a happy state of flourishing service supported by a consensus and yielding a legacy of commitment, it has realized the full flower of quality service. Greater sales and profit are its reward.

Achieving a state of affairs in which quality service becomes an integral element in the organizational culture must be the objective of every organization that truly considers service to be an essential management strategy.

A service culture is the result of careful planning and strategizing as specified in Chapters 2 and 3. It is the result of sequential development of all elements in a service strategy, from a service philosophy to service specifications for every function and every job.

A culture of service is first among the basics of quality service.

HOW TO KEEP CUSTOMERS ONCE YOU HAVE THEM

The basic function, the purpose of customer service, is to retain customers and to keep them buying.

You want to develop customers for whom loyalty is a natural instinct instead of customers like this fellow:

> "I'm the fellow who goes into a restaurant, sits down, and patiently waits while the waitresses finish their visiting before taking my order.
> "I'm the fellow who goes into a department store and stands quietly while the clerks finish their chitchat.
> "I'm the fellow who drives into a service station and never blows his horn, but lets the attendant take his time.
> "You might say I'm a nice guy. But, do you know who else I am? *I'm the customer who never returns.*
> "It confuses me to see business spending so much money every year to get me back, when I was there in the first place."

I still see businesses spending millions of dollars on advertising and store renovation and then working very hard to make sure they don't come back.

Car dealerships are a good example of this reverse logic. I see salespeople eating cookies and drinking coffee while customers walk through the dealership's show room. Or five salespeople jostle each other to reach the customer first. It's either feast or famine for customers.

As for maintenance service, I recently took my car back to a dealership for the third time with the same complaint: it wouldn't start. They charged $25 to tell me that it was necessary to replace the battery. Two months earlier they had "fixed" the same problem for $200 without mentioning the battery!

When I complained to the service manager he said: "You're wrong, but we want to keep you happy so we'll credit your account $25 toward the cost of future work."

That didn't make me happy at all. The service manager clearly didn't understand how to handle dissatisfied customers. Nor did he realize that I had no intention of ever returning to claim my $25 credit. Now I patronize a dealership that takes me five times longer to reach.

The offensive dealership exemplified poor service and poor training. This is a firm that has spent millions of dollars claiming outstanding customer service. Apparently they think their employees will see the ads and be inspired to provide the service.

Wrap your corporate arms around present customers in a benevolent bear hug. Few would disagree that customers are hard to find. So keep them. Make them want to stay.

Friendliness

The corporate slogan of Hy-Vee Food Stores is: "A helpful smile in every aisle." It may be corny, but the principal is right on the mark. [My 90-year-old mother won't shop at any other store.]

Plain, "ordinary" friendliness works.

What is friendliness? What customers interpret as friendliness is summed up by this list of friendly employee behavior:

1. Make eye contact.
2. Smile. Greet the customer. When selling in a services setting, meet every customer with a smile and a friendly greeting such as "Hello" or a sincere "How are you?" A warm smile can bring out the sunshine in a customer's face and assure a repeat visit.
3. Use the customer's name, if it's known. If it isn't known, take the name from a credit card or check, or ask for it.
4. Answer questions or obtain answers quickly.
5. Hurry.
6. Talk, act in an enthusiastic, sincere, and personal way, not in a routine, bored manner.
7. Give the customer total attention. Employees should never act impatiently, as if they want to finish with the customer as soon as possible.
8. Speak in a friendly manner. Compliment the customer. Make friendly comments.
9. Listen. Ask questions to obtain all information needed to resolve any complaint they might have.
10. Offer unsolicited help now and then. If a customer looks and acts confused, offer to answer any question he or she may have.
11. Make positive parting comments such as "We appreciate your business" and "Come see us again."

You can remember many of these friendly strategies if you remember the name of the umbrella under which most of them fit: "Treat customers as friends." It's essential for anyone in a service position to have a friendly greeting for each customer, to show sincere interest in the customer as an individual, to thank the customer for any purchases and inviting him or her to return. The same principle applies whether you are dealing with a purchasing agent or an individual run-of-the mill consumer.

One customer service training program in the hospitality industry (food, lodging, entertainment, recreation) conveys the friendliness principle by teaching employees to

Speak cordially.
Smile.
Look people in the eye.
Know guests' names and learn to remember them.
Develop systems for transmitting a guest's name to other staff members.
Go about your job professionally and cordially.
Use friendly comments at every opportunity.

How-to-do-it information can be imprinted upon employee memories with creative "training" techniques that attract and hold attention—like the board game used by Sonesta Hotels.

"The idea was to create a training tool that would grab workers' attention," says Jacqueline Sonnabend, the corporation's director of human resources and daughter of Chairman Roger Sonnabend. She concedes some workers greet the game with cynicism, but adds that the challenge, prizes, and inherent amusement quickly take over.

The game is played on a conventional folding game board. It is laid out like the children's game "Chutes & Ladders" and like a simple version of "Life." Four or five teams of two players each move their tokens with a toss of dice.

A team that lands on a "service" space must answer questions printed on cards like those in "Trivial Pursuit." The questions present situations that test the players' familiarity with Sonesta standards, and occasionally their resourcefulness.

Typically, three answers are printed on each card—a good answer, a better one, and the best one. But the players' answers don't have to be exactly the same. Their opponents rate their answers and award the appropriate amount of game money. There's a referee to settle disputes.

"We expect arguments," says Sonnabend. "It's part of the training aspect. Players have to defend what they're saying and that gets them thinking."

Players vie for their department title, worth $100, then for division title (each hotel usually has three divisions), worth another $200. Winners of each hotel's title receive $500 and a trip to Boston in September for the chain's overall championship.

Overall champions win another $1,000 and a week's stay at any Sonesta resort, plus airfare.

Sonesta supervisors suggest situation questions to Sonnabend, based on their experiences. One in Amsterdam posed this puzzler: A male rock star enters the hotel coffee shop and monopolizes everyone's attention. You're a waiter, and you notice a female patron in the corner is alone and sulking. What do you do?

"One good answer," says Sonnabend, "is to ask a male waiter to go over and talk politely with her. Just show her some attention."

The friendliness of people who are not friends or acquaintances still is so rare that it wins gratitude and a measurable increment of new business.

Nance Reb, manager of a Perkins restaurant outlet, believes that it's important to treat customers like house guests or as good friends. "Customer service is taking care of customers, making sure things are right," she says.

Personal Treatment

"I went to Sears over Christmas," says Bill Murray of Wilson Learning, a corporate training organization. "The clerk took my driver's license, gave it back, wished me a merry Christmas, then said, 'And have a happy birthday tomorrow.'"

"It was a nice surprise," said Murray. The employee checked Murray's birth date on his driver's license.

At the Norfolk Airport Hilton, where every employee receives customer service training regularly, maids actually say "Hello" to guests they meet coming out of rooms or walking in the hallway instead of acting busy or as if they don't see them.

Use the Customer's Name

We've mentioned one way to learn a customer's name—by glancing at the customer's driver's license. Credit cards may be the most frequent source of customer names for use by friendly employees.

Of course, an employee can always introduce himself or herself with "Hello. My name is Jane Smith. What's yours?"

Speak a customer's name repeatedly during a transaction. If you do you might remember it the next time the customer comes in. It's a wonderful way to win customer loyalty.

Peter Burwash, president of Peter Burwash International, management and consulting firm in Woodlands, Texas, recalls a gas station in Honolulu that asked him his name the first time he stopped there as a tourist in 1970.

"To this day," says Burwash, "no one else has ever asked me my name at a gas station. I came back two days later and they remembered it. Today, I live on the island six weeks a year and I've spent $19,000 there. I've never been to any other station in Hawaii."

"Customer loyalty," observes Burwash, "is an incredibly powerful thing. All it took was for those people to give me, a stranger, a sense of identity by calling me by my name."

People love to hear their names. But be sure that you pronounce them correctly. Addressing Ms. Smythe as "Ms. Smith" is worse than not addressing her at all.

Using a person's name is one type of "positive message." Positive communication of any kind give people good feelings about their buying experience, thereby making it more likely that they will return to buy again.

Each new employee of any of the 200 clubs operated by Dallas-based Club Corporation of America receives a copy of the company's "standards of operation," a list of 25 standards CCA uses to control service quality and consistency and corporate image. The first of these standards is that every member should be called by name at least four times while he or she is in the club. The second standard is that any member entering a club should be approached by a staff member within 15 seconds.

This is professional customer service at its best.

Every employee, from maids to desk clerks, uses customers' names repeatedly. They are taught to hurry to serve guests—and to express appreciation for their business with a warm, friendly smile.

Several years ago we introduced customer service performance standards in a four-page, 32-item form. It is important to judge employees' customer service performance by fixed standards. They must know what is expected of them if they are to be evaluated fairly.

Positive Interaction

Employees should make every customer feel like a king or queen, surely not as a serf—and certainly not as an villain sent to make their lives miserable or to waste their time.

Managers should do their best to keep employees in good moods and to make sure that they enjoy their work. When this condition exists, employees are motivated to greet customers, to offer help, to express friendly, complimentary comments, and to bid them goodbye when they leave.

Employees should find out what a customer's needs are, then react to them by making suggestions, offering information, and so on.

Always use friendly comments as "tools of the trade" just as reporters use questions as their tools of the trade.

The Friedman Group, retail training and development company headquartered in Los Angeles, teaches that contact with a customer is a social event.

Salespeople should never approach a customer with the hackneyed "Can I help you?" approach, says Marlene Cordry of The Friedman Group. Instead use a "special, creative 'opener'" that is social in nature. Refer to an article in the morning newspaper, a personalized T-shirt the customer is wearing, or a sporting event. These references are springboards to rapport with a customer.

"If a customer comes in and says that she saw 'the cutest little girls' outfit' while she was vacationing in Hawaii," Cordry says, "don't immediately ask color, size, and shape, but talk about Hawaii for a minute and about what the customer likes in children's fashions."

She calls this "schmoozing with customers."

Cordry tells trainees: "If everyone is going to be spending eight hours on the floor, why don't we have some fun."

Compliments

One customer service program emphasizes complimenting, which it calls positive feedback, and discourages negative feedback and "plastic" (phony) language. The program teaches employees to make friends of customers by complimenting, praising, and reinforcing feelings of self-worth.

Certainly it is true that millions of dollars, innovative product order-entry systems, stunning and spectacular packaging, and dramatic price cutting—all these attempts to capture patronage can be canceled out by a lack of recognition and attention.

"Is that a new suit you're wearing?" you might ask. Or say: "I've been noticing how well behaved your children are."

Compliment a customer's speaking voice, hairstyle, an article of clothing, or taste demonstrated by a purchase. By doing so, an employee reinforces the customer's feelings of self-worth.

Applying techniques such as these helped Riesbeck Food Markets maintain sales and profits despite massive layoffs at coal mines that are the major employers in its region, and despite population decline.

Richard Riesbeck proved his personal belief that in the food retailing business success or failure is determined by how customers are treated.

Here are more examples of positive statements:

"Ms. Osborne, we appreciate your business. Please call again."

"Sorry for the delay, Mr. Stevens. Nobody likes to be kept waiting."

Mr. Good! Great to hear from you again. How was your trip to Bora Bora?"

"That's a sizable order. We appreciate your business."

Negative Communication

Here are examples of negative statements:

"I'll come back when you're ready."
"Are those your kids?"
"I have no idea. Ask someone else?"
"We're busy now, can you call later?"
"Whatever possessed you to pick that one?"
"What do you expect?"
"Didn't you listen?"
"What you see is what you get."
"Wait a minute. I've got another call."
"Didn't I take care of that already?"
"That guy was a creep, wasn't he?"
"What do *you* want?"
"Speak up, please!"
"Don't ask *me*."
"Can't you just wait a minute?"
"Can't you read the sign?"
"That's not how we do it here."
"I have to go on break now. Sorry."
"Are you sick?"

Crooked Communication

And then there is "crooked" communication often uttered with a smile. Words express information that's opposite to thought or body language.

"Thanks for your business. Of course, now we have to worry about collecting from you."

"Oh, Mr. Rourke, how are you? I was afraid you'd call again."

"What a great design. It's a shame it won't work."

"Nice sunglasses. They disguise your bloodshot eyes."

"Let me seat you in the smoking section. People with your smelly habit should stick together."

"I'll do everything I can to help you. Thank goodness I'm leaving in five minutes."

Plastic Communication

Some employees become so numbed by daily routine, especially in high-traffic situations, that they lapse into a masquerade of superficial remarks, actions, and facial expressions. Customers perceive them as plastic, false, and insincere.

Employees may think that such comments are witty or cute. They usually backfire.

What customers *perceive* as a crooked or "plastic" statement *is* a crooked or plastic statement. We may not mean to be phony, but if a customer thinks we are, we've failed at our efforts to win customer satisfaction.

Learn to commend consistently and to do it consciously. Make customer recognition—and also praising of fellow workers—genuine, specific, and sincere.

Positive verbal and nonverbal communications give customers "good feelings" about their shopping experiences, making them feel important and valued by the business. The direct result is that they most likely will continue to buy.

More Friendliness

Employees should listen when a customer speaks instead of busying herself or himself with paperwork or even making an offhand remark to another employee or customer. Listening is complimenting.

Respond courteously and patiently to questions.
Be attentive and interested, always. Don't just act interested.
Be interested. If you want to you can always find something about a customer or her or his needs to be interested in.

Hustle

Clearly, you send a strong message to a customer when you hurry to complete a transaction instead of doing your imitation of the South American sloth. It's a compliment to the customer when you hurry. You declare your respect.

Be Appreciative

Take no customer for granted. Let customers know how important they are by thanking them for their purchases, in a spirited voice. Some businesspeople send a lot of thank you notes.

Recognize That the Customer Is Always Right

Of course, don't take the statement literally. Many members of the younger working generation don't take it at all. They seem to believe that the customer is always wrong. (See Chapter 5, "Don't Hire Employees Who Hate Customers.")

The phrase, "The customer is always right," has been widely disobeyed and dishonored since it was originated as the motto of the American merchant class by John Wanamaker, founder of Philadelphia's Wanamaker's department store.

You don't have to believe blindly that all customers are always right in order to act as if you believe it and to make customers think that you think they are right. Certainly, customers often are wrong: They are overbearing. They actually *intend* to use merchandise such as a new spring dress for a weekend and then to return it on Monday with an unimaginative excuse. They treat clerks and salespeople like servants required to respond to their every whim. They *insist* that they are right when you learned two years ago in a technical school run by your industry that they are wrong.

Stew Leonard's "world's largest dairy store" in Norwalk, Connecticut, does many things to develop whole company culture dedicated to producing satisfied customers. One of them is to give refunds to customers even on goods purchased in other stores.

More than 100,000 customers a week are served in the store. Sales approach $100 million a year—in one location. The store sells more of every item it carries than any other store in the world. It boasts sales of $2,700 for each of its 37,000 square feet of selling space, giving it the world's fastest-moving stock.

Still, some businesses perform as if the offensive adage, "The customer is always wrong," was their business philosophy. They react to customer complaints with the same alacrity as Stew Leonard's rock.

Truly service-driven companies with service-driven managers don't argue with the facts or try to persuade a customer that the buyer is wrong and the seller right. They listen and they respond. They hold hands. They seek out customer comments and take them to heart. And they do not consider doing so a burden or an avoidable expense.

They constantly keep in mind how it feels to be a customer.

Dependability

In service-driven companies, dependable service is a way of life. Management and employees work at it every day.

Leon Gorman, president of L. L. Bean, highly rated for its quality service, says that service is "a day-in, day-out, ongoing, never-ending, unremitting, persevering, compassionate type of activity."

In 1988, L. L. Bean won a National Quality Award for service from the U.S. Commerce Department. But the company still was dissatisfied because customers took the company up on its no-questions-asked return policy to the tune of 14 percent of annual sales—about $82 million worth in returns. It should be noted that in the mail-order clothing industry roughly 15 percent to 18 percent of basic apparel shipped is returned, according to a survey by Kurt Salmon Associates, a New York consulting firm. Alarmed, Bean hired a Harvard Business School professor as a consultant and inaugurated an 18-month, $2 million service improvement program.

The company gathered its 3,500 employees to launch the program that was given the theme: "Get It Right the First Time."

Bean scaled back expansion goals for the purpose of ensuring greater care in inspecting and shipping goods. Gorman said: "We don't mind fewer new customers as long as we do it right."

Deliver. Perform. Be quick and efficient in meeting customer needs. It's obvious that if you don't perform by fulfilling customer expectations, then complimentary language and the most attentive listening in the world won't be enough to retain a customer's loyalty.

Deliver: keep your promises.

Deliver: be dependable and trustworthy. Do this by

Telling the whole truth about the performance of your products and the effectiveness of your services.

- Making only promises that you are sure you can keep.
- Telling customers immediately about any developments that will disappoint any of their expectations. For instance, when you can't meet a deadline that your delivery people promised to meet, have those delivery people call and change the time. That's the least you can do since you are causing people a great deal of trouble even when you keep your delivery appointment. They've probably taken off from work, talking somebody into filling in for them. They may even be losing pay. When you've made an appointment with a customer, there's simply no justification for not showing up and not even calling to tell the customer that you won't be able to keep the appointment.
- Warning customers of impending service problems. Often they are allowed to discover late shipments for themselves, and also substitutions and back orders. This can be infuriating. Warn customers of service problems as soon as you become aware of them so that they can take action to minimize inconvenience or loss. In fact, go so far as to suggest alternatives and solutions to the problem that untimely delivery causes. Do not try to hide a problem hoping that customers won't notice it.
- Sharing economies and cost savings with customers. Tell managers that the company is committed to fair play in this way. Don't allow "clever" managers to decide that they're going to save the company money or realize a windfall by delaying the point at which they tell customers about their options. By the time their options are revealed, of course, it's too late to exercise them. Only

> then do such managers say, with mock surprise: "Oh, didn't you know that you could . . ." Fair play requires that you tell customers that:
> They can buy a little more and get something free.
> They will get a better price if they wait a few days to buy.
> They can buy last year's model, identical to this year's model, for 25 percent less.

A business determined to improve service standards must begin with a firm commitment not only to achieve a higher level of customer satisfaction but also to deliver this level of satisfaction *consistently* even if it means lower profits in the short run.

Dependable Service Through Planning

At an outdoor supplies mail-order company, a customer called to order a tent. The order taker did not have details needed to answer the customers' questions, so she transferred the call to a buyer. The order eventually was placed but not until 45 minutes after the initial call.

This company's order operators should have fingertip access to product specifications files to equip them to answer customer's questions.

A high-ticket gift catalog's sales during December were below plan. The company hadn't adequately anticipated its needs in setting up its new telephone system. The result was that 26,000 call attempts were blocked during that one month.

In a test, Catalog Media Corp. sent 500 requests for catalogs to mail-order companies. After three months only 65 percent of the catalogs had been mailed out by the companies. This debacle occurred despite the fact that mail-order companies had been bemoaning slow growth in the number of new catalog buyers.

That's the way it is in the customer service game: you can have profit-building customer service if you want to work for it; if you lag behind because you have too many dissatisfied customers (whether they complain or not), you have only yourself to blame.

9

Turning Your Business into a Shopping Service

BAN BANKER'S HOURS!

Satisfaction is your right. We intend to see that you get it.

— *Lee A. Iacocca, chairman, Chrysler Corporation*

The customer is always right.

—*John Wanamaker, founder of the Wanamaker's department store, Philadelphia*

"The whole store is a shopping service," says Luke Mansour, vice president of marketing for Mansour's of Columbus and LaGrange, Georgia, family-owned department and fine specialty store.

Now, that's the spirit of a customer service operation that helps out the marketing and advertising departments by delivering what advertising leads customers to expect.

For a business to provide service that imitates up-close and personal service today, it must offer service that's fast and convenient because the American life-style is fast, and convenient service saves time, thereby accelerating the pace of personal achievement.

Fast Service

NBC "Evening News" interviewed consumers for a report on customer service. The consumers complained: "They make you wait." "Clerks don't know what they're doing."

A New Bedford, Massachusetts, department store clerk found herself on national TV chatting on the phone while a customer twiddled her thumbs, waiting.

A California bank offers customers $5 if they are kept waiting in line for more than five minutes. A bank officer said: "If they stand in line, we're going to pay. If we make mistakes on their statements, we're going to pay. If we don't call them back in 24 hours, we're going to pay."

To save time for customers, Nordstrom's department stores provide such services as fetching items from other departments and wrapping merchandise at the counter where it's bought instead of at a distant counter on another floor.

So instruct your employees to hurry to get merchandise, to demonstrate it, to write up sales slips, to settle claims. "Hustle" compliments customers.

Example: Passenger claims are settled at the departure gate as passengers leave American Airlines flights. That's an improvement in pace of service over the past when a passenger needed to wade through months of paperwork before being reimbursed for a cleaning bill necessitated by spaghetti sauce and salad dressing spilled on clothing by a flight attendant.

After the inconvenience of a soiled suit that required a change into a new suit of clothes and the unexpected delays that accompanied the need to change, passengers faced the additional time-consuming inconvenience of obtaining, filling out, and filing claim forms.

It was as if business was consciously attempting to discourage complaints.

Other airlines maintain that company policy and procedures prevent swift response. All American did, though, was shift its mental attitude in regard to employee qualifications to handle claims immediately. They empowered employees.

Time Is Valuable

Today, people don't want to commit an hour to shopping any more. One reason that time is so highly valued is that both adults in many families work. When they reach home, they have chores to do; or they are intent upon scratching out a little time for hobbies or special interests.

They become quickly "annoyed," to use a gentle word, at long lines, employees who don't seem to know what they're doing and who take a long time doing it, incomprehensible merchandise presentation and organization, and products that stop working and that require frequent service.

As noted earlier, at the time that Marshall Field department store started a service-improvement campaign salespeople took an average of 10 minutes to approach a customer. Thanks to computer scheduling that puts salespeople where they're needed most, and to other changes, Field lopped eight minutes off average response time.

Bankers Hours

Here's unexpected improvement in pace of service: In deference to the high percentage of customers who are too busy during the week to do all their banking then, we are seeing the decline of the custom of "bankers hours." In the past, bankers hours were a state of affairs to which many people aspired. Now, banks are staying open on Saturdays, evenings, and during all weekday working hours.

It seems amazing, from the vantage point of the early 1990s, that banks didn't get into the swing of Saturday and all-day weekday openings until the late 1980s. A few banks, though, had begun to stay open on Saturdays as early as the late 1970s.

In the San Francisco Bay area, the Bank of America was the first to open on Saturdays, starting in March 1989. Other commercial banks such as the Wells Fargo Bank rushed to follow. Wells Fargo began extending weekday hours in 1988. Each Wells Fargo employee is expected to work one Saturday every three or four weeks.

"People are demanding more services," said Kim Kellogg of Wells Fargo. "We just opened the doors and people came sailing in." "Excellent response," said Cynthia Kasabian, director of banking public relations for Bank of America. "Overall we are bringing in 4,500 to 5,000 new accounts every Saturday."

Convenience

In the customer service game the company's convenience is superfluous. If the customer loses, even if the company wins big, then the most progressive customer service organization must understand that in the long run the company will lose.

Keep customer needs in mind. Then do nothing that impedes customers in satisfying those needs.

Some auto repair services, believe it or not, are leading the way in service convenience today. Servtech, auto repair service in Burnsville, Minnesota, a Minneapolis suburb, picks up customers' cars at their homes during the middle of the night and drives them to their garage. While customers sleep, Servtech changes the oil and filters, lubricates the chassis, checks the entire car for total fitness, and delivers it back to the customer's driveway before 6 A.M.

When Servtech makes an estimate, it sticks. And if repairs require less time than estimated, the customer is billed only for time spent. This point doesn't relate to convenience, but it relates to service: Servtech mechanics are paid on a work quality scale. Compensation is influenced also by how well they treat customers and meet their needs.

"Our mechanics have to do more than work on a car," says Steve Barnhart, owner of the business. "They have to talk with customers and handle them throughout the transaction instead of having a service manager as a go-between."

The result, says Barnhart, is a greater sense of job satisfaction for mechanics. They don't just fix a machine. They help make life easier for a person they know.

It's not surprising that, as Barnhart says, "People are just eating it up." Good service affects people that way.

"Convenience" refers to a decrease in time and trouble for customers.

Packaging

Take a look at your product packaging some day. Is it so impenetrable that it's difficult for a customer to open it? How about an elderly customer with arthritis? How about a customer who doesn't have a knife (or a pick ax) handy?

Major culprits are food wraps that can't be opened without a scissors or sharp knife, blister packaging so recalcitrant that the item inside is endangered in the opening process, and packing tape that requires a razor blade to cut.

If your packaging is designed to protect the product from marauding hordes until the year 2050 A.D., design new packaging. Make it easy to get at the product and to use it. It's in your interests to do so. Make the packaging secure but simple to open.

High on any consumer's list of inconvenient situations generated by business is long waits for service.

Long waits are bad enough in themselves, but sometimes this happens: A customer patiently shuffles forward in line until —Oh, wonderfulness! She or he reaches the head of the line and has just spoken two words to the clerk when—guess what? The phone rings. Instantaneously, the employee snatches up the phone, as if it was a cup of water and she'd been in the desert without drink for a week.

The customer is not so enthusiastic about the phone call.

Certainly, in this situation employees should ask the person on the phone to wait while they finish the transaction with the person in line. Then they should ask permission from the next person in line to answer the phone call. Then they should finish the phone call quickly.

Customers Come First

Convenience? Perkins restaurants operates an in-house training program that instills in employees the philosophy that guests come first, before anything else. Employees are taught to greet and to seat customers immediately, to offer a newspaper to single diners with no one to talk with, to check back regularly with guests to determine whether they want anything, and to avoid seating children next to businesspeople.

The restaurant also uses a "mystery shopper" who drops by occasionally to rate customer service practice. The shopper, unknown to employees, dines on different days and at different times of the day to get an overview of service.

Northwest Airlines began using mystery customers in 1989.

Long Lead Times

A customer inconvenience that goes unidentified by many businesses is long lead times for delivery of orders.

When you have long lead times that extend beyond a customer's ability to forecast his or her needs, customers experience planning problems. So the customer sometimes takes matters into his or her own hands and places "phantom" orders—orders for products or merchandise that they think they might need but are not committed to. This happens most often with infrequently bought products such as capital equipment.

The trouble that a business causes itself with long lead times is that phantom orders often are canceled. And cancelation disrupts a company's production schedule and increases cost.

Mail-order companies experience a similar problem born of awareness that sizes are not consistent in fit. Customers bracket their orders. They order merchandise one size smaller and also one size larger than their size. The purpose is to move closer to certainty that one of the orders will fit perfectly. Of course, they always return two of the orders, which means that the mail-order company must refund the payment or cancel the charge, functions for which they receive no compensation.

Is Self-service Inconvenient?

Action to reduce inconvenience for customers often is a very low priority. Consider the movement among major oil companies during the past several years to slash their networks of dealer-operated service stations and to replace them with a smaller number of company-operated convenience stores with gas pumps that offer no repairs.

Between 1981 and 1987 Sacramento County, California, for instance, lost 114 of its 459 gas stations, according to statistics from the State Board of Equalization. In the entire state the number of stations dropped to 12,855 in 1987 from 22,091 in 1972. During that same period, the number of automobiles grew by more than a third.

Over a three-year period from 1985 to 1988, the number of gas stations licensed as auto repair shops sank to 4,959 from 9,788 in California.

The trend is being fueled by a number of complex factors including customer buying patterns, quests for profits, undervalued land, fuel contamination and environmental regulations, and a need for judicious allocations of assets.

But where is the consideration for customers in this trend? The distance between garages is becoming a chasm for customers. Long waits for auto repairs are more and more common.

REPAIR AND MAINTENANCE SERVICES: CUSTOMER RECRUITMENT TOOLS

Some companies such as IBM are renowned for repair and maintenance and service in general. You can name other outstanding companies.

Managers in these companies feel that service is as much of a competitive advantage as a product that gives them a technological edge. Repair and maintenance is their secret weapon in the customer service wars. It's "secret" because competitors never seem to catch on to the fact that they are being clobbered by their competitor's customer service.

Many companies still can't figure out why IBM is a consistent high performer, even though the company freely attributes much of its success to quality service.

Sales as Service

When the sales force applies service techniques they gain an advantage over salespeople for competitors that act as if their concern with their clients' welfare ends with a name on the dotted line.

The vice president of a company offering drilling services to the oil and gas industry reports: "Our sales force visits the purchaser before every job begins. The sales engineer reviews the data and interprets it for the client's chief engineer. The sales engineer then gets back to the home office and makes recommendations on the basis of these interpretations."

That's service.

Monitor service performance of field sales and service personnel to make sure they are making a good impression besides doing good work.

Poppy Rossano of Williamsville, New York, won't allow repair technicians for her office machine business to service a customer's equipment until she has taught them to "leave the client's place neat and clean."

Contemporary Service

The home appliance repair industry has adapted to current realities such as absence of both husband and wife during the day in many homes.

Dick Jones, director of Service Operations for Maycor, Maytag's service organization, says that Maycor offers "First Call in the Morning" and "Last Call of the Day" service. That is, service people arrive at 8 A.M. and often finish before a home owner's usual morning departure time for work. Or they arrive between 4 and 5 P.M.: customers find that it's easier to leave work early than it is to go home during the day to let the service technician in the house and then to return to work.

Home appliance repair services have rarely made appointments for specific times. But appointments are becoming more common, says Joy Schrage, Whirlpool Corporation Communications marketing manager. Customers lose less time from work when a technician arrives at a scheduled time than they do when the technician comes whenever he or she finishes earlier jobs. Clearly, appliance repair services are reacting to customer need.

Business must monitor changes in customer needs and wants and be aware of social and economic changes that influence needs and wants.

"Troglodytes"

"Indeterminate" arrival times caused much customer exasperation in the past.

Dick Youngblood, outspoken business pages columnist for the *Star Tribune* newspaper of Minneapolis, brought up the subject in a column. He lambasted "those troglodytes of the service sector who insist on keeping 9-to-5 weekday hours despite the fact that more and more adults are working and thus are unable to avail themselves of such limited schedules.

"Worse yet," he wrote, "are the cretins who hold you hostage all day when you finally are forced to stay home from work to have the plumbing fixed or the stove repaired."

"Invariably, the service worker arrives late in the day—often too late to do the job, which means another weekday appointment some time later—or doesn't show up at all."

Youngblood also told the story of "sweet revenge" (the dream of millions of aggrieved consumers) wrought by a consumer who took a day of vacation from his job to wait for a telephone service worker to install a phone in his New York apartment. The installer never did arrive and New York Telephone Co. didn't bother to call the consumer and tell him that the service worker wouldn't arrive, even though there was no doubt that he wouldn't be able to make it that day.

So Bhaichand Patel, native of the Fiji Islands, took the phone company to Small Claims Court—and won. The phone company paid him $305.92, a day's pay at his job as director of the United Nations Information department, plus expenses.

Savvy Service

Besides promptness, there are other tricks of the trade in achieving customer satisfaction by means of service.

Instruct employees never to say cheerfully, "If it doesn't work, just bring it back." Instead they should say: "If it doesn't work, give us a call and we will bring it back for you and leave you a new one." The best warranties include promises similar to this.

When a customer hauls in his washing machine to your shop, that's fine for you. But it means a lot of trouble for your customer. Here are other instances of savvy service: When a distributor sends out a serviceman, the serviceman bring along the right part so he doesn't have to interrupt the job to run back to the shop to get the part. He works without disrupting the customer's business. And he cleans up before he leaves.

Customer Relations in Service

Quality service may involve "customer relations" ability. For instance, a customer may need repair work on a product, expect service immediately and be angry because she can't get it. The service employee must be able to practice the placating techniques described in Chapter 11.

In the case of a big-ticket item, the employee may have to deal with an irate customer who really believes that because the item was so expensive, regular maintenance and repairs should be free—regardless of whether the product is under warranty.

Warren Blanding, a leading customer service consultant, admits to being a customer who does not buy again when service is rotten: "I have a Canon copier, which is great, but when we needed a larger copier for the office, we didn't go to Canon because the dealer was so 'snotty' about providing service." He meant that the dealer was slow and uncooperative when Blanding requested service.

IN PRAISE OF OUTGOING WATS

In 1988, the Technical Assistance Research Corporation (TARP), the leading customer service research firm in the United States, updated a 1983 study of 800 number systems in cooperation with the Society of Customer Affairs Professionals (SOCAP). The 1988 study confirmed findings of the 1983 study: in many industries, between 60 and 80 percent of customers who have questions but do not request assistance would do so if a readily accessible 800 number existed.

Customers whose needs are not satisfied (whose questions are not answered) are time bombs under a company's bottom line.

Breaking Down Barriers

So use an 800 phone number to break down barriers that customers perceive as impeding requests for assistance or for answers to questions. It is in an organization's best interests to know what customers want and need. When the company knows, the knowledge neutralizes the illusory and erroneous impression among executives in many companies that customers are satisfied and will continue to patronize their company indefinitely. Naturally, when the CEO and other senior executives see no reports of a major customer complaint problem, they assume customer satisfaction.

Of course, it happens that the result of installing and publicizing an 800 number sometimes is the same as opening the flood gates in a dam. But isn't this the way it should be? It is very difficult to manage successfully with your head in a sack.

Loyalty

Customers who know that they have easy access to a company are more satisfied. And more loyal.

Industry specific research by TARP shows that an 800 number is more effective than a correspondence-based system in maximizing customer loyalty. Significantly more customers who contact an 800 number are satisfied with results of the contact-handling process. Customers value the timely response that is the distinctive characteristic of 800 number systems.

Early Warning Device

An 800 number often tips you off early to problems such as product deficiencies, policy mistakes, and customer difficulties. Once a problem begins to appear, customers who call an 800 number can be questioned at once and in depth to obtain detail needed to identify root causes of problems.

Consumer reps answering 800 line calls often can pick up nuances of customer attitudes that do not emerge in formal studies. This is valuable information because most companies do little of the kind of research that reveals what drives consumer satisfaction.

So develop a reporting and review system that locates these problems among the calls received on the 800 line.

Fine Points of 800 Service Management

Training of telephone communicators, discussed shortly, is vital, to the success of an 800 phone system. But N. Powell Taylor, manager of the GE Answer Center in Louisville, Kentucky, carries management of his system much further.

His service representatives wear professional dress. Male reps wear coats and ties and women wear dresses and suits. Why? Self-confidence that shows up in the sound of the reps' voices over on the phone.

Taylor motivates his people with messages that appear out of nowhere on computer screens—messages such as: "Put a smile in your voice." He employs incentives—clothing, sporting goods, and trips to Disney World. The Disney World trips are an outgrowth of a Taylor visit to that entertainment mecca. It was there that he learned some of his ideas for the Answer Center—at Disney University where Disney employees are trained.

Self-Confidence

The self-confidence principle comes into play in the hiring practices of Maurice Maio, San Diego plumbing tycoon and president of Maio Plumbing. He hires attractive, self-confident females for his phone work and then installs mirrors along the walls of the telephone area so that they can indulge in self-admiration. A woman who feels good about her appearance as a result of frequent self-assurance in the mirror is likely to be friendly and outgoing on the telephone, Maio believes.

Mirrors also are placed in positions where the women can see themselves while they are on the telephone—and notice whether or not they are smiling. According to Maio's theories, an individual's voice is naturally more pleasant when the individual is smiling.

To maintain the winning edge, Taylor and his GE staff evaluate service reps three times a year. If reps score 80 percent on productivity, attitude, attendance, and quality of service, their new goal becomes 85 percent, and so on. Many top reps move on to field offices as sales managers.

Both quantitative and qualitative measurements are taken. Computers count calls automatically. The result is the quantitative measurement. Qualitative evaluations are taken by managers listening in on calls. The atmosphere at the Answer Center is cheerful, but it's clear that supervision is tight.

Toyota, a company that puts extraordinary emphasis upon customer courtesy, ranks phone reps daily on productivity. Original Research II, which conducts customer satisfaction call-backs for major clients, grades "communicators" daily on five measures of telephone and vocal effectiveness.

Cost

The cost of incoming WATS (800) often is offset by an increase in employee productivity: studies show that customer contact personnel require less time to respond by phone than by letter.

John Goodman, president of TARP, says of 800 numbers: "They are very low risk. If you don't get many calls, then you don't incur very much cost.

"We find that each minute you spend on one of these calls probably is going to more than pay for itself in terms of enhanced profits and sales."

The American Management Association reports that the average 800 line service costs a half million dollars a year, for the largest users.

Average expenditure for 800 number operations is well over $250,000. Oscar Mayer spends an average of $6 per call. Chesebrough Ponds spent $800,000 during one recent year.

More than half of all companies with more than $10 million in sales use 800 numbers to handle complaints, inquiries, and orders, according to the American Management Association (AMA).

Case Histories: 800 Systems

Companies fashion their 800 systems to suit their needs, in working toward customer satisfaction and loyalty. The GE Answer Center currently operates the state-of-the-art system, many customer service experts believe. The system, which went on-line in 1983, handles more than 3 million calls a year and costs about $10 million per year to operate.

All 150 customer service representatives (three quarters of them female) are college graduates. Their starting salary is $20,000 a year. About 40 technical representatives in the Answer Center have at least four years of field repair experience and earn considerably more than $20,000.

A giant data base stores about 750,000 answers to questions about 8,500 product models in 120 product lines. Answers are accessed through millions of key words.

The data base "makes every rep an expert," says Taylor. GE reports that its people can solve 90 percent of complaints or inquiries on the first phone call.

The Answer Center receives up to 15,000 calls a day, a total of 3 million a year. Each representative talks to about 20,000 customers per year. In a recent year the Answer Center directed some 700,000 callers to GE dealers.

Many calls cover the same ground over and over, but some calls are "originals." The Center has received calls from the crew of a submarine off the Connecticut coast asking how to fix a television monitor, from a homeowner who wanted to convert a black-and-white TV set to color, and from technicians on a James Bond film who needed help to get their underwater lights to work.

Calls from Prospects

Roughly a third of calls are from people who are on the verge of buying a GE product and want some information. These calls produce the Center's biggest returns. Reps use the opportunity to tell customers about upgrades or new options and more. GE dealers appreciate it because they like working with customers who know everything about the product they're going to buy and need only discuss color, price, and availability.

Another third of the calls spring from difficulty or confusion in operation of a product, and the final third involve repairs and service.

Whirlpool's Consumer Assistance Center, formerly called Cool Line customer service phone system, established in 1967, employs 49 technical consultants. They are experienced employees or retirees from the manufacturing, engineering, service, sales, and home economics divisions.

Photographs courtesy of Whirlpool's Consumer Assistance Center.

800 Calls Head Off Returns

Answer Center Manager Taylor figures that calls to the Center head off a significant number of problems that would otherwise result either in a product under warranty being returned for service or in a home service call by a repairperson. Problems with installation, for instance, can be handled over the phone frequently.

The Answer Center yields at least twice the return GE predicted in its planning for the Center. The company spends an estimated $2.50 to $4.50 on a typical call—15 percent of them complaints—and reaps two to three times that amount in additional sales and warranty savings.

A company that wants to learn how GE does it can find out by purchasing an audiovisual presentation at the current cost of $12,000. Coca-Cola installed its 1-800-GET-COKE lines to promote feedback. Roger Nunley, manager of Industry and Consumer Affairs at Coca-Cola USA, says some studies indicated that only one unhappy person in 50 takes time to complain. "The other 49 switch brands, so it just makes good business sense to seek them out," he says.

Without toll-free lines, Coca-Cola might never have understood the depths of its error in trying to replace old Coke with new Coke. Immediately after the company launched its reformulated new Coke in 1985, calls on the phone system skyrocketed from an average of 400 a day to more than 12,000 per day. Nine out of 10 were from customers who said they preferred the old cola to the new drink.

On the day after old Coke's return as Coca-Cola Classic, 18,000 people called.

An 800 Number for Each Rep

The 800 phone system on WATS lines at the Textile Fibers Department of E. I. du Pont de Nemours and Co., Inc., is the ultimate in accessibility. Each customer service representative has a different number.

Efficiency is the watchword at Bio-Lab. Call activity is monitored and the number of lines are increased when business warrants it. This way customers don't get busy signals.

Bio-Lab's Customer Service Department has "universal call director" and recorder equipment that prevents incoming calls from ringing at representatives' desks while they're already busy talking to customers. This equipment also prevents incoming calls from being randomly answered.

A billion-dollar chain of convenience stores spent $200,000 on an 800 line to field customer queries and complaints, according to an AMA research report, "Close to the Customer." Sales revenues increased for the company in one year by 19 percent, the report stated. This company installed its 800 system even though it does all its selling to local stores.

A mid-sized chemical processor spent $350,000 to leap over its retailers and put salespeople directly in touch with consumers by phone. By doing so the company increased sales by 20 percent.

A computerized voice response system simultaneously routes a call and a data screen to a workstation operator when a touch-tone phone caller requests personal assistance. Simultaneous voice/data transfer capability allows requests to be handled quickly. (Reprinted courtesy of the Service Quality Institute.)

After-Hours 800 Number

The company that manufactures Humming Bird fish locators has an 800 number listed on its products for Saturdays and Sundays—times that are convenient for its customers. This is an organization that understands the power of customer service characterized by customer-friendly hours and knowledgeable, helpful employees on the phone.

Some companies tailor systems and procedures that make it convenient for the companies but inconvenient for customers.

Robert Pastorini, Claim Customer Relations director for Allstate, says that the future of the insurance industry belongs to companies that are accessible and ready to take action 24 hours a day, that do not just take messages and provide help when convenient but instead when it is needed.

Standard Rate & Data Service, Inc., that publishes directories listing advertising rates and specifications for periodicals, prints a direct line phone number for each of its top officers, including the president, near the front of its directories.

The Canada Post Corporation (CPC), Canadian equivalent of the U.S. Postal Service, uses a computerized phone system that gives employees who answer the phones instant access to information on postal codes, rates, products and services, and other subjects customers often ask about. In 1989 the system handled about 9 million calls.

In the old days, trying to phone the Post Office was comparable to using the phone system in a Third World country. It was difficult to get the right number. When you did find the right number, the line seemed to be busy all the time. If you were lucky enough to get through, the person answering often seemed unable or unwilling to deliver a straight answer.

800 Service Training

The most intensive and comprehensive training of phone communicators on earth probably is done by Original Research II of Chicago. The company operates Original Research II Merit University, a role model for all business. Original Research conducts customer satisfaction surveys for major clients by phone.

Communicators are college students who work only an average of 9 to 11 months. Yet they are trained for four weeks with full pay before they call their first customer.

After they start work following the first four weeks of training, supervisors work with communicators for four weeks more "to make sure all their questions get answered and all the bases are covered," says Denise C. Foy, senior vice president for operations.

Supervisors listen to every phone call for the second four-week set. Several trainers continue to support the communicators during this period.

After graduation from the eight weeks of training, communicators still are continuously supported and trained. Nobody ever really graduates from training.

Explaining why the training program is so comprehensive, Foy says simply: "Our customers are that important to us."

At Procter & Gamble, new customer service representatives spend four to five weeks in classrooms learning to defuse anger as well as to solve problems.

New GE Answer Center representatives are trained for five weeks, full time. "We teach them to recognize different personality profiles in 10 seconds or less and to change their personalities to complement that of the caller," says Taylor. If a customer is angry, the rep will be businesslike and alert. If a customer begins by talking about the weather and moves on to leisurely questions about refrigerators, the rep will try to match that pace and tone.

Customer Personality Profiles

All representatives receive 50 hours more of training each year, to keep them sharp. GE identified seven different customer personality profiles that are assumed by role models in practice sessions.

Consumer Relations Telephone Tips

When a customer has an inquiry or complaint it is important to handle the matter quickly and courteously. Following these simple steps will make your telephone communications go more smoothly and increase the chance of satisfying the customer.

1
LISTEN attentively to the caller. Don't interrupt. The caller's first goal is to be heard. This also gives you a chance to determine what the problem is.

2
REMAIN CALM, composed and polite regardless of the caller's language or approach. Treat the caller with respect.

3
EXPRESS CONCERN or regret if appropriate and a desire to help. Be emphatic and sincere. Use the caller's name.

4
ASK QUESTIONS to obtain the necessary details. It is important to determine the next step necessary to resolve the problem. Ask the caller to clarify the requests or statements you don't understand.

5
RESTATE the question or problem using the caller's words. This allows you to take control of the dialog. Ask the caller if you've interpreted the question or problem correctly.

6
FORMULATE A SOLUTION. Tell the caller what action you will take. Make sure the caller understands why you have made your decision.

7
GIVE your name and phone number to the caller.

8
CLOSE on a friendly, helpful note. In the few cases where the caller wants to talk to someone else, refer him/her to Consumer Relations in Long Grove.

The Kemper Group of insurance companies provides a tent card bearing these "Telephone Tips" for each customer service telephone station. "Following these simple steps will make your telephone communications go more smoothly and increase the chance of satisfying the customer," according to a sentence on the card.

Besides how-to-do-it training, Answer Center reps attend periodic stress management seminars. It is acknowledged that customer demands, tempers, and ignorance can cause stress.

Some companies use training provided by telephone companies. A free training program, "Speaking of Courtesy," is offered by U.S. West Communications. "The program has grown in popularity because companies realize that the most direct contact they have with many of their customers is over the telephone," says Hazel Newman, manager of the training program.

One telephone trainer teaches basic telephone techniques that may seem routine to some people but that are unknown to many employees:

- Use the hold button, when you put the phone down for any reason, to silence background conversations. Talk overheard by a customer may be embarrassing or may even reveal confidential information.
- Ask customers if you can put them on hold before doing so. Some employees ask but slam down the phone before hearing the answer. This practice enrages some people, according to surveys. In a similar situation, say that an employee has been taught to

pick up a phone before the third ring. In cases where the employee must, however, finish with a transaction before conversing with the caller, that employee is likely to say, in mock courtesy, "Would you mind holding, please?" Cut-off! The caller is left with her or his mouth open, about to respond. That's how to make a customer mad.

- Never eat or drink while on the phone.
- Remember that your speaking voice is affected by your attitude. If you roll your eyes toward the heavens or grimace while talking, the customer may "hear" it.
- Speak with a smile on your face to project confidence and enthusiasm through your voice. It's a trick used every day on the job by radio disc jockeys.

LITTLE THINGS THAT MAKE A BIG IMPRESSION

Million-dollar automated answering systems play an important part in a company's overall service program, but so do "little things." Remember: Dumping tea into Boston Harbor might seem like a little thing from the distance of a couple hundred years, but it played a major role in the American Revolution.

Here are some "little things":

1. Helpfulness. When a customer has a question, patience and a courteous response are essential. This is a chance to help, and to win a customer's commitment. Learn the needs of regular customers well. Anticipate them, if you can.
2. Honesty. Example: A waitress coming right out and telling restaurant guests about a backlog in the kitchen and that their meals will be delayed, instead of telling them little white lies calculated to keep them happy.
3. Reliability. Return phone calls promptly. Be on time for appointments. Call customers promptly when ordered merchandise for him or her arrives.
4. Extending yourself. Do more than customers expect. A customer who needed his order on Saturday so he could be up and running early Monday probably would remember for years that you got the order out of the warehouse for him on Saturday.

   It is being reliable when employees still fill out an order when a computer that ordinarily handles that job is not functioning. When an employee claims that he or she can't take an order because they'd have to write it, they're saying to a customer: "I don't want to help you if it means I have to work at it."

¿TIENE ALGUNA PREGUNTA SOBRE EL USO SEGURO DE LA ENERGIA ELECTRICA?

La respuesta podría obtenerla por teléfono, gracias a los Telemensajes Sobre Energía de Wisconsin Electric.

Telemensajes Sobre Energía es un servicio de información sobre energía al alcance de sus dedos, que incluye una biblioteca de mensajes grabados. Un especialista en energía le pondrá la cinta que usted quiera escuchar y le responderá las preguntas sobre energía que tenga.

Puede escuchar los Telemensajes Sobre Energía, de lunes a viernes entre 9 a.m. y 6 p.m., o los sábados entre 9 a.m. y 1 p.m.

Llame y pida cualquiera de las cintas sobre el uso seguro de la energía eléctrica (disponibles en inglés y en español):

NUMERO DE CINTA	TITULO DE CINTA
213	Uso y operación segura de los calentadores unitarios supletorios
800	Seguridad con la secadora de ropa
801	Operación segura de las cocinas eléctricas
802	Operación segura de las secadoras de pelo eléctricas
803	Operación segura de planchas eléctricas
804	Seguridad con el refrigerador
805	Seguridad con los árboles de Navidad
807	Qué hacer cuando percibe el olor del gas natural
808	Seguridad de los alimentos
809	Precaución con las antenas
812	Seguridad del sistema eléctrico en el hogar
813	Monóxido de carbono: El asesino invisible
913	Poda de ramas de árboles sobre líneas eléctricas
914	Línea de emergencia del excavador
MENSAJES GRABADOS PARA NIÑOS (DE 6 A 12 AÑOS)	
10	Cuidado con la electricidad
11	El Capitán Energía habla sobre la seguridad del sistema eléctrico
12	Sy Malone y el secador de pelo travieso
13	Qué hacer cuando percibe el olor del gas natural
14	¿Qué es una interrupción del servicio de energía?

Tenemos un número mayor de selecciones de cintas grabadas sobre una variedad de tópicos relacionados con la energía eléctrica (incluyendo grabaciones para niños).

Wisconsin Electric
POWER COMPANY

The common electric company practice of providing energy facts by means of recorded messages adds an increment of good will to the reputations of the companies. Spanish-speaking customers, particularly, would appreciate this list of tape titles. (Reprinted courtesy of Wisconsin Electric Power Company.)

5. Taking personal responsibility: No "hand offs" allowed. At the Norfolk (Virginia) Airport Hilton Hotel, anyone collared by a guest complaining that he or she doesn't have enough towels will go to Housekeeping and get the towels and deliver them to the guest themselves, immediately. Even if the employee that the guest approaches is the sales manager.

The general managers of Continental Management's Ramada Renaissance hotels have outlawed the phrase "It's not my job." Anyone caught with those words on his lips is likely to receive an ultimatum similar to the U.S. Navy's saying, "Shape up or ship out."

Management would much rather hear employees say: "I'm sorry, sir, but I don't have the facts on this situation. But I'll get the facts, and I'll take care of this for you myself, right away."

The objective of the Ramada Renaissance is expressed by a spokesperson: "We're trying to avoid giving the impression that what the employee is doing is more important than what the guest is doing," he says.

At The Rivers Club in Pittsburgh, Pennsylvania, General Manager Jack Kimball says: "We handle complaints with overkill. For example, if a member is unhappy with his meal, the table eats free."

Day-to-day actions of support employees, unnoticed internally, can create a sense of silent antagonism by the customer toward the company. Service reps, billing clerks, and other internal staff members have the most frequent dealings with customers, yet these employees—even people whose assigned job is "service"—often unwittingly sabotage the corporate image.

Lower and midlevel employees, operating out of sight of both management and the customer, undermine the effect of millions of dollars spent on marketing and advertising.

Insulting collection notices, unfriendly phone operators, and bills that sound like accusations make enemies out of customers every day.

The "little things" loom large in a customer's memory.

They help make a store, manufacturer, supplier, or service organization seem like "a shopping service" to customers.

10
My Customer, My Friend

HOW TO KEEP YOUR FRIENDS

Do things right the first time, every time, and on time.

—Robert Pastorini, Claims Customer Service Manager, Allstate Insurance Companies

Service demands constant attention. It is something good that managers must think about every day. New customer service programs inevitably stall after about a year to a year and a half without renewal. No matter how much energy and organization go into a program, managers and employees are unlikely to work as hard on service months or years after the bells and whistles kick off as they did during the first bloom of excitement and enthusiasm.

Award programs grow stale. Team leaders lose interest. The easy problems have been solved. The first round of training has ended. So the program declines to a slow shuffle after a year or so. It is at this point that many companies lose their zest for service.

Service: A Dynamic Strategy

To prevent the decline and demise of service culture and practice in your organization, view customer service as a dynamic strategy. The needs and wants of your customers are sure to be dynamic. Your service program should be dynamic too. It should be dynamic because trends come and go. Social and economic standards shift. The population undergoes major demographic changes, so new needs develop.

The following standards are part of the essential foundation for a continuously effective customer service program:

- Vigilance for changes in needs and in effectiveness of current programs.
- Creativity in developing new customer service responses.
- Persistence through periods of declining interest or unyielding difficulties.
- A mechanism for constantly renewing the spirit of commitment.

Instead of letting their service program waste away, managers should grit their teeth and dream up new ideas that pump life into it.

Managers and employees must come up with new ways to provide service.

Products, services, and entire markets should be "recalculated" as demographics and social and economic standards change.

Remember that a customer service strategy should be a moving, changing strategy. Expect to change programs and the people who administer them. The best programs change continuously.

WARNING SIGNS

The eternal vigilance that is the price of consistently superior service still may not be enough to prevent service declines unless you know exactly what you're supposed to see in all your vigilance.

The following common pressures to reduce your commitment to service are some of the storm flags that you should notice when they fly from the mast of the corporate ship of the line:

1. The finance department recommends cost reduction measures. If they are adopted, the result is sure to be a reduction in service delivery capability.
2. The business becomes a monopoly or reaches a point where all competitors in a marketplace offer mediocre, poor, or inconsistent service.
3. The business offers a product for which there is heavy demand or for which there is undersupply.
4. Management or ownership changes or the number of staff members or their experience or training decline.
5. Business grows so quickly, requiring investment of large amounts to expand facilities and production, that resources needed to pursue exceptional customer service are depleted or diverted to "more important" uses.
6. Profits increase. Business becomes self-congratulatory. Executives lose touch with the service system and with the reality that service has declined in direct proportion to company profitability.

These developments must be recognized as the warning signs of declining service that they are so that deterrent action against their effect can be launched.

MONITORING SERVICE LEVEL

Every business that's serious about maintaining a high level of service forever must put in place a system that will sound a loud J. Arthur Rank Productions' gonging sound when service declines for any reason.

If a company is to maintain a high level of service it is elementary, my dear Watson, as Sherlock Holmes says, to stay abreast of customer reactions to products and services for the purpose of detecting customer dissatisfaction quickly. Stay up to date with changes in your customers' opinions and attitudes and in their values, their needs, and their wants.

Monitoring the quality status of customer service should be one of the ongoing projects in any service program.

There are four general methods of gauging customer opinion and service status:

Surveys of employees

Listen to what employees say about customer mood. "My first message is: Listen, listen, listen to the people who do the work," says Ross Perot, chairman of Perot Systems, Inc. Conduct open-meeting key-account reviews with all employees attending.

Convene employee focus groups in which a leader asks questions and stimulates responses. Focus groups must include all functions and all levels of seniority.

Ask standard, quantifiable questions such as "How many complaints did you get in the first 90 days after the product went on sale?" Also, put energy into devising ways to quantify answers to qualitative questions such as "What is the reaction to the product that you hear most often from customers?"

Report to employees findings from employee surveys and also from any customer surveys. Good news and bad news both motivate most employees. In a forward to its research report, "Close to the Customer," the American Management Association (AMA) suggests keeping the people who actually do the customer contact work—front-line salespeople—well informed. Employees, for instance, should receive a consumer comment/complaint report, the AMA recommends. Everyone should be let in on the results of 800 number survey calls.

You might consider running focus groups of employees on the topic: "What is it like to do business with us?" They know the answer to that question well. Videotape meetings of the group and show the videotapes to everyone.

Surveys of customers

Measure customer satisfaction in customer terms such as time spent waiting. Emphasize intangibles such as willingness of employees to answer questions. These intangibles seem to have the greatest effect upon emotional reaction of customers.

Measure satisfaction regularly for all customers in the distribution channel. Don't be satisfied with a single measure or survey instrument, though. Coordination and cross-checking among many survey formats is necessary.

The chief roadblock to success in customer surveys is the natural human inclination to do easy surveys. So force yourself to move beyond obvious measurements to use difficult-to-articulate, controversial variables that determine long-term customer satisfaction and business growth. The distance that customers must walk to reach a service counter, the prevailing temperature level, decor, and similar things all impact long-term customer attitude.

Conduct formal surveys of customers every 60 to 90 days. Less than 90-day frequency is risky. Customer preferences often change even faster than that.

Do informal surveys monthly, at least—telephone surveys, for instance, or samples of customers as they are buying. Domino's Pizza surveys every week.

A major annual image survey should be the backbone of the customer survey program. It should be done by a third party.

Other formal customer survey programs consist of

1. Customer focus groups. Informal focus groups of a few customers that should be convened not only in marketing but in manufacturing, distribution, and accounting departments, too.
2. "Debriefings" of key accounts. Employ "open-ended" discussions. Just asking customers what they are satisfied with and what they are dissatisfied with usually yields valuable information. Annual or semiannual debriefings should include formal survey questions and open-ended discussions with all levels and functions.
3. Customer attitude surveys, with random samples of customers similar to a program conducted by Puget Sound Power & Light Co. The firm analyzes media coverage and listens to customer feedback from field personnel. In analyzing the media, the company looks for awards to the company and other civic recognition as means of assessing whether the community thinks the company is doing a good job.

Computerized information systems

Customer compliments and complaints both can become more valuable sources of information about real, generalized customer opinion if they are managed after the fashion of General Mills' procedures.

Irma Cameron, manager of customer relations at General Mills, reports that the company automated customer response functions, using a mainframe computer, in the 1970s. About 300,000 contacts with customers per year are recorded to the computer. At the end of each month and each recording cycle all customer comments are cross-referenced by product, compliment, and complaint. Printouts of the resulting report go to department managers.

In addition, a word processing package is tied into the main frame computer, enabling GM to do paragraph assembly. With one key, customer name and address and brand number are entered in files and printed with any of about 1500 possible paragraph responses.

"Creative" methods of obtaining information on customer opinion and attitude:

1. Visit your best customers when your customers are businesses. No better way exists for obtaining insight into customer needs and means of satisfying them than observing the work that goes on.
2. Prepare summaries of customer complaint correspondence, too.
3. Post key customer satisfaction standards in every part of the organization. Update them. Change them.

Follow up on lost customers or lost sales. Find out exactly why you lost the customers or the sales. More often than you might think you'll find that an "intangible" such as emotional reaction to service or incompatibility with an employee was involved.

Systematic "lost sale" follow-up programs are a must.

Once you know why you lost a sale, action needed to prevent further losses for the same reasons usually become clear.

Results Measurement

Measurable results that contribute to the bottom line figure are very important to most executives. Executives of companies that I work with throughout the world always ask what results they can expect from a customer service program.

One of the foremost reasons that service measurement is important is that without it management tends to lose interest in a customer service program within three to four months. On the other hand, hard, quantifiable results win and hold their support. That which gets measured gets done, said one anonymous sage.

The attitude of management changes quickly when they are expected to judge the worth of a customer service program on the basis of a manager's embarrassingly subjective report that "People seem to like it" or "I have had some positive feedback."

If management is to commit resources to customer service training and to a quality service program itself, they will require regular, updated results reports. The most important yardsticks are sales, amount of average sale, customer count, number of repeat sales, employee turnover rate, and so on.

If statistics prove that the number of new employees required within a quarter was 80 instead of 100 and the cost of replacing employees declined from $100,000 to $80,000, then the financial benefit of a service program that improves employee morale is $20,000. If, then, the cost of the quality service training and the program itself was $5,000, let's say, the net result of a customer service focus is $15,000 a quarter.

Usually companies want to do their own measurement. But, when they do, after six months measurement still hasn't begun, usually. If a company does measure results, the information is shared only with top executives.

The complications and obstacles in obtaining the cooperation of clients in measuring the results of customer service programs is one of my most frustrating experiences since I began my quality service training program in 1980. The most perplexing part of the problem is that whenever scientific measurement is done, results show great benefit to a company.

Yet the only way to achieve consistent measurement is to do it ourselves at no cost, we found. The first two clients whose service program results we measured were Nutrition World and St. Paul Book and Stationery Co. They still use our technology.

When companies actually do measure service results, they often measure the wrong things such as employee satisfaction with training. A sophisticated measurement program would find sales rising, turnover dropping, and complaints disappearing. Without measurement by the customer service function marketing or advertising department will take credit for the benefits of customer service.

What ought to be done is to measure results of a customer service program monthly and to distribute the findings to the entire management team. If this isn't done, the "warning signs" listed earlier may advance to real breakdown.

But, if this *is* done, the department responsible for customer service would find itself with a larger budget and greater authority and influence.

Northwestern Bell Telephone Co. (now U.S. West) put thousands of employees through our customer service training and measured results monthly. Every month service levels measurably improved.

Two retailing firms in Dallas measured results of our program, "Quest for the Best: A Professional's Guide to Selling and Service," developed with Stanley Marcus, retailing guru. Stanley Korshak, high-fashion retailer, increased sales 54 percent from June to November over sales during the same period the previous year. The Gazebo high-fashion retail stores found, in measuring results of their customer service program, that sales increased in successive months 18 percent, 13 percent, 12 percent, 10 percent, 9 percent, and (during the Christmas shopping season) 28 percent. If training departments and human resources departments would more diligently measure results of customer service training, they might be able to greatly expand their budgets and their influence upon the corporate decision making. Moreover, results conveyed to executives help maintain commitment to a customer service program.

The most important measurements are customer census and sales volume.

You might want to measure the impact of a professional customer service program upon employee turnover. Withhold all other influences upon turnover during the training period. Then record training cost; cost of employment; advertising; and cost of interviewing, testing, and training. You will usually find that the cost of replacing employees occupying the lowest positions approaches $1,000.

Impress management with a report that *interprets* the benefits of reduced turnover. For instance, "The customer service training program reduced turnover by 20 percent. That means that we reduced annual hiring quota from 100 to 80 and that we saved $1,000 per position. That's an annual saving of $20,000. Our investment in customer service training and implementation was $5,000. That means that we saved $15,000, a 300 percent return on our investment, *the first year.*"

In evaluating the effect of a service program upon customer complaints, assign a money benefit to each customer retained as a result of complaint resolution. For example, if you know that the average customer spends about $100 per month and shops once a month, and if you know, too, that the average customer stays with you for seven years, each customer saved would be worth about $8,400 over seven years ($1,200 per year X 7 years).

You can also do this calculation for customers that you save by fast complaint resolution that satisfied *the customers*: You know that a customer is worth $8,400 in income over seven years. If you save 100 customers you have made $840,000 in increased income.

It's this type of hard, measurable results that excite executives. To them employee motivation, reduction in turnover, a service-driven staff—all this is meaningless unless results can be measured in more dollars.

It is my conclusion that superior customer service is the most profitable business strategy that an organization can adopt.

EVALUATE EMPLOYEES ON SERVICE PERFORMANCE

Managers of departments with the highest levels of customer satisfaction should be paid more than managers of departments to which customers give low scores. That is, tie compensation and performance scores for managers and supervisors to customer satisfaction.

Every performance evaluation also should include an assessment of the executive's degree of "customer orientation."

Every job description should incorporate a qualitative description of the executive's connection to customers. For instance, satisfaction levels on surveys should be consistently high or they should rise. For product managers, one job standard might be obtaining feedback from focus groups and 800 lines.

Jerre Stead, president of Square D Company of Milwaukee, said that the company "changed the mentality by which most people had consistently been rewarded and promoted."

"We changed our measurement program," he said. He gave as an example the fact that beginning in 1987 "our managers have been measured on customer service and quality."

Profit at the Expense of Customers

Stead said that when he took over as president some managers justified certain anticustomer practices by saying: "You're rewarding me to make a profit."

Square D doesn't pursue profit at the expense of customers anymore.

In the past, says Stead, all functions of the company reported individually to him. "The only time sales, marketing, manufacturing, and engineering came together was in my office." It was up to him to see connections, trends, and implications in the information shoveled into his "in" basket.

"I'm certainly not as smart or as quick as I need to be to pull all that together," said Stead. So Square D reorganized into businesses handling the industrial, international, and construction sectors "to better concentrate on meeting our customers' needs," said Stead.

Rank-and-file employees also should be evaluated. Develop a quantitative scoring system for

1. Individuals such as salespeople and service persons.
2. Groups (a dispatch or reservation center team, for instance).
3. Facilities (factory or operations office or store).
4. Divisions.

Tell every employee involved just what you find out.

An example of a personal evaluation standard, for people who repair or service merchandise, would be elapsed time between customer call and arrival of service, and also quality of repair: Did the repaired device *stay* fixed?

FINE-TUNING AND UPDATING SERVICE PROGRAMS

Creative Ideas

Call Three Customers Each Week

All senior managers in all functions should call at least three customers a week. Then they should share data generated by the calls.

Summarize Complaint Correspondence

Make statistical reports, letters, and phone call transcripts available to all senior managers.

Conduct Exit Interviews for Employees

Maurice Maio, president of Maio Plumbing, a large San Diego company, routinely conducts exit interviews of employees who are leaving to get the employees' opinions of the operation, including service aspects. These sessions are valuable, Maio believes, because workers tend to be very candid when they are leaving a company.

HERE'S HOW SOME COMPANIES KEEP THEIR SERVICE LEVEL HIGH

Robert Pastorini, Claims Customer Service Manager for Allstate Insurance Companies, says that the future of the insurance industry belongs to companies committed to doing things right "the first time, every time, and on time."

Pastorini recognizes that any company's good service reputation is only as good as the latest good service.

Armstrong Tire Co's. Bill Gamgort, director of Quality Assurance & Customer Affairs, says that the Field Intelligence Project that is part of the customer service program is used to determine whether Armstrong is satisfying needs and requirements of the customer base.

The Field Intelligence Project combines these fact-gathering methods:

- Review of product returns under warranty. Information is compiled by product line.
- 800 phone lines available to both wholesale and retail customers, that is, for dealers and ultimate consumers. About 70 to 75 percent of calls request technical information. About 25 percent express clear product problems. Armstrong strongly encourages questions.

WHAT IS A CUSTOMER?

A CUSTOMER IS THE MOST IMPORTANT PERSON EVER IN THIS COMPANY - IN PERSON OR BY MAIL.

A CUSTOMER IS NOT DEPENDENT ON US, WE ARE DEPENDENT ON HIM.

A CUSTOMER IS NOT AN INTERRUPTION OF OUR WORK, HE IS THE PURPOSE OF IT.

WE ARE NOT DOING A FAVOR BY SERVING HIM, HE IS DOING US A FAVOR BY GIVING US THE OPPORTUNITY TO DO SO.

A CUSTOMER IS NOT SOMEONE TO ARGUE OR MATCH WITS WITH. NOBODY EVER WON AN ARGUMENT WITH A CUSTOMER.

A CUSTOMER IS A PERSON WHO BRINGS US HIS WANTS. IT IS OUR JOB TO HANDLE THEM PROFITABLY TO HIM AND TO OURSELVES.

L. L. BEAN, INC.
FREEPORT, MAINE

Motivational messages such as the copy on this "What Is a Customer?" poster are effective in maintaining a high level of service. (Reprinted courtesy of L. L. Bean, Inc.)

- Phone solicitation of the comments of major customers. People in the Quality Assurance & Customer Affairs group solicit randomly selected major customers (dealers) monthly, asking for their comments. They are given opportunity to report the good things and the bad things about products.

Information acquired this way is presented formally at monthly executive staff meetings that include the company President. Then the information is issued in report form to key appropriate management—vice presidents of marketing and sales, vice president of manufacturing and finance, and the director of employee relations.

The Textile Fibers Department of E. I. du Pont de Nemours and Co., Inc., stays in touch with its customers with a different WATS line (800 number) for each customer service representative.

Grace Richardson, director of consumer affairs at Colgate-Palmolive, reports that the company maintains a high service level by using tactics such as mystery shoppers who do conniving things like asking for change for a $100 bill and observing the reactions of salespeople.

Those whose response is "Are you kidding!" are likely to be perusing the want ad section soon.

Says Richardson: "We're doing a good job of communicating with the consumer and telling the company what we hear the consumer saying."

Customer Comment Response cards at Mervyn's are available in two or three plastic holders at every service counter in every store of this company.

The short-run purpose of the response cards is to provide information that prepares the company to react immediately to customer dissatisfactions.

The long-run goal is obtaining enough feedback from customers to get a feeling for how merchandise is serving their requirements.

In the early 1980s, a patient care survey showed that Humana Hospitals was perceived as highly professional and efficient, but that it received low marks on the way employees interacted with patients. Employees needed to be more empathetic and personal.

Humana responded with a special employee training program called "Humana Care." It is based upon a series of films that portray the hospital experience from a patient's point of view. The theme is: "Treat each patient as you would a member of your own family." Humana's success is based on the premise that health care is, above all, a service.

But patients are not their only "customers," Humana believes. Other important customer groups are physicians, who usually choose which hospital their patients use, and corporations, that pay for employee health care benefits.

Humana listens carefully to all customers. "Our strong suit is our ability to hear all that chatter out there and to come up with a clear focus," says Chief Executive Officer David Jones.

REINFORCEMENT OF TRAINING

There is no such thing as having "arrived" in ones commitment to quality service or in one's knowledge about how to deliver it.

Once a person feels that he or she has "arrived," the world will begin tipping and they will begin sliding on a Teflon surface toward disillusionment.

Good customer service habits must be reinforced, continually.

This can be done by offering new customer service training programs. A program that employees have never seen before will appeal to some employees who were not "turned on" by earlier programs. Different emotional appeals and factual arrays will comprise a communications approach that will attract attention and induce retention of some employees who got virtually nothing from earlier programs.

Compare customer service seminars and training programs to movies. Some people will love a movie that their friends hate. So a variety of programs spaced over a period of months will have a greater cumulative effect upon employee service behavior that the same program repeated.

The Value of Variety in Training

Some quality service programs incorporate "follow-up and review" sections. They can be used to maintain employee awareness of service practice at a high level.

After initial presentation of a quality service program, periodically remind employees how customers should be treated. Review main customer service points in employee newsletter articles, in bulletin board or poster messages, with oral communication from supervisors, and in any other ways that you normally communicate with employees.

At Hershey Foods Corporation, Quality Through Excellence workshops stress the importance of making everyone responsible for quality by teaching employees what quality means, why it matters, and how to attain it. These workshops, along with other programs, help maintain a customer orientation in all facets of work, encourage continuous improvement, reward initiative, and facilitate problem solving by individuals as well as by employee teams at all levels.

In their daily relations with employees, supervisors and managers can do a great deal to maintain commitment to service. They can do it by congratulating employees on good service and by offering suggestions.

Managers as Day-to-Day Role Models

Above all, they should be role models for good service. They must practice the service tactics that they expect their employees to practice.

If, on the other hand, they treat customers like unwelcome guests, employees are unlikely to treat them like friends.

Furthermore, managers must remember to show employees that they (the managers) care about the well-being of the employees. Managers should maintain good relationships with their employees, if they expect employees to work at winning customer satisfaction.

Service Renewal Ideas

Certified Collateral Corporation of Chicago, which provides 3,000 insurance company claims centers with estimates of the repair and replacement costs of damaged vehicles, reports to employees daily on how they are doing in their service performance. But first, the firm makes sure that new employees know precisely what is expected of them, service-wise.

Hyatt Hotels Corporation buoys on-going service quality with a forum of Hyatt executives from hotels recognized for quality service. They convene regularly to exchange ideas and concerns over service issues in the 1990s. The forum is part of Hyatt's much applauded "In Touch for the '90s" program.

At Albertson's, Inc., supermarket chain headquartered in Boise, Idaho, employee meetings are held every three months to discuss problems and to provide solutions. Albertson's customer service training program is called "Fast, Friendly Service:" Employees wear blue ribbons that say, "I promise fast, friendly service."

For more ideas on how to keep the quality service program going, see Chapter 6 and Chapter 12. Information in these chapters will help maintain a level of service delivery that prevents customer dissatisfaction.

11

Win by Losing: A Complaint Is an Opportunity

SO, SOLICIT COMPLAINTS

> Those who buy support me. Those who come to flatter please me. Those who complain teach me how I may please others so that they will buy. Only those hurt me who are displeased but do not complain. They refuse me permission to correct my errors and thus improve my service.
>
> —*Marshall Field, Pioneering Merchant*

If your organization receives virtually no complaints this is not a sign that you are blessed with the most efficient and intelligent employee force on the face of the earth. It is far more likely that the few complaints that you receive are the tip of a submerged iceberg of complaints.

That's the picture revealed by an A. C. Nielsen Co. study, which found that only 1 in 50 dissatisfied consumers takes the time to complain. So to find out how many customers out there are dissatisfied, multiply the number of complaints received by 50. The result is more likely to represent the true picture in your organization.

Another way of looking at the significance of the number of complaints actually heard is to consider the fact that the ratio of complaints heard at headquarters to the instances of complaining in the marketplace (articulated or not) yields a number called the "multiplier." It ranges from 6 to 1 for serious problems, when there is no field or retail contact organization available, to 2,000 to 1 for less serious problems when an extensive field service organization is active to receive and to absorb problems. So if you have a well-established, professional complaint system in place, and you receive only two complaints last month, you should understand that it is likely that 4,000 customers felt like complaining but didn't.

The existence of a multiplier is the reason that you should solicit complaints, smooth the way for complainers, and even reward customers for complaining. This is what you would do if your objective is total customer satisfaction and its bottom-line benefits.

It's far better for an organization to yank its head out of the sand and to open its eyes to face complaints and complainers than it is to pull a cloak of smugness around its shoulders. Dissatisfied customers are going to strike back, eventually. The company that is aware of complaints will be equipped to take action to prevent the consequences of the complaints.

Employees at all levels need to understand why it is important to solicit, to accept, and to handle and satisfy complaints effectively. They should be assisted in understanding the relation between productive complaint handling and your strategic thinking.

Shycon Associates, Inc., found in a customer service study that almost 70 percent of corporate purchasing agents would take immediate punitive action against a company without complaining to either a salesperson or to a sales manager. They said that it was just easier to switch vendors than to complain. This is a very good reason for soliciting complaints.

The Technical Assistance Research Program (TARP) found that for major problems where there would have been an average loss of $142, about 31 percent of individuals who encountered the problem did not complain.

Nielsen found that for small problems that resulted in loss of a few dollars or a minor inconvenience, only 3 percent of consumers complained. Thirty percent returned the product. Furthermore, 70 percent of consumers encountering this type of problem either would do nothing or would discard the product.

Results of a survey of 1,000 businesses conducted by TARP indicated that 42 percent of companies that encountered problems with a car rental company didn't complain to anyone—even to the counter clerk. You can see the flaw in measuring effectiveness of service by the few number of complaints received.

By the way, the Council of Better Business Bureaus says that complaints about auto repairs top the list of the nation's service problems followed by gripes about home improvement contractors, mail-order companies, and landlords.

Ask Customers for Complaints

Original Research II of Chicago is the model for complaint solicitation. The firm calls customers and asks if they are satisfied with the service or product they receive. If they are dissatisfied, they are asked why they are dissatisfied.

British Airways has video complaint booths at Gatwick airport where customers can vent their anger on videotape. Consideration was being given to installing them in other airports. This is complaint solicitation at its most convenient.

The following incidents indicate how frequently customers refrain from complaining and how serious a problem must be before they complain:

- After production of a $20 bra that tore during its first use, only 1 in 2,000 was returned by either the customer or the retailer.
- Fewer than half of residential customers who experienced a billing problem with a telecommunications supplier told the company about it. What's more, corporate clients have been found to complain to service technicians rather than to account execs because of perceptions that marketing staff is powerless to solve technical problems.
- A business customer of a major computer company complained to the company about system failures. But the computer company's headquarters was flabbergasted when the dissatisfied customer placed an ad in *The Wall Street Journal* and was joined by 300 other companies in legal action. The dissatisfied customer took this drastic action because he got no response to his complaints: the computer company's regional sales reps and management had decided that the problem was "customer incompetence" and not a system failure—because they had actually heard only one or two complaints.
- The average customer who complained to the headquarters of a major credit card company had tried to use routine channels an average of six times.

Break Down Barriers to Complaining

Anybody who's been treated as if he has halitosis, body odor, and ringworm when he or she had the temerity to express a complaint knows about barriers to complaining.

By breaking down consumers' perceived complaint barriers, "unarticulated" dissatisfaction and its resultant negative word of mouth references are lessened.

Make Complaining Easy

Instead of maintaining barriers to complaining, make it easy for customers to complain. Make it as easy as a bad habit. Then the company might discover a flaw in corporate policy or performance that otherwise would be left to alienate large numbers of customers or clients for months—or years. The function of a complaint service is to find wounds in the body corporate and to dress them before gangrene sets in and causes loss of a limb or an organ—a product line, an entire market—or an entire company.

Besides keeping track of the content of customer calls, the General Electric Answer Center stays in tune with what manager N. Powell Taylor calls "the emotional dimensions. You may have a new product with two problems that have surfaced," he says, "and you may want to know which one to fix first. Our people can step in and say 'The consumer is going to be much more emotional about problem A than about problem B.'"

The most nearly effortless complaint procedure in the country may well be the one maintained by the Quill Corporation, a family business that began at the back of a chicken store. Now, this mail-order office supply house is one of the largest companies of its kind in the nation, employing more than 1,100 and occupying 442,000 square feet of office, manufacturing, and warehouse space in Lincolnshire, Illinois.

Quill's complaints procedures are

1. When Quill sends out an order, the package contains a "preauthorized return form." This form, which lists the products that the package contains, allows the customer to complain by simply checking one or more boxes—"damaged merchandise," for example, or "not as advertised" or "needed merchandise sooner."
2. The preauthorized return form includes a section in which the customer can indicate action expected of the company—replacing an item, giving credit, or sending a refund, for instance.
3. Complaint instructions are posted in the place of business and on printed materials to instruct customers in complaint methods.

So a Quill customer needn't call to complain. The complaint form, within each package, is already in the customer's hand. It completely does away with the need for customers to write down order number, account number, or other bothersome data because all of that already is printed on the "preauthorized return form."

Any company could add such a preprinted complaint form to invoices as a tearoff, as a copy in a multipart form, as an extra ticket, or as a loose sheet packed inside packages and boxes, Quill's procedures.

Quill reports that employees often receive compliments on the preauthorized return forms, not complaints.

HOW TO EARN BACK THE COST OF COMPLAINT HANDLING

Bemiss Rolfs, president of National Car Rental, attests to the value of positive resolution of complaints. Says Rolfs: "For every $1 spent in courtesy adjustments, we receive $5 in business."

Companies profit from complaint resolution because they earn customer loyalty that way; so customers continue to buy instead of deserting to competitors.

Profit is a result, too, of sales made in the wake of satisfaction. For instance, Marva McArthur of Waddell and Reed Services in Kansas City says: "When we've turned unhappy customers around, they've said something like, 'Say, what about this other mutual fund that I hear you're coming out with?' We make more sales."

Here are formulas for figuring bottom-line differences between resolving and ignoring customer complaints:

- Resolving a complaint: Profit from resolving customer complaints equals profits from future purchases plus profits from referral purchases.
- Ignoring a complaint: Total loss from failing to resolve a complaint equals loss from future purchases plus loss from word-of-mouth comments minus savings from not resolving one-time complaints.

"During 1980," says a report on a White House study of complaint-handling procedure, "1.56 customers were gained as a result of positive word of mouth for every customer lost because of negative word of mouth."

But Warren Blanding, a leading customer service consultant, apparently believes that negative word of mouth by dissatisfied customers has a greater impact upon sales than does positive word of mouth. He said: "On the average, a company loses four times as many sales through negative word of mouth as it gains through positive word of mouth."

I've found that effective complaint handling policies can virtually reverse these figures to the point where positive word-of-mouth can gain three customers for every two lost as the result of negative word of mouth.

On the other hand, in one study customers who felt that their complaints weren't satisfactorily resolved told a median of 9 to 10 other people about their negative experiences. More than 12 percent of complainants told more than 20 other people about the response they received.

Complaint Resolution Pays Off

Long-term financial benefit from customer loyalty means so much to leading customer service companies such as L. L. Bean, Inc., that they are willing to endure large short-term loss in the interests of customer satisfaction. In 1988, Bean accepted return of $82 million worth of goods—about 14 percent of $588 million in sales. The returns cost Bean $18 million in shipping and handling costs that it could have avoided by denying liability. But that would have been like denying the company a future.

Bean's management knows very well that the company probably wasn't at fault for a large proportion of those returns. Bean feels this way because of the conventional wisdom in the mailorder industry that a significant proportion of shoppers "bracket" their orders. That is, they order the same item in three sizes or colors and return two of them after trying them all on and saving the one that's the best fit and color.

Actually, only a small percentage of merchandise is returned because of defects, Bean reports.

TURNING COMPLAINTS INTO OPPORTUNITIES TO KEEP CUSTOMERS

If service level falters now and then, as it is sure to do because human beings are fallible, all is not lost. Complaints that often result from bad service can be opportunities—opportunities to retain a dissatisfied customer despite a complaint.

Lorna Opatow, president of the New York marketing research company that bears her name, says that customers who complain "are doing us a favor. They're giving us an opportunity to keep their business.

"Whether or not they're nice about it is irrelevant," she says, acknowledging the resentment of employees for customers who insult them.

Just to keep customers, British Airways gave full refunds averaging $3,200 in August 1988 to 63 passengers on a Concorde flight from London because a technical problem left customers grounded in New York. And that's not all: After passing out letters of apology, the airline chartered planes to fly the passengers to their destinations. "We'd rather spend money and keep customers than initiate complaint procedures," says John Lewis, vice president of customer service.

Complaints Expressed Equals Sales

Here's proof that complaints are opportunities. A landmark TARP study for the U.S. Office of Consumer Affairs, entitled "Consumer Complaint Handling in America," found that people given the opportunity to express complaints are more likely than noncomplainers to do business again with the offending company, even if a problem isn't satisfactorily resolved.

If a complaint is resolved, the study found, between 54 and 70 percent of customers who register complaints will do business with an organization again.

That figure rises to 95 percent who will buy again if customers feel that their complaints were resolved quickly.

What we've said here is this: A customer who's never had a complaint or who has never been involved in a customer service complaint situation with a company is not as loyal as a customer who's had such an experience and has been satisfied with a company's handling of it.

Hawthorne Effect Reborn

This seems to be a manifestation of the Hawthorne Effect, so named for pioneering research in employee motivation at Western Electric's Hawthorne Works near Chicago. As noted earlier, the Hawthorne effect is the benefit of "paying attention" to people. Paying attention by servicing a complaint produces customer satisfaction because people love to be noticed. It's similar to a celebrity saying, "I don't care what you say about me. Just get my name right."

The U.S. Office of Consumer Affairs study found that 70 percent of complainants will buy again from the same source if merchandise involved in a complaint costs $5 or less and if the complaint is resolved in a manner satisfactory to the customer. But if an item or service costs $100 or more, only half the complainants will buy again. Still, repeat business from half the disgruntled is better than none.

Use Complaints

Sometimes, companies pour millions of dollars into making sure that their customers have a chance to complain, but then they forget the value of communicating the number of customers who have complained and what they've complained about. They let dearly won and valuable complaint information lie in a computer file when they should be rushing into action a plan to make strategic use of the insights conveyed by the complaints—that is, by taking action to prevent them.

The same negligent companies often fail to provide complainers with satisfactory responses. They either aren't convinced of the financial impact of constructive complaint handling or they don't know how to handle them. So they ignore them. These are the same companies that spend many thousands of dollars on advertising and price cutting to get new customers that improper complaint handling lost.

Customer service is less expensive than is customer replacement. Companies rush in to handle complaints with 800 numbers, service representatives, and consulting firms that measure complaint numbers and impact. But these measures handle only a small percentage of the problem since few dissatisfied customers complain.

That's why the very foundation of quality service is complaint prevention through quality—quality in design and engineering, in manufacturing, in sales practices, in accounting, and in other activities fundamental to a business operation.

When complaints are prevented by doing work right the first time, a company saves the money that doing the same work over again costs.

Getting it right the first time is far more important to customer satisfaction and repeat business than is making good on a product or service that doesn't live up to expectations or to its warranty. The U.S. Air Force and the U.S. Navy Medical Commands, Federal Express, and thousands of other organizations have substantially reduced complaints by training all employees in customer service.

HOW TO PREVENT COMPLAINTS

Drain the swamp instead of constantly fighting the alligators.

Firnstahl's First Rule is: "Always deal with complaints before they're made." Firnstahl is Timothy W. Firnstahl, founder and CEO of Satisfaction Guaranteed Eateries, Inc., of Seattle.

The fact that dissatisfied customers relate experiences to twice as many friends as satisfied customers do is certain proof of the value of preventive customer service.

There is even more preventive value in eliminating the reasons for complaints than there is in providing customers with unlimited opportunity to complain so that the discontent of customers doesn't fester and swell. This is the rationale behind strategies aimed at consistently meeting and exceeding customer expectations.

Do It Right the First Time

The substance of a study by the U.S. Office of Consumer Affairs completed by TARP is the finding that doing the job right the first time and thereby preventing complaints, together with effective complaint handling, yield increased customer satisfaction and brand loyalty.

Well-managed companies see customer complaints as a way to learn: "What lesson can we derive from this complaint that will improve our service in the future?" executives ask.

They also see complaints as opportunities to impress customers by going to any lengths necessary to resolve a situation to a customer's satisfaction. In other words, successful companies pay attention to complaints, but they dedicate most of their efforts to preventing whatever caused the complaints.

Celebrate Success

They categorize, summarize, and distribute complaint data to the people who have the responsibility to change the things customers complain about. They make sure there's a comparable method for collecting, analyzing, and publicizing positive feedback from customers—bouquets or complimentary letters, comments, and data. They celebrate success.

In the reasons for most complaints lies the knowledge needed to prevent them. The most knowledgeable experts seem to agree on the leading causes of customer complaints from a manufacturer's point of view:

design problems, marketing or delivery problems, problems caused by customers, and production defects. The first three are said to cause two-thirds of customer complaints. These causes arise because manufacturers haven't analyzed or made allowance for reasonable customer behavior.

In preventing complaints, American Express's Office of Public Responsibility deals with issues such as

1. What are customers' key expectations?
2. How well is American Express meeting customer expectations? What are the bottom-line implications of not meeting them?
3. What policy or procedural improvements are needed to assure that service meets customer expectations?

John McCormack and his wife, Maryanne, who own 16 Visible Changes hair salons, based in Houston, had a total gross of $20 million at end of a recent year. Quality service is the secret of their success, says McCormack.

The McCormacks work to prevent complaints by recording them and assigning individual salon managers to review them with the employees who are the subjects of the complaints. An employee named in three or more complaints within two weeks must meet with John McCormack at corporate headquarters in Houston. "Usually it's a personal problem," he says. "I give them time off to work things out." He doesn't "discipline" them.

Northern Telecom, Inc., is a paragon of effective complaint prevention activity. The company's Customer Satisfaction Program encompasses all contact between the company and its customers, from presale to ongoing maintenance and repair service.

The Polaroid Corporation maintains a "complaint data base" as part of a program to correct the root causes of customer problems. Progress of the corrective action program is reported to senior corporate management regularly. What's more, a Technical Hotline Unit solicits complaints.

Timothy Firnstahl's first complaint system didn't work: His restaurants would give a free dessert to any customer who complained about slow service, pick up the cleaning bill when an employee spilled the soup on the customer, and send certificates for complimentary meals to customers who wrote in to complain about reservation mix-ups or rude service.

But customers were further inconvenienced in the process of obtaining satisfaction. Usually they had to wait for satisfaction: giving out the free dessert required approval from a manager, for instance. Getting a suit cleaned meant filling out a form and getting a manager to sign it. Some people felt that they had to write in with their complaints to get satisfaction.

Firnstahl asks: "What good is a guarantee that makes complaining an ordeal for the customer?"

But most of all, responses to complaints didn't appear to effect the number or the type of complaints received. "We were on a treadmill, going nowhere."

Identify System Failures

A complaint system, says Firnstahl, should accent areas of system failure that must be corrected to prevent complaints.

He says: "Every dollar paid out to offset customer complaint dissatisfaction is a signal that the company must change in some decisive way. A guarantee of good service (that Satisfaction Guaranteed Eateries offer) brings out a true, hard-dollars picture of company failures and forces us to assume full responsibility for our output.

"Every dollar you give away (in a complaint satisfaction program) is a plus. It puts your finger on a problem you can fix.

"Only the huge cost of a new (complaint satisfaction) strategy revealed that customer problems were gutting profits," says Firnstahl. "Suddenly, we had a real incentive to fix the systems that weren't working, since the alternatives—sacrificing profits permanently or restricting the power to enforce our guarantee—were both unacceptable.

"The trick is to reject Band Aid solutions, to insist on finding the ultimate cause of each problem and then to demand and to expect decisive change."

Firnstahl describes with anecdotes how his new system works: "Our search for the culprit in a string of complaints about slow food service in one restaurant led first to the kitchen and then to one cook. But pushing the search one step farther revealed several complex dishes that no one could have prepared swiftly.

"In another case, our kitchens were turning out wrong orders at a rate that was costing us thousands of dollars a month in wasted food. The cooks insisted that the food servers were punching incorrect orders into the kitchen printout computer. In times past, we might have ended our search right there, accused the food servers of sloppiness, and asked everyone to be more careful.

"But now, adhering to the principle of system failure, not people failure, we looked beyond the symptoms and found a flaw in our training.

"We had simply never taught food servers to double-check their orders on the computer screen, and the system offered no reward for doing so. Mistakes plummeted," Firnstahl says, "as soon as we trained people properly and handed out awards each month for the fewest ordering errors and posting lists of the worst offenders."

Profits Will Improve

As for cost of a guarantee system such as his for handling complaints, Firnstahl says: "As you find and correct the ultimate cause of your system failures, you can reasonably expect your profits to improve.

"But," he says, "you can begin to tell if you're succeeding even before you see it on the bottom line. Remember, costs will go up before they come down, so high system-failure costs and low phone survey complaint rates probably mean you're on the right track.

"Our own system failure costs rose to a high of $40,000 a month two years ago and then fell to $10,000 a month. Meanwhile, sales rose 25 percent, profits doubled, and the cash in the bank grew two and a half times."

In 1989 *Chief Executive* magazine surveyed 1,000 chief executives, and the results confirmed Firnstahl's on-the-job conclusions. The survey sample was slightly skewed toward larger companies and toward the manufacturing sector. One of four key messages concerning customer satisfaction that emerged from the survey was: don't just train employees to deliver service. Get more fundamental: change how you do business. In other words, generate customer satisfaction.

LONG-TERM VALUE OF FAST, FAIR COMPLAINT HANDLING

Procter & Gamble, the nation's largest producer of consumer products, prints an 800 number—543-0485—on all its products. During a recent year, P&G answered about a million telephone calls and letters from customers, according to Dorothy Pucini, manager of Consumer Services. Only a third of these replies dealt with complaints. (Among complaints were those about product ads and the plots of soap operas sponsored by the company.)

The long-term value of competent complaint handling is revealed in the projection that if only half the P&G complaints were about products with 30 cent margins, and if only 85 percent were handled to the customer's satisfaction, annual benefit to the company would have exceeded half a million dollars.

Financial Benefit

This result is reached with a formula for calculating financial benefit of complaint resolution activity that was developed by TARP. The formula projects that when customers are completely satisfied, 9.9 percent of them buy more and 84 percent of them buy at the same rate. That is, they are retained as customers.

When customers find service merely "acceptable," 2.7 percent still buy more, but 31.5 percent buy less, compared with only 5.2 percent who buy less when they are completely satisfied. When service is only "acceptable," 59.6 percent of these customers buy at the same rate.

Predictably, when a customer is not satisfied with service, 75.3 percent (3 out of 4) either stop buying or buy less.

What's more, they tell at least nine others about their bad experience, according to a study by the White House Office of Consumer Affairs.

Here is a reason for maintaining good service.

An 800 number or any other well-established means of responding to consumers provides a friendly human contact and, often, a quick solution—remedies to consumers' unhappiness with faceless corporate monoliths.

What's more, consumer response setups increase the speed with which information reaches customers and the speed with which a repair is completed or a product is delivered—all of which contributes strongly to customer satisfaction.

NINE TECHNIQUES FOR COOLING DOWN AN IRATE CUSTOMER

"Irate." It means infuriated, enraged, indignant, angry, mad. Retail salespeople everywhere, and their supervisors, know these meanings well. They've seen them acted out many times by customers who were displeased with service or merchandise.

They may sell ladies fashions in an exclusive department store or groceries and gas in a neighborhood convenience store. They may sell face to face or over the phone.

No matter what or how they sell, they have been confronted by people who were merely displeased or mildly disappointed, by people who were spluttering and turning purple, and by people who were speechless and embarrassed by their anger.

No matter what their own emotional reactions, salespeople should stay in control of themselves.

When employees notice storm clouds gathering, they should head off complaints at the pass with concerned comments such as "Thank you very much for waiting. I apologize for the delay" or "Thank you for being so patient."

A warm smile can push storm clouds aside to reveal blue sky.

Handling irate customers coolly and intelligently is the real test—the final exam—in the college of customer relations. Take the offensive with kindness and tact when faced with the ticking time bomb that is an irate customer.

When customers have a specific complaint, follow these steps:

1. Listen actively. That means make responses that show that you are listening, responses such as "I see" and "I can appreciate your problem." Make certain a customer receives either an apology, if deserved, or an explanation —at once.
2. Empathize. Be courteous and helpful. Sprinkle genuine, sincere, friendly comments through your conversation. "Sir, I can appreciate your concern" or "I don't blame you for being upset." Once customers feel that they are talking to a real human being who understands and who sympathizes with their problem, the door opens to rational discussion.

QUALITY SERVICE TECHNIQUES

Four Methods for Defusing a Difficult Situation

- SMILE: give the customer a warm, sincere hello with a smile.
- ANTICIPATE: the customer's complaint and head it off with a sincere, concerned comment. (Take the offensive with kindness.)
- APOLOGIZE AND ASSUME RESPONSIBILITY: take the blame for the customer's situation and empathize with them for their problem on behalf of your organization.
- ACTION: solve the problems promptly.

Six Keys to Cooling Down an Irate Customer

- LISTEN: carefully and with interest.
- EMPATHIZE: put yourself in the customer's place. Use Warm Fuzzies that are:
  Genuine
  Specific
  Timely
  Sincere
- ASK QUESTIONS: in a mature, non-threatening way, that requires the customer to think about his/her answers.
- REPEAT: back to the customer your understanding of their problem, then suggest one or more alternatives to answer their concerns.
- APOLOGIZE: without blaming.
- SOLVE the problem: identify solutions to satisfy the customer's needs or find someone who can.

FEELINGS

COMMUNICATION TECHNIQUES

Positive Strokes:

Communicating in a positive manner through Warm Fuzzies that are:

- Genuine (Real)
- Specific (Definite, Precise)
- Timely (Give immediate feedback)
- Sincere (Without deceit or pretense)

Negative Strokes:

Communicating in a negative manner through Cold Pricklies (Any negative word or action). Additional categories of Negative Strokes are:

- Zero (Absence of any communication technique)
- Crooked (Positive communication followed by a negative remark)
- Plastic (Comments given as a ritual)
- Hostile (Aggressive, threatening communication style)

Quality Service:

Providing excellence in customer service through six methods of human interaction:

- Feeling Good About Yourself
- Practice Habits of Courtesy
- Speaking (Verbal and non-verbal communication)
- Listening (Anticipating, reading between the lines, asking questions, getting involved, caring about your customer and their needs)
- Performance (Providing quality work that is prompt and accurate)
- Learning (Job growth through knowing more about your customer, company and products)

A pocket card lists "Four Methods for Defusing a Difficult Situation" and "Six Keys to Cooling Down an Irate Customer." (Reprinted courtesy of the Service Quality Institute.)

3. Ask questions that require logical thinking by the customer to try and pull the person out of the irate state. Keep asking questions and listening to the response until the customer has cooled down.
4. Don't become emotionally involved. Learn to understand that you, personally, are not the target.
5. Identify the problem as quickly as possible. For instance, obtain facts about a situation from the sales rep or from the person who told a customer that a job would be finished on time, though it was destined to be late from the beginning. Also ascertain current status of the job.
6. If you are at fault, take the blame immediately. Apologize. Say: "I'm sorry for making you wait so long. I'm new in this position." "Unfortunately, I haven't mastered this cash register yet." "Thanks for being so patient."
7. Make a sincere, positive statement such as: "Mrs. Jones, you have been doing business with our firm for four years and we are going to take care of you." This way you make the person feel important.
8. Find ways to minimize the problem like farming out a job that might be delivered late so that it can be delivered on time.
9. Solve the problem. Get help from a supervisor, if necessary. And let the customer know what you plan to do.

It is very important that the customer walks away thinking that she or he came out on top of the deal, even if it costs you money.

Stephen Brobeck, executive director of the Consumer Federation of America, says: "In my experience, almost every consumer who is upset has some justification and is complaining rationally. Very few consumers get angry unless they're ignored or are turned away when they try to explain their complaint.

"A smart businessperson says calmly, 'We will try to resolve your complaint.' Then they lead the customer into his or her office, sit down, and ask the person to explain the problem. They don't argue."

Jan Charles Gray, senior vice president of Ralph's Grocery Co. in Los Angeles, says: "One of the main things is to try and not take complaints personally. Understand that there is a lot going on in the customer's mind. People get most irate when they aren't greeted with a smile or with concern about their problems."

Here's an alternative complaint handling "matrix":

1. Accept responsibility. The last thing a customer wants to hear is: "That's not my department." If you are the person the customer has chosen, you are the one, at that point, who is the organization's representative. It's up to you to listen to and to understand the problem and then to take the customer to the person who can ultimately solve the problem. At that point, you are the customer's

advocate. Stay with her or him until you are sure that the problem will be taken care of.

2. Show your concern. The primary way to accomplish this is to listen, with empathy. Ask yourself how you would like to be treated if you were in the same situation. Never interrupt or assume that you know what the problem is before the customer explains it. You may have heard the same complaint a hundred times before, but this is probably the first time the customer has voiced it. He or she may have even rehearsed his or her story and will sorely resent an uninterested attitude by you.
3. Stay calm. Sometimes a person with a complaint gets excited or even angry. Occasionally, he or she will take out their frustrations on you. Try to understand the situation from his or her point of view. Don't get pulled into a shouting match. Reassure the customer that you are concerned and will try to resolve the problem.
4. Be sure you understand the complaint. One of the keys to handling a complaint successfully is to be sure that you know exactly what the problem is. Put it in your own words, and ask the customer if you are understanding it correctly. If the customer doesn't spell out the resolution he or she is looking for, ask what he or she wants. This will assure the customer that you care enough to see the problem solved.
5. Solve the problem. Either take the problem to whoever can solve it or solve it yourself. In either case, it is up to you to stay with the customer until the problem is resolved.

Remember: You are the one the customer has chosen.

Employees must learn to separate their job roles from their personal identities. Through effective listening, reflection, asking effective questions, avoiding impossible promises, negotiating, and handling complaints, they must develop the ability to assess their personal levels of tolerance, to understand their feelings, and to match their behavior to the needs of the situation.

Here are more tips for dealing with irate customers.

- Do not respond to attempts by a customer with a complaint to "bait" you even if the customer is making preposterous and outrageous statements.
- Even if an irate customer is wrong and you are right, don't go overboard trying to prove it. Concentrate, instead, upon gathering enough information to solve the problem.
- Get the person to focus on the specific complaint that's at the root of any general complaints.
- Never blame another employee or another department.
- Avoid use of the pronoun "you" or language implying that the customer caused the problem. The most common example—"You failed to enclose payment"—leaves no room for the possibility

that the check was lost, misposted, or stolen and places unnecessary blame on the customer. The object is to get the check, not to assign responsibility.

You can "neutralize" such a statement by saying: "The check appears to have been omitted. Has it turned up there?" This no-fault approach suggests that an abstract third party (not "you") simply may have forgotten to enclose the check.

Another useful neutral approach is to call an error to the customer's attention through rephrasing and paraphrasing: "Let me see if I have this right." Often, the customer will immediately see the error without prompting, by virtue of having heard it phrased differently by another person without using any judgmental language.

Market-driven companies don't argue with the facts or try to persuade a customer that the buyer is wrong and the seller is right. They listen and they respond. They seek out customer comments and take them to heart. And they don't consider doing so a burden or an avoidable expense.

HOW TO DETERMINE IF A COMPLAINT SYSTEM IS NEEDED

Apply research techniques described in Chapter 4. However, if you don't have a complaint system, it is a safe assumption that you need one, judging by results of a *Wall Street Journal* 1989 annual survey. The "aspirations and attitudes" of more than 4,000 consumers from all walks of life were surveyed and a lot of "peevish shoppers" were found.

"Shopping has become such a chore," the *Journal* commented, that some people actually hate taking a trip to the supermarket more than doing housework, the paper reported.

The "in-depth probe of the consumer psyche," as the *Journal* labeled it, was conducted in two separate polls by the Roper Organization and by Peter D. Hart Research Associates Inc.

Peter Hanlon, 32, a computer analyst in Spokane, Washington, was quoted as saying: "I'm happier as a person than as a purchaser. I live in the best country on earth, so I guess I'll put up with high prices, mediocre quality, and poor service."

Only 5 percent of the people in Hart's part of the study think that American business is listening to them and trying to do its best. Almost one-third think companies and executives are too greedy, a view that's popular with white-collar professionals and executives earning $35,000 to $50,000 a year.

One of the top peeves of America's stressed-out consumers, reports the *Journal*, is waiting in long lines while other registers or windows are closed. The newspaper also reports that many consumers seethe when they hear a recorded solicitation message while in a store.

It turns out that if you want to drive people crazy—especially working women—have your service or delivery people fail to show up when they say they will. Joan Tinsman, a 52-year-old nurse in Topton, Pennsylvania, is still fuming at how a Kenmore washing machine repairman failed to show up at her house, even though the event occurred a decade ago. Ms. Tinsman, a respondent in the *Journal* survey, recalls: "He showed up a week late and said, 'Lady, maybe you'd better buy a new machine.' I thanked him for his suggestion—and bought a Westinghouse."

ORGANIZING THE COMPLAINT-HANDLING FUNCTION

A complaint-handling department should consist of two coordinated functions: operations, to respond to complaints on a day-to-day basis, and support, to assist in identifying and eliminating causes, to ensure that consumers know where and how to complain, and to see that complaints are handled according to established procedures.

Operations Functions: Input

1. Screening: Sorting complaints, directing to appropriate offices for resolution.
2. Logging: Recording information on each complaint.
3. Classification: Coding complaints according to preselected categories thereby defining problem areas.

Operations Functions: Response

1. Investigation: Examining in-house records, telephone research, written correspondence, field research.
2. Response formulation (the most important step in complaint handling): Formulating responses according to legal responsibility, expectations of complainants, compromise, marketing benefits, concepts of equity, and when necessary third-party arbitration.
3. Response production: Preparing text of final response and transmitting it, which includes decision and rationale. If response goes against expectations of the complainant, delineate appeal procedures. When responses are verbal, notes should be made on conversations.

Operations Functions: Output

1. Distribution: Sending out final response to complainant. Do it promptly.
2. Storage and retrieval: Maintaining files of complaints.

COMPLAINT INFORMATION FORM

Kemper GROUP

2-4 OFFICE | 5, 6 CO. | 7-10 MO. YR. | 11-14 SEQ. NUMBER | 15-20 DATE RECEIVED

21-46 COMPLAINANT'S NAME—LAST | FIRST | M.

STREET ADDRESS

CITY | STATE | ZIP CODE | PHONE NO.

POLICYHOLDER, IF OTHER THAN ABOVE

47, 48 CIRCLE STATE WHERE COMPLAINT ORIGINATED

AL	AK	AZ	AR	CA	CO
CT	DE	DC	FL	GA	HI
ID	IL	IN	IA	KS	KY
LA	ME	MD	MA	MI	MN
MS	MO	MT	NB	NV	NH
NJ	NM	NY	NC	ND	OH
OK	OR	PA	PR	RI	SC
SD	TN	TX	UT	VT	VA
VI	WA	WV	WI	WY	ON
QU					

49 FUNCTION | 50-52 REASON | 53-55 LINE TYPE | 56-58 SOURCE | 59, 60 HOW TRANSMITTED | 61-73 POLICY NO.

74-88 INSURANCE DEPT. NO. | 89-104 CLAIM NO. | D/L

105, 106 CO. DISP. | 107-112 DATE CLOSED | CLAIM REPRESENTATIVE/UNDERWRITER NAME

AGENT/BROKER NAME

NATURE OF COMPLAINT

FINAL DISPOSITION

The complaint information form used by the Kemper Group of insurance companies includes the original copy for the home office and carbons for the division affiliate, for the reporting unit. The fourth sheet is a "change/deletion copy." The back side of the sheets contains a list of codes identifying the subjects of complaints, the company and function involved, and the sources of complaints. (Reprinted courtesy of the Kemper Group.)

Support Functions: Control

1. Internal follow-up: Setting and monitoring standards for response time and quality. Correcting deviations from standards.
2. Referral follow-up: Applying time and quality criteria to responses of other departments, the field, and other organizations or agencies. Do it by requesting copies of final responses. Ask for all responses or for samples.

Support Functions: Management

1. Statistical generation: Use statistics in policy analysis and evaluating performance of complaint-handling office.
2. Policy analysis: Interpreting data to uncover root causes of complainants' problems, key issues, trends. Costs associated with not eliminating problems can be quantified and solutions proposed.
3. Evaluations: Determining whether performance objectives set for the complaint-handling department are being met, identifying performance problems that need attention, and addressing these problems. Whenever possible, evaluation should be done by an outside firm. If this isn't possible, in-house evaluators from other departments are acceptable.
4. Planning: Setting priorities for the complaint-handling department. Planning should cover setting goals for complaint satisfaction and assuring that new problems are identified and integrated into the system. Tools for achieving goals can include staff training, consumer education, and so on.
5. Accountability: Assigning complaint-handling and prevention responsibility to specific people and offices.
6. Creating a reward and/or punishment system to encourage proper handling of complaints and prevention of future problems. Rewards can be economic or noneconomic (plaques, praise).
7. Staff selection, empowerment, and training: Choosing people who have the appropriate personal skills, giving them authority to make immediate problem-solving decisions, and training them in the technical skills needed to perform their jobs adequately.

Employees should be trained so well that they apply the appropriate service instinctively. It helps if they possess personal characteristics that equip them for this work—pleasant voice, optimism, ability to listen, flexibility, and patience.

Fidelity Bank of Philadelphia consolidated its complaint-handling systems. There had been a system for each of 14 different business segments.

Copy To

Date

To

From Consumer Relations, Long Grove, F-6

Previous
Comm

Regarding

______ A corporate officer has received the attached communication concerning a consumer complaint. I am indicating to the consumer that a company representative will be in touch. Please copy me in on any pertinent correspondence, in addition to returning a "Complaint Information Form" properly completed.

______ I am forwarding the attached complaint to you for handling. We have acknowledged receipt to the Insurance Department/complaintant. Please copy me in on any pertinent correspondence, in addition to returning a "Complaint Information Form" properly completed.

_____ I am attaching further correspondence on this complaint, originally sent to you on __________________________. Again, please copy me in on any pertinent correspondence.

Thank you for your assistance.

art 20

9057R
(0270r)

When a consumer sends a complaint to a corporate officer, the consumer is likely to receive a prompt and efficient response. When an employee receives a communication such as this from a corporate officer, reaction usually is fast. (Reprinted courtesy of the Kemper Group.)

Now customers with problems involving savings accounts, auto loans, and credit cards call one telephone number. Clients with major problems write to the office of the president. The president reads all the letters as well as summaries of the bank's other complaints and inquiries, about 120 per month. In 1989 87 percent of Fidelity's customers said that they are satisfied or highly satisfied with service compared with 57 percent in 1986.

Sometimes, really listening and reacting to customers can trigger massive changes. Bell South Corp. was reacting to customer input when it decided to recombine its business services and its equipment sales and maintenance operations. They had been scattered into separate subsidiaries as part of the original Bell System divestiture plan. On January 1, 1989, it restored "one-stop shopping" for business customers. It became the first of the Bell companies to recombine its services and equipment sales and its maintenance staff under new FCC rules.

"We took this step because customers told us time and again that this is what they wanted," says Jere Drummond, senior vice president of Marketing for Bell South.

COMPLAINT-HANDLING CASE HISTORIES

Conrad Hilton of Hilton Hotels always sent apology letters under his own name. The letters included enough detail to make the recipient feel that Hilton knew about his complaint. For instance: "Please accept my apology for November 13. The fact that you were kept waiting and then obliged to use another hotel is distressing to us."

In some of the best customer service-driven companies, an executive personally resolves a service quality problem. A complainer receives prompt, personal attention and often special gifts that demonstrate earnest concern for the customer's situation. In this way an organization can convert a complainer into a loyal, life-long customer.

Connie Bell of C. C. Bell Electronics in St. Louis, established a Zero Defects Customer Complaint Policy. It consists of

- Employee attitude.
- Use of the customer's name.
- Fast service.
- Quality service.
- Fair price.

When a consumer arrives for service, says Bell, the consumer already is unhappy because the product no longer works. He or she resents spending money to restore the appliance to its promised performance level.

It is important, at this point, to assure the consumer that the problem is understood. It's also necessary that store employees provide whatever help is needed to resolve the problem.

The service person at the counter must project a sincerely friendly attitude and conduct the transaction positively.

Bell emphasizes importance of using the customer's name repeatedly. In most cases the last name should be used with the Mr. or Mrs. prefix, unless the service person knows the customer on a first name basis.

Service Delay? Communicate

When a customer delivers a product to the service center, Bell notes, she or he is most interested in getting it back quickly. He advises that it is the duty of a service manager to monitor progress on the repair. When completion will be delayed, the service manager should call the customer before he or she comes in to pick up the appliance.

Jerry Stead, CEO of Square D Company of Milwaukee, says that the company began using role model examples. "Originally we had 'corporate officer of the day.' It really meant the junior citizen in town got all the complaints. Instead, we put in a complaint phone under my desk and I answer it."

But, said Stead, "I hope that as our other systems get better, I won't have to."

TARP did a study for Coca-Cola that found that a complainer denied a request over the phone is 30 percent more likely to remain brand loyal than a buyer who receives the same message in a letter. That's because a phone conversation is more personal and gives the service rep a chance to explain the company's position and to woo the customer back.

Not only is answering complaints by phone faster. It usually saves money. American Express spends five to ten times as much replying to a letter as it does answering a complaint over its toll-free lines. The company often ends up calling a letter writer anyway to get more information about a problem.

TELLING MANAGEMENT THE WHOLE TRUTH

Employees often have a stake in not reporting complaints to management. That's another reason why some managements have a rosy picture of their complaint situation.

Complaints aren't reported because correcting the problem that's causing the complaint might inconvenience employees or reflect negatively on their performance.

For example, if customers complain that they can't reach the company after 5 P.M., an employee who doesn't want to work after 5 o'clock might not tell his superior about the complaints.

Both medical products and insurance companies have found that field sales reps tend to pass on complaints only when doing so ingratiates them with an important customer—or when a product is of such low margin that the sales staff would rather see it discontinued. Complaints, of course, provide a good rationale for discontinuing a product.

Only 1 in 50 Complain

Retail outlets and field offices of manufacturers filter out *and discourage* complaints. Complaints that reach headquarters definitely are no measure of the degree of customer satisfaction. The A. C. Nielsen Co. survey referred to earlier found that, for package goods companies, only 1 person in 50 who encountered a problem wrote a letter to the manufacturer. So a package goods manufacturer hears only about 1 out of 50 problem experiences at headquarters, the same proportion referred to at the beginning of this chapter.

TARP's studies found that less than half of those who complained at the retail level were satisfied by the company's response. However, less than half of those who were dissatisfied bothered to escalate to the retailer's headquarters or to the manufacturer.

A retailer or field service may stop a complaint from going further, whether they handle or mishandle a complaint. So to get a true picture of the extent of complaints, you must extrapolate the actual number of complaints, using a multiplier such as the 50 to 1 multiplier dictated by the Nielsen finding that about 1 of 50 customers dissatisfied with a package goods manufacturer complain to headquarters.

Managers need to generate enthusiasm about getting feedback from customers and passing it on to management so action can be taken to prevent problems.

Training

A vital part of all training programs for employees (the subject of the next chapter) is training in handling complaints. If you want burnout one hour into employees' shifts, don't train them. You can't tell employees that they ought to encourage customers to complain without training them to handle complaint situations and to defuse them. If you toss employees to the customer wolves without training, you will demoralize the work force and accelerate turnover rate.

When employees don't know how to handle complainers, they avoid customers who complain. Or they deflect complaints by saying something like: "My supervisor should handle this problem and he or she isn't in now."

An effective service system is able to satisfy many consumers who experience problems and who would otherwise have been dissatisfied. But first, it's necessary to reach them which means that first they must complain.

That's the point of service setups: they are designed to reach dissatisfied customers so they can be satisfied, but most of all, service systems should prevent dissatisfaction.

12

Customer Service Pros Are Made, not Born

TRAIN FRONT-LINERS AND EXECUTIVES ALIKE

> Business in general spends too little time training and motivating front-line employees whom they treat as the lowest workers on the ladder.
>
> —*Time Magazine*

> You train dogs and bears. You educate employees.
>
> —*Stanley Marcus, Chairman Emeritus, The Neiman Marcus Company*

What are the basic, bottom-line benefits of quality service training? One of them is added effectiveness of marketing activities, including advertising, sales promotion—all those things that are done to coax customers to buy.

Training equips sales and support people who are untrained in service to earn customer satisfaction and loyalty—and future purchases. Without customer service skills, employees can cause customer defection—and waste millions of dollars spent on marketing. Marketing efforts bring people in, but poor service immediately turns them away, encouraging them to buy from a competitor.

Trained people with specific customer service skills and customer service orientation are more productive in terms of both time and results of transactions, too.

Training Reduces Employment Cost

Warren Blanding, leading service consultant and president of the Customer Service Institute in Silver Spring, Maryland, performed these calculations: under conditions of typical productivity in customer service operations, an employee earning $6 to $7 an hour has an actual fully distributed cost of as much as $20 to $25 an hour. Making that employee 10 percent more productive through training reduces the cost range to $17 to $22, a savings of about $20 per employee per day and $100 weekly. That's roughly $5,000 annually per employee. For a company with 20 phone employees, a one second reduction in all customer service inquiry and complaint calls, a result of training that makes employees more efficient, produces annual savings of more than $3,500 per employee.

Training Retains Employees

Employee retention aspects of service training, alone, give training a value at least five times its cost. The basis for this calculation is the generally accepted fact that attracting new customers costs five times as much as keeping customers you already have by practicing customer satisfaction techniques.

A service mentality, conveyed by employee training, adds credibility to the marketing mix. If customers develop a disapproving attitude toward a company because of the way they're treated—or not treated—the company loses credibility. Customers are unlikely to react to marketing messages in the ways intended.

I saw a TV ad for a New York hotel with front desk people singing in the street and a bellman greeting customers warmly and toting luggage. But, when I stayed at the hotel there was no bellman to pick up my luggage or to greet me. The commercial bore no relation to reality.

How important is credibility? If you don't have it, you have nothing. No matter how good your product, people still won't buy it if they're treated like consumers obligated to buy unquestioningly.

But, if people smile when they hear the name of your company or your brand name or your service because they are recalling your friendly, helpful, knowledgeable employees and how fast and uncomplicated it is to buy from you, then they will react well to your marketing messages. Your marketing budget will be spent efficiently.

The positive impact of quality service upon the effectiveness of your marketing program is one of the primary reasons why you need service training for your employees.

Actions Speak Louder Than Words

The best way to illustrate the close connection between quality service and marketing effectiveness is to ask an admittedly far-fetched question: Is a customer who has learned by experience that your employees are indolent, insolent, ignorant, insincere, indifferent, and aloof going to rush in and buy just because your advertising claims that you treat each customer as an individual and as a potential friend? The answer is "No." The customer will flee from you. Sometimes they'll go to outrageous lengths to avoid buying from you, even if it means doing without a service or product that they can't get anywhere else.

Prospects react in generally the same way to claims about product value when they've been treated with the same personal care given store mannequins, repeatedly.

When your actions contradict your words, your marketing messages not only become unbelievable but also subjects of ridicule.

Furthermore, future marketing messages, in ads and commercials, for instance, are questioned. An atmosphere of distrust and of discounting of ad claims can persist for years.

To attain a valuable symbiotic relationship between service and product, in-store training programs and on-the-job training are indispensable.

Values of Training on Site

Managers and supervisors can be trained to conduct customer relations training for employees. Some companies prefer to have managers and supervisors train the employees who report to them. When they train their own employees, managers and supervisors can convey to them their personal commitment to service and present themselves as role models.

Supervisors and managers must model, coach, and reinforce the attitudes and behavior they expect of subordinates. Without active support, education in customer service is a risky investment.

Low-Cost Education

Using your own managers and supervisors to convey education at the job site makes it unnecessary for employees at distant, scattered locations to assemble at a central point that might be thousands of miles from their jobs. Transportation cost and time are saved, too.

The resulting low cost education makes it practical to present a review of customer service education every few months when turnover is high.

Travel costs have become excessive. So use technology to educate employees. Labor cost is the most expensive component of work force education.

For the past 40 years we have defined "good training" and "bad training" in terms of number of training days. Clearly, 5 days of training were better than 4—and 4 days better than 3.

There may be validity to this view of executives or salespeople who are being trained. But, if an entire dynamic work force is being trained, then 5 days of training is costly and difficult logistically without disrupting business.

Leader Guide Text

> Note: The information in the boxes must be conveyed to the participants. You may read it or you may convey the information in your own words. Additional instructions to you are printed outside the boxes.

In welcoming the participants to this program, you may want to tell a bit about yourself and your job responsibilities. Whichever way you proceed as Group Leader, please remember that the objective is to generate discussion among the participants.

> Welcome to Session One of the AT YOUR SERVICE Customer Service System. For those of you who don't know me, I'm (give your name), and I'll be acting as Group Leader during the training sessions. As Group Leader, I'll be providing some framework for our discussions, but each of you will be helping one another as we go along. Now that you know me, how about introducing yourselves. Please share with us your name and job function.

(Allow time for each participant to introduce themselves.)

> Thank you. For the next few seconds, I'd like each of you to think about something you've done, either in your work or personal life, that gave you satisfaction—some accomplishment that really stands out in your mind, that you really enjoyed. Okay, close your eyes and think about it for a second.

(Please wait five or ten seconds until you start seeing some smiles.)

A successful leader guide is user friendly—easy for course leaders to follow. It contains all the information a leader needs to conduct a class while permitting any additions a leader wishes to make. This sample is from the leader's guide employed by Service Quality Institute, formerly Better Than Money Corporation.

That felt good, didn't it? That warm feeling is what AT YOUR SERVICE is all about: feeling good more of the time, and just as important, making others feel good, too. There's more to AT YOUR SERVICE than making people smile more often. Our moving company has decided to use this system for a very simple reason: to improve the quality of service we deliver to our customers.

As an Allied Agent, our company's success depends upon the personal success of each of us. So it stands to reason that anything which helps us will help the company. We all benefit. During these sessions, you'll be hearing some statistics about the positive and negative impact of customer service, or lack of it, on businesses.

The success of any business today depends upon the quality service it provides. It's no different for us. The feelings that our customers have about Allied, (name of your moving agency), other agents, and about each of us, directly impacts the bottom line. Like any other business, we need customers. Think about it for a moment. What does being a customer mean?

(Participants will likely say that being a customer means spending money to buy something.)

In the moving business, we generally refer to our customers as shippers. Throughout these sessions you will hear both terms, customer and shipper, used interchangeably. From a customer stand-point, we need to think about how the word "shipper" affects our customers. It doesn't sound as personal as the word "customer" does it?

One goal of the AT YOUR SERVICE System is to bring continuity to the Allied system. We, as part of that Allied Family, have the power to change attitudes and increase the level of service we give our customers. Let's begin our commitment to excellence by making a conscious effort to use the word "customer", especially when dealing personally with those very people who choose to use our moving services.

Let's think about our customers for a moment. What kind of customers do we have?

(Our customers are varied. They come from all walks of life and expect us to provide them with a professional move of their household belongings, business equipment, or storage of their possessions. Hopefully, some participants will say that fellow employees, families, and friends are customers in many senses. If this point comes up, allow it to continue. If not, don't worry—it will be covered.)

So, I think we've established that being a customer covers a lot of ground, but as we'll see, the word "customer" has a very broad definition. Let's think about the customers we meet every day. How about sharing with our group some positive or negative customer experiences you've had.

(Ask a couple of people to share positive experiences they've had as customers; then, ask a couple of people to share negative experiences they've had as customers.)

Analyzing experiences like these is the basis of the AT YOUR SERVICE System. Much of what we're going to talk about in these sessions won't be anything new to you. The system is based on some very simple ideas. Most of us know these ideas, but statistics and surveys show that many people often don't put them into practice, especially in a work environment.

With your help, AT YOUR SERVICE will teach us the skills we need to deliver quality customer service. The system will give us a real workout, in much the same way that athletes are trained to improve their skills. AT YOUR SERVICE will help us understand why we do what we do and give us tools to help us to do our jobs better.

(Distribute copies of the participant book as you speak.)

That's why we're here. The copies of the AT YOUR SERVICE Participant Book you're receiving now are yours to keep. We'd like you to read the book as we go through the sessions. The material in it will help stimulate discussion and start us thinking about the concept of customer service.

These sessions will be structured around our group discussions and the videotaped scenarios we'll see. The skits in the videotapes were structured to get us to think about the issues presented. There will be questions based on the situations shown and on your own experiences. There are no right or wrong answers to these questions, so don't be concerned. Our goal is to look at what we're doing now, and find better ways to deliver quality service to our customers. We're going to learn skills that will help us in our personal lives as much as they will help us on the job.

Let's start the videotape.

(Please turn on the videotape; Session One, Section A.)

I believe strongly that user-friendly course leader material is necessary. It equips virtually any committed person with peer respect and enthusiasm to conduct a program of employee education in customer service. But most learning programs have been designed for implementation by their authors or by highly skilled facilitators. They need to be flown to various locations, at great expense, to conduct the training.

With employee turnover rates typically at 50 to 100 percent, the facilitator must be sent on his or her costly way every three to six months.

Too often facilitator material is designed to protect training jobs instead of making them user friendly and capable of on-site implementation.

The sample leader guide format printed here was developed by Better than Money Corporation (now Service Quality Institute) for Allied Van Lines. It was formatted so that virtually anyone in any of the 750 Allied agent offices can implement a customized customer service system called "At Your Service."

The cost of implementing a customer service program in terms of facilitator salaries and travel costs become so high that many organizations never get around to committing to service education.

Service education should teach employees that actions speak louder than words. Service representatives, billing office employees and others have frequent dealings with customers, yet they often unwittingly sabotage the messages conveyed through advertising, display, and public communications. Insulting collection notices, unfriendly phone operators, and bills that sound like accusations all create a sense of silent antagonism by the customer toward a company. But the company often is unaware of what is going on.

Despite havoc wrought by uneducated employees, on-site and on-the-job service education is not common. A survey of 20 major organizations found that they devote less than one day of education to people in service positions. Most of this education is misdirected. It is aimed at teaching people how to run equipment and how to smile when handling angry customers.

A study of more than 200 corporations by Zenger-Miller, Inc., found almost the same thing. Education efforts are, at best, marginal, and they focus mostly on teaching front-line employees how to cross-sell and how to handle irate customers.

EDUCATE EVERYBODY

The most effective service quality education programs reflect an understanding that service quality is produced by an entire organization and only delivered by the front line. That's why service education programs must be developed for all employees.

The rest of the company is resource for the front line.

This, I must say, is revolutionary thinking.

Still, some of these internal resources provide services directly to customers. Among them are billing, delivery, production, marketing information, sales, maintenance, security, and the switchboard operator.

Internal Service Resources

However, a front-line employee often is unable to provide good service even if he or she wants to provide it, when service cannot be obtained within the organization. Say that a new DOS operating language personal computer is being sold and the customer asks how to convert old-fashioned C/PM operating language files to DOS. If the computer sales firm's marketing department or the service department has never taken the time to locate a company that provides conversion service, the computer salesperson will deliver poor service even if he or she is eager to provide good service.

Everyone Contributes to Service Quality

The common practice of making service quality the sole obligation of front-line people is similar to making the loading dock worker responsible for product quality. Long-term consequences of this practice for both effectiveness and morale are predictably low service quality.

When customer-oriented values are taught only at the front line, then a company runs the considerable risk of creating employee frustration because the rest of the organization is not operating with service quality in mind.

"Companies spend a lot of money teaching their salespeople 'the message,' including standard answers to sensitive questions. But they may forget to teach those same answers to technical reps, field service people, and customer reps who deal with the same customers as the sales reps do," observes Brenda J. Weimer, North American customer service manager for Polystar Ltd. of Leominster, Massachusetts.

Certainly, the sales representative makes the only contact with the customer during the selling process. But after the sale, then a customer comes in contact with receptionist, secretary, billing clerks, and others.

The process of providing service quality begins far behind the front line of an organization. So improvement in service should not be the sole responsibility of front-line employees.

If an organization is going to be service driven, everybody, whether they work part time, full time, or temporarily and whether they have been on the job for a week or for five years must be trained. And they must be trained repeatedly.

This has been a difficult message to convey to managements.

Managers Only

Sometimes companies feel that employees below management level are not worthy of education.

To imply from the significance of management in the service scheme that only management needs education constitutes a significantly counterproductive oversight, no matter how elegant the rationalization supporting it.

The reason is that 95 percent of the factors that determine reputation of a company among customers and prospects, I estimate, are in the hands of front-line service employees.

But unfortunately, *Time* magazine was right: "Business in general spends too little time educating and motivating front-line employees whom they treat as the lowest workers on the ladder."

But even to management that harbors low esteem for the personal qualities of front-line workers, the fact remains that they deliver service. They create impressions. And impressions form an organization's reputation.

Getting Started

If you are responsible for service education and you must deal with less than enthusiastic support by top management, the pilot course/demonstration idea is a good way to sell the benefit of education.

Find out what skills and behaviors your customer contact people and supervisors need. Pick one deficiency and develop a pilot course that applies good learning principles. Put a cross section of new hires through it. Compare performance of the employees who were trained with a sample of employees who were not trained. You can expect that results will demonstrate the effectiveness of education.

Motivate Employees

It has been noted earlier that highly visible management commitment to quality service is more effective than anything else in motivating employees to provide service (see Chapter 6). Management commitment to service includes commitment to educate employees.

Employees should see management participating in education: in some organizations managers teach the quality service education course or, at least, they deliver an opening message; it's a way to strengthen relationships between managers and their employees.

To prepare managers and supervisors to teach service education classes, conduct special sessions for them in which top management lays out the organization's strategies and objectives for service. Doing so helps managers and supervisors who teach the service education course to develop objectives.

Any service education that you design should include these additional motivational elements:

Personal Growth

Choose a customer service concept that's successful largely because employees see opportunity for personal growth in it and, therefore, are motivated to learn and to practice good service. Employees cannot be taught anything unless they want to learn and unless they feel good about themselves.

They become motivated when they discover that they benefit from service education and from application of service techniques. The reason that they benefit is that the same friendly, considerate, helpful behavior that they are taught to use in customer service also wins and keeps friends.

Personal growth as a result of quality service can be the key to success for service programs that otherwise would founder upon the rocky shoals of employee disinterest.

A personal growth segment of an education course should teach employees to value themselves and the work they do. One result is that their self-concept improves and they derive more satisfaction from their work.

The rationale for teaching employees to feel good about themselves is that once they are at peace with themselves, then they are far more likely to value their customers and to treat them with greater respect.

Accumulated impact of the self-interest aspects of customer service education usually results in class sessions that reverberate with enthusiasm and lively discussion.

The Quality Service Institute is a joint effort of Texas Air Corp. and Scandinavian Airlines System, the Swedish carrier that is now a marketing ally of Continental, Texas Air's main carrier. SAS is renowned for its service. The goal of the Institute is to teach all Continental employees the secrets of the SAS approach.

The Institute offers a smorgasbord of pop psychology, pep talks, and game playing to put workers in touch with themselves.

"We want people to attend not because it's good for Continental but because it's good for them," says Jan Lapidoth, the Swedish president of the Institute.

If people feel good about themselves, the theory goes, they will provide better service.

Education as a Means of Achieving "Internal Customer Satisfaction"

Many employees will be more interested in education when they see it as a means of helping their peers, employees in other departments. By doing so they improve the quality of service to the end customer, of course.

The principle of "internal customer" satisfaction is seen as having the greatest chance of capturing employees' attention and commitment.

Timing: When to Train

A Citicorp study found that education is most effective during an employee's early job experience with an organization. Attitudes and practices are most easily conveyed when employees are in a learning mode as they are when they are beginning a new job. When customer service standards and skills are taught at the beginning, quality results from employees are achieved from the start.

Many organizations feel they ought to wait 90 days, to train employees after they are hired to increase the likelihood that they will stay a while. (If they've stayed 90 days chances are better that they'll become long-term employees than when they started.) Only after a "waiting period" will they consider investing in a new employee.

But if a new employee works five days a week and offends only one customer a day because of poor attitudes or skills, they can lose 65 customers in 90 days. If each of those customers could be expected to spend an average of $5,000 during the next five years, that one, "lowly," new hire could deflect $325,000 worth of business.

Untrained or poorly trained employees are expensive. They tend to leave more frequently, too, a significant fact in a day of labor shortages.

STRUCTURE AND CHARACTERISTICS OF EDUCATION

An effective education process starts with performance analysis. Analyze what must be done to service the customer well in your organization. Then spell out the knowledge, attitudes, and skills required of the people who deliver the service.

In designing an education program, plan to employ emotional appeals. Include the pleasures of dealing with satisfied people as opposed to the repugnant job of soothing angry, distrustful, or sarcastic customers. Discuss the self-satisfaction of doing a good job. Promise rewards such as bonuses and gifts or gift certificates for outstanding service.

In customer relations education, it is important to reach employees emotionally before conveying information. Get their commitment first. Convince them that the most important part of their jobs is taking good care of customers.

Tell Employees What You Expect

Then clearly describe exactly what you want trainees to be able to do when they've finished the education program. Establish objectives for them. It's not only unfair but also absurd to conduct exacting evaluations of employees who have never been told explicitly what the bases for evaluations will be.

Choose either the "team" or the "cross-section" approach to the makeup of education classes.

In the team concept, all employees in one department go through education together. Team education boosts team spirit. Enthusiasm and commitment to service improve.

Companies that practice the team approach believe that they get a much greater "bang for their buck" as a result of participation and interaction of employees who work together.

On the other hand, there is value in a cross-section concept, too. When representatives of several departments participate in the same class, a consensus often develops. The departments represented in the class begin working harmoniously toward the same goals.

Decide between cross-section and team makeup of classes based upon corporate culture, nature of your business and service delivery system, and personal preferences of managers.

ATTRIBUTES OF EFFECTIVE EDUCATION SYSTEMS

Effective education is characterized by attractive packaging, technology, simplicity, and entertainment value.

Technology

Technology reduces education time, the biggest expense in education. With the appropriate technology you can reduce training hours while retaining high impact. As a result, technology also helps keep down labor costs.

For instance, in some industries such as the insurance industry, it has become common to train employees with computer-based interactive video education systems. With equipment such as this it's possible for your own managers and supervisors to conduct education for any number of employees at many different locations simultaneously.

Good technology such as the latest audio and video equipment and attractive "packaging" of learning materials equip managers with little experience in education to run classes themselves.

What is not meant by reference to advanced technology is a VCR and a monitor on which employees view education films by themselves in a dimly lighted room. This may be a reasonably effective way to convey information. But it's not going to change attitudes. To change attitudes groups of people must be thrown together in a class and they must interact emotionally.

Packaging: Video and Print

Packaging is communication. Packaging can be slides and overhead projector presentations. It can be sound and music. It can be video and film. It should emphasize visual presentation, case histories, role playing, group discussion, and review.

Create value in the participants' eyes. Use material that is typeset, keylined, and professionally printed. Use covers that are professionally designed with at least two or three colors, but preferably four colors.

During 11 years of evaluating in-house training programs, I find that this is an area where many firms fail. I am amazed to see how far some companies will go to save 50 cents to $2 apiece on production. The result is small type, cramped layout, poor design—a printed piece that nobody but the sponsor would read.

General Mills and Kellog offer breakfast cereals that outsell generic cereal products though the products cost 30 to 40 percent more. A major reason is attractive packaging, the companies say. A sample of attractive packaging in the customer service education field is printed here.

Good packaging strengthens acceptance of education materials.

One of the values of packaging is that it can be standardized so that education can be implemented and sustained in widely separated job sites.

It's fundamental if you want good packaging to hang an "Off Limits" sign on the copy machine, though. Well-designed, original printed materials done in two or more colors are required.

Sophisticated Simplicity

In service industries, available transaction time often is no more than 15 to 30 seconds—maybe as much as a minute. What employees in these real-time situations need are skills, ideas, techniques, and tools that they can use in that brief time. You are talking *fundamentals* here.

In athletics, why do you think that coaches stress fundamentals over and over again? Why does the Army have drills every day, reviewing and practicing fundamentals? Why do lawyers and CPAs and medical personnel and most other educated people attend refresher courses? Answer: To regain lapsed knowledge of the fundamentals. If you forget the fundamentals, thinking that you are beyond the fundamentals in knowledge, that's when you get into trouble.

Doing More Than The Minimum

Think back to the last holiday season. How good did you feel after a day of shopping? Were you ready to go out and spend another day in the stores? Was the experience an unpleasant chore instead of a pleasure?

Perhaps the holiday example is a bit extreme, but it's a high-volume time that produces a lot of stress in everyone. Think about the last time you went shopping. Was it enjoyable? Chances are you vividly remember the way you were treated by someone in a store. Whether the encounter was positive or negative, you remember that personal contact.

Our Right To Expect The Best

As customers, we expect fairness, courtesy, openness, and pleasant, friendly service. When we receive positive communication, we feel good.

On the other hand, when we're high-pressured, ignored, or processed like a number, we react strongly to negative communication.

"Attractive packaging" means that materials for participants in education sessions should be pleasing to the eye and easy to read like this chapter from the Service Quality Institute handbook, *Feelings*.

This holds true for all interaction with people. If we give poor service to the people we deal with in a business environment, they simply have the option to go elsewhere.

Losing one customer doesn't make or break most businesses, but if it happens repeatedly, a business will fail. Even if we don't have direct contact with customers, our failure to interact positively with co-workers will ultimately have the same result; it damages everyone.

Success Keys: Courtesy, Honesty, Fair Play

The most successful human enterprises build their success on a foundation of courtesy, honesty, openness, and fair treatment of customers and employees. Everyone working in such an environment takes pride in their dealings with customers and each other.

Today, we see the traditional values of courtesy, honesty, openness, and fair play being overlooked by many companies. The fact that you are participating in this program shows that your employer believes in those values.

Good values make good business sense. Customers still appreciate employees who do a good job, who show they care, and go out of their way to do a little bit extra. We can all do the minimum. We can also do more than the minimum.

Quality Service: A Winning Attitude

It's no mystery. You know your job better than anyone else. You can easily think of ways to improve your personal service to customers and co-workers. With this attitude, you'll be successful wherever you work; whatever you do.

When you adopt the attitude of doing more than the minimum, you'll find that your value -- to yourself and everyone else -- increases.

No job is perfect. You may dislike your supervisor, or resent something a co-worker did or didn't do, or a customer may have irritated you. You aren't responsible for their performance or behavior. You're responsible for doing your job and doing it well.

By applying yourself and doing more than just enough to get by, you will be performing beyond the bare minimum. You will advance more in your job, gain more satisfaction from doing it well, and feel good about yourself.

CHAPTER FIVE REVIEW

Points To Remember

- People value courtesy, honesty, openness and fair play.
- Doing more than the minimum required by our jobs leads to job satisfaction, pride and advancement.
- Each of us has the ability to find ways to improve what we do and the way we do it.
- Each of us has the responsibility to find ways to improve what we do and the way we do it.
- Everyday, we need to improve what we do and the way we do it.

Customer service education programs should be written for front-line employees who want to learn what they can do to get better results tomorrow without being bored to death by detail and complexity in the learning process today.

Some managers object when an education program is not complex and highly literate. When a course throws around terms such as "psychosocial behavior change in customers" to describe what happens when customer relations techniques are practiced, these managers love it.

But few employees remember complicated concepts. Virtually none of them applies such concepts.

Complexity Is Unnecessary

But education materials needn't be complicated to be effective. In fact, the opposite is true: the more complicated they are the less effective they are.

Simple, uncomplicated materials are sophisticated. They are sophisticated in their effectiveness at teaching new behavior. Sophistication is simplicity. We can go so far as to say that if education material is not simple, then it isn't sophisticated.

Anyone can create a presentation that no one can understand. But it takes talent and its sophisticated application to couch complicated concepts in simple terms.

Less Is More

The superiority of simplicity is not an original concept, to be sure. In the sixteenth century, Andrea del Sarto, a Florentine artist, said: "Less is more." It's a simple but powerful concept.

Simplified education is employed by some of the most sophisticated organizations such as Scandinavian Airlines. Jan Carlzon, president of SAS, writes: "The most powerful messages are those that are simple and direct and can serve as a battle cry for people across all organizational levels. The message does not need to be lofty or even original."

SAS published a small red-covered booklet called "Let's Get In There and Fight" and distributed it to its 20,000 employees.

Says Carlzon: "Many people thought the little red book was far too simplistic for SAS's many intellectual and highly educated employees." Simplistic or not, the little red book was an effective communications tool internally.

"Having done away with our older, hierarchical structure," Carlzon says, "we couldn't order our employees to do things differently. Instead, we had to convey our vision of the company and convince them that they could and should take responsibility for carrying out that vision. The little red book's pictures and words did just that."

Entertainment Value

The education that you develop should be fun for participants. It should rank, in appeal, beside TV, VCRs, quadraphonic recording and hot tubs if you're to have any chance whatsoever of influencing employees to willingly, perhaps even enthusiastically, pursue customer satisfaction. The education that you develop should be fun for participants.

Unfortunately, a high proportion of managers still feel that an education program should be conservative in content and presentation, informative, and always in "good taste." (Practically speaking, "good taste" turns out to be "dull," which is not to say that all education with entertainment value is in bad taste.) Managers forget about those two words, all important to children of the video and slick entertainment age—"perception" and "communication." Before a message can be communicated it must be perceived. That means, for most of the young working generation, that it must be entertaining. Design materials for communication with participants not to please management.

Guidelines: How to Conduct an Education Session

Invite participants to education sessions with a personal letter. Invite line, office, and support employees, supervisors and managers, and part-time, seasonal, and full-time employees.

Education, best led by an immediate supervisor, should be relaxed and informal. The "facilitator," as we shall call the group leader, should be a supervisor. Relations between supervisor and supervised are improved by the kind of frank and open discussion that often goes on in these customer service education sessions. What's more, employees are motivated by the interest and enthusiasm of their supervisors.

All employees, new and experienced, should be invited to participate in the first education sessions of a customer service program.

Education Setup

Conduct education sessions in a comfortable, well-ventilated room. Make arrangements to prevent interruptions. Provide all participants with paper and pen or pencil.

Allow room for audiovisual equipment. Test equipment before the first session begins. Avoid inferior loudspeakers and faded visual images.

If the facilitator does not know all participants by their first names, list participants' names on a sheet of paper that can be referred to easily. To help identify participants for the convenience of the facilitator, provide name tags. It's a way to promote communication among participants, too.

The facilitator should speak clearly and distinctly and with sufficient volume to be heard by everyone in the room.

The facilitator (group leader) should function as a coach, not as an expert. At the beginning of each session, the "coach" should encourage everyone to share good and bad personal experiences in customer relations with the group to get the sessions moving.

The facilitator should actively encourage participation by every class member. Ask questions of individuals. Establish eye contact with each member of the class. When discussion begins, guide it into the right channels.

Team Atmosphere

Yet work to build a team atmosphere. A team will be more successful than individuals in implementing customer service principles.

Use "open-ended" questions, the kind that require anecdotal responses and opinions and that require more of an answer than "Yes" or "No." A class on customer service is not effective if it is merely a lecture session.

If a facilitator receives no response to a question he or she should just continue to ask open-ended questions. Eventually someone will speak up.

Emotional Involvement

Learning occurs most readily when participants' feelings are involved. So both facilitator and "students" should enjoy the class. Promote enjoyment by presenting the customer service education as a way to improve personal skills. And encourage everyone to speak freely and candidly.

Here are ways to promote an enjoyable atmosphere, thereby improving the learning process:

- Ask each participant to introduce himself or herself, referring to job accomplishments, the feature of the person's job that is enjoyed most, family, and so on.
- After the first sessions, ask participants to share their job successes. For the customer service education to be most effective, class members must feel good about themselves.
- Call on students to name jobs in the company that they would like to know more about.

Don't worry about objections and disagreements. It's more important to maintain an open, sharing atmosphere than to achieve full agreement. Allow the group to comment on and to answer objections.

Keep the sessions moving. By maintaining an efficient pace, participants will remain alert and active.

Questions should relate to problems and job situations that class members are familiar with. But throw in references to service that employees are likely to experience off the job, too.

Prevent domination of a class by a single person. Domination such as this threatens others, particularly subordinates or employees with little experience, so they will avoid participation.

When a participant strays from the topic, nudge her or him back to the subject being discussed by asking the person a question related to the topic.

Total agreement among participants is not necessary. But avoid and discourage shouting matches. To defuse such confrontations, stand between the debaters so they can't see each other. Then, involve other people in discussing the topic by rephrasing it and asking the group for opinions.

When some people do not participate, ask them questions, using their names. Get them to talk about their personal experiences and opinions.

To promote participation, ask for suggested solutions to a problem, for an analyses of a situation, or for a reason that something is important or unimportant. Ask for a story to illustrate a point. Ask individuals to explain how they feel about a topic or a point of view.

How to Handle Questions

The best way to handle questions is to answer with another question. The objective is to induce group participation as a way to enhance learning.

- Reword a question and ask for detail.
- Pass a question to another participant for answering.
- If a participant responds with an answer that's out of line or counter to the service strategy, don't disagree with it. Ask still another participant (who you're quite sure will answer more productively) to respond.

How to Ask Questions

1. Avoid questions that can be answered with a simple "Yes" or "No." Instead, ask questions that require respondents to compare, contrast, list, organize ideas, and so on.
2. Use open-ended questions that require participants to apply responses to their experiences.
3. Employ probing questions, inducing participants to do the "lecturing."
4. Apply questions and phrases such as these to encourage group interaction:
   "Why?"
   "Analyze."
   "Give us your own story."
   "How would you have done it better?"
   "Solve this problem."
   "Would you explain to us how you feel?"

Heighten Awareness

Adapt program flow and pacing to fit the needs of your group for the purpose of maintaining a high level of attentiveness.

Vary media—audiovisual, flip chart, participant literature, role playing—and alternate pace. Speed up and slow down.

Even moving from one location in the room to another can vary the mood and interactiveness of a group. The facilitator can walk from the front of the room to the sides, to the back, and then walk among participants.

PREPACKAGED PROGRAMS

Often an organization will need to supplement internally developed education with a prepackaged program produced by a leading customer service consulting organization.

If you are concerned that employees will not identify with an "off-the-shelf" program, that it might lack influence and credibility because the video or film presenter is unknown to employees, consider customization.

When we customize our service programs for an organization, the result looks very much as if it has been produced by the organization's own staff.

Customization

Workbook covers are printed with the company's logo and a typical photograph of company operations or people on the front.

A statement from the chief executive appears on the back cover with his or her photo.

The first portion of the first videocassette is introduced with videotaped statements by corporate and facility executives.

Course completion certificates bear the company logo—and so on.

This off-the-shelf package includes a leader's guide that explains how to run group discussions, that describes material needed, and that includes transcribed copy from three audio cassettes that accompany the material.

Also included are professionally recorded audio cassettes that employ dramatic case history capsules and music, blended with the narrative.

To prepare, leaders read a leader's guide and the participant's workbook twice to become familiar with material.

Education is conducted every 30 to 90 days, though the period is determined by turnover levels. Even if no new employees are hired, this education program is presented for review every 6 to 12 months to present employees.

Packaged customer relations programs work well for some companies. They are an especially good resource for owner-managers who lack the time or the motivation skills and the knowledge needed to develop their own programs.

EDUCATION CONTENT

Too many companies limit their service-improvement programs to the kind of education that ensues after an executive suggests: "Let's round up the employees and give them a little training."

Other organizations work on developing commitment in employees, thinking that committed employees will learn how-to techniques on their own.

Skill Training

But skill training is important. It can significantly enhance the quality of service. Conduct an educational program for employees that is very specific about actions that employees must take in order to win customer satisfaction every time.

Telling employees to be "nice to customers" is meaningless unless you define exactly what "nice" means in the context of your type of organization.

Employee Viewpoint

But as important as they are, specific customer service skills should not be the total content of education, either. Also teach fundamental viewpoints that become the framework and the foundation for practical skills. One of these fundamental viewpoints is that the customer is all important to employees themselves.

I believe that the secret of successful customer service education is teaching employees

- To derive satisfaction from winning friends for the company.
- To derive satisfaction from meeting the challenges of complaints and other pressures.
- To identify with the company and with coworkers.
- To understand and to appreciate importance of customers to the livelihoods of the employees.
- To understand and to appreciate the importance of their jobs, no matter what they are.

Teach employees to respect themselves, the work they do, and their employers. When they believe in themselves and what they're selling, then they find it much easier to treat customers with respect.

The result, then, is friendly, constructive reaction from customers. This gives employees more satisfaction from their jobs and motivates them to continue to practice professional customer relations techniques.

Employees also need to understand the standards against which their performances will be measured as well as their accountability for meeting those standards.

The customer service program of The Pacific Institute (PI) of Seattle, Washington, is called "Investment In Excellence." Its goal is to teach employees to understand how they and their peers think, how self-image is formed, and how self-image affects performance. The program teaches the realization that each of us has the ability to change inappropriate beliefs and attitudes.

Pacific Institute's program is built around 15 to 20 videotape segments on topics such as comfort zones, self-image, goal setting, and possibility thinking. The PI program is about two and a half days long. It uses one of the retailer's own managers to lead sessions. During sessions, employees answer five reflective questions in a workbook after each video segment in order to "inventory themselves," says PI.

Whereas PI teaches motivation as an input, Mohr Development of Stamford, Connecticut, teaches it as an output—a result of skill education.

Says Michael Patrick, Mohr's director of business development: "When employees see the benefits of applying a skill, they get excited and they use it again and again until it becomes habitual. They keep using these skills because it feels good to do so."

Friendliness

This is a basic concept in education.

A customer-friendly system is one that by its basic design makes things easy for the customer.

Smiling is important for a sales clerk. It establishes a positive mind-set that will be displayed throughout a transaction. It gets a transaction under way positively.

Unless she or he is smiling, a sales clerk's body language may say, "I'd much rather be doing something else." These "vibes" are noticed by customers. And resented. That's why the first five seconds of a sales transaction are extremely important.

As time passes, employees may be sure that they'll meet some of the same people. It's more pleasant to meet an old friend than an old enemy made when they treated a customer as an antagonist.

Employees should be taught to put aside concern that a customer might scowl in response to a smile. Friendliness by people who have not yet become friends is so rare that it will be noticed and it will win gratitude and, often, more business.

Bob Hynes, of American Hardware Supply Company, develops in his education the idea that salespeople should treat customers as human beings instead of as tedious interruptions of other activity. Employees should be taught to become friends of customers, to make them feel important, and to perfect the store's reputation, so customers will return to shop again.

Texas American Bank of Ft. Worth developed this checklist of friendly actions used in its education:

1. Acknowledge the customer's presence with a smile.
2. If you know the customer's name, use it in your greeting. If you don't know it, obtain it from a check or credit card, or ask the customer what it is. Don't overuse it, though: you could risk sounding phony.
3. Listen carefully without interrupting or allowing yourself to be distracted. Ask questions to obtain all information needed to resolve any complaint.
4. Identify the customer's need by restating the facts as the customer tells them.
5. Don't lecture.

6. Offer solutions. Don't tell the customer to do anything.
7. Provide referral for additional service.
8. Close with a smile and use the customer's name again.
9. Invite the customer to return.

Here's a different list of basic skills to practice in face-to-face customer service:

1. Make eye contact.
2. Answer questions or obtain answers quickly.
3. Hurry.
4. Talk and act in an enthusiastic, sincere, and personal way, not in a routine, bored manner.
5. Give the customer your total attention. Never act impatient, as if you just want to finish the transaction as quickly as possible.
6. Speak in a friendly manner, complimenting, making friendly comments.
7. Offer unsolicited help now and then.
8. Make positive parting comments such as "We appreciate your business." And "Come see us again."

Internal Service

Show employees how to use and to contribute to good service internally. Show them how to mobilize service within the company and to render service to those who deal directly with customers. Roland Dumas, former research manager of Zenger-Miller, Inc., of Cupertino, California, leading customer service research and consulting firm, says that front-line employees "must be given the skills not just to deliver quality service but to obtain it from their internal suppliers, their fellow employees upstream."

Richard Riesbeck, president of Riesbeck Food Markets in Ohio, believes that employee relations is the foundation of his customer relations success. "We need to realize that good relationships within the store have a lot to do with how successful we are in treating customers well."

Yet internal service might as well be a theorum in nuclear physics for the amount of awareness of it that many managers display.

After Zenger-Miller conducted a study of quality service programs, Roland Dumas, then director of research, reported: "Virtually all service quality programs that we encountered focus on resolving issues or handling situations with people external to the organization. None handles internal service issues or the relation between internal service quality and external customer satisfaction."

Helpfulness

Hurry to help. Anticipate needs. Offer information.

Edwin Hoffman, chairman and chief executive of Woodward & Lothrop, well-known Washington, D.C., department store, says that he was shopping at Nordstrom's Westside Pavilion store in Los Angeles when a saleswoman offered to place a long-distance call for him—on Nordstrom's tab.

"A tear came to my eye," said Hoffman.

Importance of the "Little Things"

Many customers are lost to competitors because of little human oversights—not returning a phone call, being late for an appointment, failing to say "Thank you" or in other ways indicating that an account or a retail customer is taken for granted.

Little things can be the difference between a very big success and failure for a company. The reason is that people react emotionally to small insults. Yet they hesitate to complain about them for fear of being seen as unreasonable.

Customize Service Style to Customer Personality

Convey to employees in education that it makes no sense to treat everyone alike. Some people might react well to the bartender's personality, a slap on the back and a hearty laugh. Others would be appalled by such treatment.

Learning to read body language and developing listening skills are part of "Fast Forward," a Sears, Roebuck and Co. service education program for new employees.

Fit your type of service to the personality of the customer. Learn to pick up on subtle cues and to react to your experience-based instincts.

". . . observe the customer's 'social style' to determine the way he or she would prefer being treated," says Bill Murray, a vice president of corporate learning at Wilson Learning Corp.

"Is the customer amiable/responsive? Is he or she a hard driver who doesn't want to waste time? Expressive/talkative? Analytical/quiet? Nonresponsive? You can tell in 30 seconds by the pace of speech and the vocal tone," Murray claims.

Telephone Tactics

Employees convey their feelings, their attitudes, and an impression of their probable off-telephone behavior with vocal nuances during phone conversations. In other words, the things that they say and the way that they say them create either a positive or a negative impression.

So education should include tips on talking with customers on the phone.

The American Management Association's self-education study course on telephone communication includes these directions: "Listen carefully

. . . take notes . . . get the caller's name and phone number before hitting the hold button . . . avoid transferring calls. . . ."

Employees should become aware of exactly how they sound to others on the phone and how to communicate a more positive impression. Specifically, they should learn to convey positive feelings to customers on the phone. After all, customers buy, stop buying or switch their buying to competitors as a result of their perceptions of a business's service level based on employees' telephone manners.

Whether or not an employee "means" to give a customer the impression that the company is run by rude, unfriendly people is not the point. If the customer derives that impression, that's all that counts in the world of competitive business.

There is no such thing as creating no impression on the phone.

Be Sincere

Employees should be taught to engage customers in sincere conversation by saying something like: "Were you able to find what you were looking for?"

The key word is "sincere." Watch out for ritualistic, sing-song expressions recited by rote such as the knee-jerk, "Have a nice day." They do more harm than good because customers are as quick as cats to catch on to insincerity.

A sincere attitude demonstrates to customers that employees don't care only about "number one." It indicates that they want to provide good service, that they care about their work, and that they are determined to do their work in a professional manner.

Personality Skills

Spend a little time during education in discussing personality skills. Emphasize importance of maintaining good relations with peers and supervisors. This is important groundwork for friendly relations with customers. When an employee gets along well with his or her supervisor and coworkers, then that employee is more likely to be in the kind of mood that enables them to deliver good service.

The Customer Viewpoint

A fine general rule that could be taught to employees, as an umbrella concept, was expressed by Tom Peters writing in *Thriving on Chaos*: "Every action, no matter how small, and no matter how far from the firing line a department may be, must be processed [by employees as if they were seeing it] through the customer's eyes. [Employees should ask]: 'Will this make it easier for the customer?' 'Faster?' 'Better?' 'Less expensive?' 'Will the customer be more profitable because of it?'"

If employees learn nothing else in education but how to process information as if they are customers they will learn to react in ways that win customer satisfaction.

DURATION OF EDUCATION, FOLLOW-UP

How long is long enough in education time? Most service education programs last less than eight hours. Often they last only a couple hours. And there's no follow-up, no integration with performance management systems, no management support.

Service education for front-line people must be at least six solid hours long with a follow-up session a month or two later if you are to expect a reasonable amount of behavior change and commitment to service standards.

At L. L. Bean, Inc., intensive education goes on for three weeks. Performance of employees who have been trained is monitored periodically.

At Procter & Gamble the customer service education course is four to 6 weeks long and 40 hours per week for each "clan" (as they are called) of new hires.

CASE HISTORIES: SUCCESSFUL QUALITY SERVICE EDUCATION

Dow Chemical USA

The education focus for Dow Chemical USA is individual, particularly in two areas:

Problem Resolution Education

Dow operates in a "continuous quality improvement" mode that requires all departments to find ways to solve problems that prevent them from achieving perfection in their responsibilities. "I have a manager of quality improvement," notes Mitchell J. Kern, manager of customer service resources for Dow Chemical USA in Midland, Michigan. "He works with our people to develop standards, policies, and procedures for customer service and to analyze how we are doing in these areas. We have 'instrumented' the customer service process, much like a car's dashboard is 'instrumented,' allowing everyone to see how they're doing."

Once gaps are found between actual service levels and expected service levels, investigations take place to determine causes of the problems. If one cause turns out to be lack of education, individualized education is introduced to bring an employee up to speed.

Advancement Opportunity Education

Supervisors and their employees regularly discuss career advancement opportunities for employees and identify additional education required for each employee to advance to the next appropriate level. Employees can take advantage of Dow's internal education courses as well as external courses.

Dow's customer service organization developed a "college catalog" of courses that employees can use in choosing education programs that will be of most benefit to them in advancing to the next levels in the organization.

Miller Brewing Co.

Miller has won for itself a bank full of good will among its distributors, and the management and employees of the distributors' customers (bars, restaurants, and clubs), with an inexpensive customer service education program.

In trade magazine ads, Miller pictured a "Grump," an unfriendly, inconsiderate service employee in the form of a seedy-looking waitress with hair flying, chewing on a toothpick, and a bottle opener dangling from her left ear lobe.

The Grump program teaches service employees in restaurants and bars (the wait staff) how to win customer satisfaction. Waiters, waitresses, bartenders, and other front-line employees are motivated to learn customer service principles with the promise that satisfied customers will tip better than dissatisfied ones.

"When satisfied customers tip better and react more positively to waiters and waitresses," says Don Beaver, who developed the program, "then employees are happier with their work and they change jobs less often."

The primary focus of the "Grumpbuster" education program, as it is called, is to reduce employee turnover, one of the major problems of restaurants, where a great deal of Miller beer is sold.

Linde

Linde, supplier of industrial, medical, and specialty gases to the Canadian market, determined through customer research that it had an opportunity to differentiate itself through superior customer service. So the company devised a 2-pronged education attack to improve employee customer relations skills and to "reorient the culture" of the firm's senior executives. By reorienting executive culture the company hoped to increase executive commitment to service.

During an 18-month period, more than 700 employees attended two-day service orientation workshops. Linde's top 35 managers attended leadership management workshops to assess whether their behavior set an example that encouraged other employees to place more value on customer relationships and service. Managers also learned how to give better feedback to employees, to remove corporate bottlenecks to customer service, and to reward employees for outstanding performance.

Giant Food, Inc.

This Landover, Maryland, company calls its customer service program "People Who Care." Education programs are conducted in stores with groups of 10 to 30 employees and the store manager. A two-hour workshop that incorporates an illustrated manual is included in the program.

"We use 'role reversal' that works out very well with new people and with older employees as a refresher. It reinforces their desirable customer contact behavior," says Mark Roeder, Giant's public affairs coordinator.

Ramada Renaissance Hotels

Ramada Renaissance Hotels is determined that employees will remain intensely aware of professional guest relations practices. After initial education, service is emphasized in day-to-day supervision, in an employee evaluation system, and in quarterly reviews of the education course that the company uses. Performance reviews are scheduled every 90 days for every employee.

HOW MUCH SHOULD EDUCATION COST?

Citicorp. conducted a study of 17 "role model" companies recognized for superior customer service and found that each made major investments of up to 2 percent of gross sales in formal, on-going service education programs.

Education is paid in present dollars, but it offsets selling costs that will be paid in tomorrow's more expensive dollars.

Index